Single Adult Passages

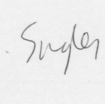

Carolyn A. Koons has become a spokesperson for a generation of unmarried Christian adults, frequently addressing their needs at conferences and seminars. She is the author of *Beyond Betrayal, Tony: Our Journey Together,* and *Unstuck: Risking Change in Adult Life Passages.* She is associate professor of religion at Azusa Pacific University and holds an M.R.E. degree from Talbot Theological Seminary.

Michael J. Anthony has written or edited four other books: *The Effective Church Board, The Short-Term Missions Boom, Foundations of Ministry,* and (with H. Norman Wright) *Help, I'm a Camp Counselor.* Associate professor of Christian education at Biola University/Talbot School of Theology, he holds an Ed.D. degree from Southwestern Baptist Theological Seminary and a Ph.D. from Claremont Graduate School. He is a frequent speaker at camps and conferences for single adults.

Single Adult Passages

Uncharted Territories

Carolyn A. Koons

and

Michael J. Anthony

BAKER BOOK HOUSE
Grand Rapids, Michigan 49516

© 1991 by Baker Book House Company

Published by Baker Books
a division of Baker Book House Company
P.O. Box 6287, Grand Rapids, MI 49516-6287

New paperback edition 1995

Second printing, January 1996

Printed in the United States of America

Library of Congress Cataloging-in-Publication Data

Koons, Carolyn A.
    Single adult passages : uncharted territories / Carolyn A. Koons and Michael J. Anthony
      p.   cm.
    ISBN 0-8010-5219-X
    1. Single people—United States—Religious life. 2. Church work with single people. I. Anthony, Michael J. II. Title
    BV4596.S5K66   1991
    248.8'4—dc20   91-2162

We would like to dedicate this book to . . .

Leaders of single adult groups in the United States and Canada who labor diligently each week, offering the gospel of hope, love, and redemption to millions of single adults.

Christian educators who are involved in the quest to better understand single adult development.

Counselors who are actively involved in helping single adults, especially those who are suddenly single (divorced and widowed), make the transition to single living. Their faithfulness reminds us that we serve a God of second chances.

Contents

List of Illustrations

Acknowledgments

A survey of this nature needs the significant contributions of many people. We express our appreciation to our fellow members of the National Association of Professors of Christian Education and the National Association of Single Adult Leaders for providing us with a forum to present our findings and to offer constructive critique of our conclusions.

Dozens of single adult leaders in the United States and Canada helped by allowing us to distribute our lengthy "Singles in America" survey in their single adult fellowships. Obviously, this book could never have been accomplished without such valuable input.

Roy Carlisle, president and publisher of Page Mill Press, gave his professional expertise and support throughout the entire process of this research. His commitment to our vision and his personal involvement, which contributed to the fulfillment of our dreams, is much appreciated.

Our appreciation is extended to Allan Fisher, director of publications at Baker Book House, whose commitment to provide the church with valuable ministry resources has resulted in the publication of this manuscript. We also wish to say thanks to Betty De Vries, managing editor, and her editorial team for their work on making this dual-author manuscript a smooth-flowing book.

Finally, we would like to acknowledge the valuable contribution of Todd Jennings, director of our five-member research team, for his leadership during the enormous amount of tabulation, data entry, and statistical analysis that was required to produce this work.

Carolyn A. Koons
Michael J. Anthony
June 1991

Preface

When the dream to write a significant book on single adults began, little did we realize the challenges that would surface. The phenomenon of single adults today is so common and research is so limited, we felt as though we had set sail into uncharted waters. As we continued our project, the "uncharted waters" feeling returned again and again.

We do not feel that there are predictable stages or passages for single adults. And we do not intend to force singles into unrealistic or nonexistent modes simply to foster research data. So little is known about the single adult. The underlying reality is that we have all been single at one stage of life or another. Those who responded to our survey were single at the time the survey was conducted. Some had never been married. Others were separated, divorced, or widowed. Traditionally we have tended to classify all singles in one category, but the singles who have never married differ in some major respects from those who once were married and through often tragic circumstances now find themselves single again.

Single Adult Passages is the first indepth historical and sociological study of Christian singles in America. We assume that the attitude of Christian singles toward singleness, as well as their behavior, is influenced by their spiritual life and the teachings of the church. Comprehensive in scope, our survey is a valuable resource tool for Christian singles themselves, as well as for those who minister to single adults.

We surveyed almost 1400 singles of all ages, of various educational levels, in a wide variety of occupations, and living in forty different states. For the record, 1363 singles returned usable surveys. However, 20 singles skipped checking the gender box; the female category was checked by 884 while 459 checked the male category. Therefore, for questions related to gender, we could use only 1343 responses. This will explain the occasional variance in survey totals. We have also interviewed hundreds of singles and included data from the interviews in the book.

Our aim is to challenge readers to get in touch with the uncharted territories of single adult life. Since there is so little quality material available for leaders of singles ministries, we have included information on how to establish programs which address major concerns of singles.

The Christian singles who openly and honestly participated in the study have provided reliable documentation on many facets of singleness not previously researched. Their messages are an urgent plea to all of us to minister effectively to an often ignored or neglected segment of the family of God.

One

An Overview of Singleness

I n an age of reducing hard questions to simple answers, there is hardly a shortage of material intent on enhancing our understanding of ourselves, our fellow humans, our culture, and—for a Christian—how best to fulfill one's individual potential in light of the divine purpose. Many of the current publications that have examined "singleness" are enlightening to one degree or another, but usually according to whether or not the author considers being single an acceptable lifestyle, rather than an incomplete, less-than-perfect state of existence. Whatever one's view on that particular matter—and whatever truth can be sifted from the flawed generalizations and subjective data in this array of information—it is incontrovertible that more and more adults in our society are unmarried, either through choice or circumstance. Many of these singles are content with their lifestyle; others harbor doubts and fears about whether personal fulfillment is possible unless (or until) they fit the expectations of a culture that continues to idealize the family model of husband/wife/children.

This section will first briefly survey the cultural implications of "the singles phenomenon" evidenced in the rising population growth of this segment of contemporary American society. Next, chapter 2 examines the "validity," or "normalcy," of being single, in light of some general theories about the human developmental cycle. Chapter 3 will take that concept one step further by presenting our rationale and plan for undertaking the research study that is foundational to the observations and recommendations to be outlined in later sections of this book. Finally, in chapter 4, we offer a philosophical review of what we call "The Quest for Identity"—the dynamic process that underscores an individual's mind-set and life choices, with special reference to gender differentiation and role modeling as they apply to single versus married issues.

1

Implications of the Singles Phenomenon

The singles population is increasingly a factor in modern society, and it is apparent that this trend will not be reversed in the foreseeable future. Millions of unmarried adults are creating nontraditional lifestyles that are in turn affecting every aspect of American culture. This phenomenon is by no means geographically restricted. All across the world, even in the so-called undeveloped nations, adults are choosing to postpone marriage until certain personal goals have been attained, whether educational, professional, economic, or emotional. Some may never marry; others, for either personal or financial reasons, remain unattached after a divorce or spousal death.

This trend has far-reaching effects on business, government, jurisprudence, and personal relationships. It seems clear that, perhaps indefinitely, we will all be living in a world heavily influenced by single-adult concerns. It has been estimated, for example, that single Americans are worth $200 billion to firms with the "right" products. Singles are setting the tone for much of what is available in the marketplace—on television, in the fashion world, in restaurants, and in leisure activities. Ethical standards, too, have been heavily influenced by the singles lifestyle. This translates into new perspectives on sexual mores, property laws, public policy, time-honored traditions, and value systems.

One important factor in the rising singles population has been the steadily increasing divorce rate, which has had a major impact on both the makeup and dynamics of society. The National Center for Health Statistics reports that between 1900 and 1965 the divorce rate (divorces per 1,000 population) rose from 0.7 to 2.5 and that by the year 1975 it stood at 5.0. In that year the annual number of divorces first passed the million mark; there was approximately one divorce for every two marriages—up from one divorce for every six marriages in 1930. This means that between 1950 and 1982 this component of the singles population increased by 385 percent (from 4 million to 19.4 million). Figure 1.1 charts the percentages of the three major "unmarried" population groups from 1970 to 1986.

Fig. 1.1

The Single Population in the United States

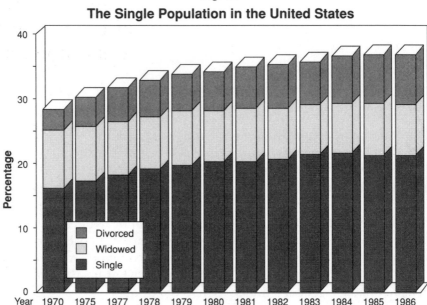

From U.S. Bureau of Census, Current Population Reports, series P-20, No. 418. *U.S. News and World Report,* Sept. 19, 1988, p. 72.

The never-married adult faces challenges different from those of the newly single after a divorce or death of a spouse. The time between twenty and thirty years of age has always been marked by a struggle for self-identity and independence. Around every corner are discoveries about one's physical, sexual, emotional, and social identity. Since modern life is never a constant and is usually confusing, the challenge to develop and maintain a positive self-image is more pressing than ever before. Millions of today's young adults, for example, are not settling on a marital partner early in life, although that has been the traditional time for pairing off and settling down, usually to raise a family. Unfortunately, if they do marry, some couples do not regard this as an irrevocable lifetime commitment. Today's young people are asking searching questions about their own personhood and their relationships and, indeed, about cultural and religious standards regarding "proper" behavior patterns. Even when facing the same basic issues confronted by their parents, they are refusing to accept pat answers. The culture's recent emphasis on self-discovery and on exploring one's options has made young adults more reflective than previous generations in evaluating the choices available to them in a changing world.

There are *new* issues as well. Baby-boomers are dealing with realities unknown to their parents: gender equality, civil rights, medical breakthroughs that have lengthened the life span, expanding educational and career opportunities, and a more progressive view of governmental responsibility in the human-services area. Yet, when these issues are seen in the light of the problems—the growing national debt, fears of recession, increased distancing between haves and have-nots, a drug-related culture, global unrest, and what is seemingly a breakdown of morality—young people are understandably confused about their place in society, if not worried about their economic survival. Whereas one of the major concerns of their parents might have been "*How* can I find a perfect life partner?" (implying a high degree of urgency), this generation may be asking, "*Why* should I get married?" (implying that there might be a better lifestyle than the traditional one).

The communication media has shaped a national concept of the singles lifestyle as a pleasure-filled, "grab it while you can" existence unhampered by the need for personal accountability or longtime planning. But the "swinging single" image is simply not a reality for most single adults. Much of the hyped propaganda portrays the unmarried adult as selfish, hedonistic, irresponsible, if not unstable. Yet, despite a flood of myths and misconceptions to the contrary, most young adults yearn to discover a way of life that will not only fulfill their own needs but also validate their place in the general culture.

This search has led many single adults—whether never-married, widowed, or divorced—to popular literature for some meaningful answers. The majority of books and articles that address the concerns of singles are either first-person narratives ("This is what happened to me!"), psychological studies that purport to understand the singles phenomenon, or self-help manuals on coping with the related problems of being single. Many of the latter concentrate on how-to-find-a-mate advice, implying that that alone is the main concern of all singles. Such material often fails to view the facts and issues through the eyes of a single adult. Some studies actually perpetuate damaging half-truths and stereotypes.

We believe that singleness is a valid lifestyle and that comprehensive

research about today's Christian singles is missing from contemporary literature. In addition, sociologists, human-development researchers, psy-
chologists, educators, and church leaders must address the singles phe-   -
nomenon from new perspectives. As long as these authorities continue
to regard the single adult as somewhat of an anomaly—an exception to
the "normal" or traditional pattern of human development—little will be
accomplished in helping this significant population group find the right
answers for themselves and for society's opinion-shapers.

Obviously, a comprehensive study of "singleness" is needed—both to
understand why increasingly large numbers of adults are opting for this
lifestyle and then to establish this group's alignment in the mainstream of
the culture. It is hoped that the findings presented in this book will add
to that body of information. To accomplish our purposes, we have drawn
from a wide variety of sources: psychosociological studies of "human
development," statistical data, analysis of 1343 (459 male, 884 female)
responses to our "[Christian] Singles in America" survey, and personal
narratives. Both the facts and the theories have far-reaching implications
for the single individual (who may be struggling with his or her self-
image), for their married friends, and for our cultural institutions,
including the church (which often remains distant from the cutting edge
of social change).

It seems appropriate here to mention the church's responsibility for
addressing this modern challenge in a more forthright and positive manner than has yet been evidenced. In particular, religious authorities who
have been too deeply entrenched in the tradition that *only* marriage-and-
family is the proper model for a Christian must rethink their "theology of
singleness" (see chapter 7). If (as we believe) being single is a biblically
acceptable way of life, church leaders and the fellowship of believers can
no longer ignore this group's need for spiritual nourishment. As will be
amplified in later chapters of this book, singles should be welcomed
enthusiastically at the local level of the church through programs tailored
to meet their special concerns. Some congregations already pursue such a
ministry, but in many respects the church has lagged behind in acknowledging the existence of singles in the mainstream. As in other aspects of
the cultural scenario, the church must maintain a degree of flexibility
when confronted by economic and societal changes that do not violate
general scriptural guidelines. On the premise that singleness is a valid
lifestyle, whether by choice or by matter of circumstance, any Christian
single is fully entitled to the church's best efforts and full attention.

2

Perspectives on Human Development

Although one might not agree with Aristotle that "educated men are as much superior to uneducated men as the living are to the dead," it is hardly disputable that knowledge can (and should) increase understanding. A certain college sophomore walked into the office of his faculty advisor to discuss his schedule for the coming semester. His program would include courses needed for his major and a few general electives. As he read down his schedule, the student's eyes stopped at a listing that elicited a strong response.

"Art appreciation!" he cried. "Why do I have to take an art course? I don't know anything about art and have no interest in that kind of stuff!"

The advisor explained that this was precisely the reason for his having to take the course, but the student concealed neither his skepticism or his displeasure. "Okay," he responded, "I'll take the course since it's required, but I'm not going to like it."

At the end of the school term the student once again kept an appointment with his advisor. Remembering the young man's response regarding the art-appreciation course, the advisor asked how he had fared in the class. The student's eyes brightened as he began to explain how much he had learned about art. He spoke with an air of excitement as he told about the lifestyles of some of the artists he had studied. Learning about the background of the artists and the cultural conditions under which some of their work was done had given this student a deeper appreciation for specific paintings and art in general.

Our appreciation of human development can be similarly enhanced. The more we know about human maturation and behavior patterns—the more we investigate potential explanations for stages in the life cycle of a typical human being—the greater can be our appreciation for the manner in which we have been created. As we acquire comprehensive understanding of the changes that are likely to occur as we progress from birth to death, this knowledge gives us tools for identifying and solving some of life's challenges. Knowing what is "normal" and what is not can make a real difference during crisis moments and as we make choices that will determine our future.

The growth and development of a child from birth through adolescence is far more predictable than the complex process of adult behavioral cycles over a span of many decades. Adult "development" is less uniform and its stages are more ambiguous. What is one person's experience at thirty may not be another's until forty-five, if at all. Some adults get married right after high school and begin to raise a family while they are in their twenties. For others that scenario is delayed until midlife or even later. Some remain single until they die.

The Theorists

The psychology of human development is a paradoxical mixture of fact and theory. "Theories" are statements formulated to explain a set of observations. They can allow us to understand something that was once a mystery, or they can help us predict future events. In the fields of "pure" science—chemistry, physics, botany, biology, for example—theories derived from precisely controlled observations and accurate statistical analysis usually yield predictable results, time after time. The predictive ability of any generalization about human nature, however, is far less reliable because of the complexity of human physiology, the importance of nonmeasurable emotional and mental components in human decision making, and (above all) the uniqueness of every individual.

With that qualifying disclaimer in mind, we will present in this chapter a brief overview of some of the more prominent theories of human development. None of these theories can be considered definitive, and some have elements that contradict the hypotheses of other respected researchers. Since there is some element of enlightenment in all the theories, however, they are a starting point, or, rather, a foundation on which we will attempt to overlay a "theory of singles development."

Sigmund Freud

Psychoanalytic theory generally attempts to attribute human personality and behavior to deep-seated and usually unconscious forces that operate within an individual. Perhaps no other individual has received as much acclaim in this area as Sigmund Freud, the Austrian neurologist known as the founder of the psychoanalytic school of thought. As a physician, Freud brought a wealth of medical knowledge and clinical observation to the study of human development. His earliest studies involved the use of hypnosis, but he soon branched out into areas of free association of ideas and dream analysis, which he believed were a more accurate measure of the human psyche and an expression of one's subconscious feelings and motivations. Freud saw the psyche as being comprised of three parts: the *id* (the unconscious), consisting of largely hidden impulses and desires; the *ego*, the completely conscious personality that interacts with society; and the *superego*, or conscience, the partly conscious reflection of parental guidelines and society's rules.

One of Freud's most significant contributions to the field of human development was his theory of psychosexual stages. Freud believed that a person's sexuality was a powerful force from birth onward, the lens through which to interpret human development. This theory proposes five distinct stages, passed through sequentially: oral, anal, phallic, latency, and genital. Each stage identifies specific tensions or needs that must be addressed. If the needs at one stage are not met, Freud suggested, the individual is unable to progress to the next. An individual matured into "healthy" adulthood to the degree he or she was able to move through each stage without undue detours along the way. Freud's approach formed the basis for subsequent psychoanalysis in the twentieth century.

Erik Erikson

The work of Erik Erikson built heavily on Freudian theory but with a number of significant revisions. Whereas Freud saw human development from the perspective of one's sexuality, Erikson saw it in reference to one's social condition. His views came to be known as psychosocial stages of human development. Freud built his theory mainly by attempting to understand abnormal personality development, but Erikson concentrated on examining the characteristics of a "normal" personality.

Erikson viewed the human life cycle as a series of eight stages, during each of which there were major issues to be confronted (see fig. 2.1). Although the ages cited to represent each stage are approximate and may vary in individual cases, the principle on which Erikson based his conclusions is that each developmental stage is seen as a crisis, a conflict situation that must be dealt with before it can serve as a stepping-stone toward "normalcy." In childhood and adolescence, the challenges are as follows: trust versus mistrust (birth to 1 year), autonomy versus shame and doubt (1 to 2 years), initiative versus guilt (3 to 5 years), industry versus inferiority feelings (6 to 11 years), and identity versus role confusion (12 to 20 years).

Adults, too, according to Erikson, must resolve distinct stages of developmental crisis. The first is early adulthood (20 to 35 years), where the prevailing issue is intimacy versus isolation. Optimal development comes about as one develops the ability to maintain intimate personal relationships. If a person is not able to establish relationships of openness and mutual transparency, isolation is the natural and painful consequence.

In middle adulthood (35 to 65 years), the "crisis" is generativity versus self-absorption. This was described by Erikson as the tension between developing an interest in and concern for others—a family, community, and worldwide orientation versus a selfish, egocentric complacency. A life characterized by altruism would indicate successful progression through this stage.

The final stage, late adulthood, is seen as a struggle between integrity and despair. Healthy adjustment in this stage depends (in general) on being successful in resolving the issues met in prior stages as well as having accepted the ultimate conclusion of one's life without morbid fears about death or feelings of failure.

Fig. 2.1
Erikson's Stages of Human Development

Stage	Year	Development
1. Early Infancy	0–1	Developing a sense of trust while overcoming a sense of mistrust
2. Later Infancy	1–2	Acquiring a sense of autonomy while avoiding a sense of doubt and shame
3. Early Childhood	3–5	Acquiring a sense of initiative while combatting a sense of guilt
4. Middle Childhood	6–11	Acquiring a sense of industry and avoiding a sense of inferiority
5. Adolescence	12–20	Acquiring a sense of identity while avoiding a sense of identity diffusion
6. Early Adulthood	20–35	Acquiring a sense of intimacy and avoiding a sense of isolation
7. Middle Adulthood	35–65	Acquiring a sense of generativity and avoiding a sense of stagnation
8. Late Adulthood	65–	Acquiring a sense of integrity and fending off a sense of despair

From *Childhood and Society,* Erik H. Erikson, 2nd ed. © 1950, 1963 by W. W. Norton & Co., Inc. Used with permission.

Erikson continued to further our understanding of human development. Perhaps one of his greatest contributions was his hypothesis that lack of complete resolution in one stage of development does not inevitably determine the outcome of future stages. Many people navigate the adult stages with confidence, success, and a fulfilling sense of achievement despite painful childhood and adolescent experiences.

Jean Piaget

Freud's and Erikson's theories are primarily concerned with human personality development. Other theorists have sought to explain developmental progress as a matter of mastering intellectual stages of growth. Chief among these theorists was a Swiss psychologist, Jean Piaget. Although trained as a zoologist and skilled as a practicing epistemologist, Piaget studied the mental reasoning processes of children. His theories were summarized into what he called stages of cognitive development. The process is sequential, with each stage building on the preceding one.

Piaget believed that successful development into adulthood occurred throughout these stages as a function of adapting to environmental pressures. These stages are *Sensorimotor* (birth to 2 years), *Preoperational* (2

Fig. 2.2

Piaget's Stages of Human Development

Stage	Year	Some Major Characteristics
Sensorimotor	0–2	Intelligence in action
		World of the here and now
		No language, no thought in early stages
		No notion of objective reality
Preoperational	2–7	Egocentric thought
		Reason dominated by perception
		Intuitive rather than logical solutions
		Inability to conserve
Concrete operations	7–11 or 12	Ability to conserve
		Logic of classes and relations
		Understanding of number
		Thinking bound to concrete
		Development of reversibility in thought
Formal operations	11 or 12 to 14 or 15	Complete generality of thought
		Propositional thinking
		Ability to deal with the hypothetical
		Development of strong idealism

to 7 years), *Concrete Operational* (7 to 11 or 12 years), and *Formal Operational* (11 to 15 years). Piaget's theory has been applied primarily to early development, since children were the focus of his experiments. He believed that most intellectual "development" occurring during the adult years is of a quantitative rather than qualitative nature and is influenced by one's environment and experience rather than biological factors.

Robert Havighurst

Chairman of the department for human development at the University of Chicago for many years, Robert Havighurst explained human development in terms of seven stages. Each stage is characterized by a set of achievements or "tasks." Successful progression through the seven stages depends on one's ability to exhibit the qualities portrayed in these tasks. According to Havighurst, an understanding and mastery of these tasks allows one to be prepared for whatever challenges life will bring in the years ahead. They are predictable and for the most part, unavoidable. A summary of these age-related achievements appears in figure 2.3.

Daniel Levinson

A significant contribution to the study of human development was made in recent years by Daniel J. Levinson, psychology professor in the department of psychiatry at Yale University's School of Medicine. He brings a unique integration of psychology, medicine, and sociology to the field. His book, *Seasons of a Man's Life*, is an overview of male adult development between the ages of 18 and 47. Levinson's sequence of stages is displayed in figure 2.4.

Levinson suggests that each of the three major adult stages is preceded by a five-year period of transition that enables an individual to shed the dominant behavioral characteristics of previous stages and become a more mature individual. Levinson describes the life cycle in terms of crisis management, with major tasks to be achieved during stages that last approximately fifteen years. Adult development is seen as a systematic and sequential progression through these predictable stages.

Gail Sheehy

Passages, a book on human development written by Gail Sheehy, achieved best-selling status in the general marketplace. It was based on a research study of 115 adults, most of whom were either married or divorced. The people Sheehy chose as subjects belonged almost entirely to what she described as "pace setters" of American society, the urban middle-class professional. Although her approach is more balanced than

Fig. 2.3

Havighurst's Stages of Human Development

Stage	Development
Infancy and Early Childhood	Learning to take solid foods
	Learning to walk
	Learning to talk
	Learning to control the elimination of body wastes
	Learning sex differences and sexual modesty
	Getting ready to read
	Learning to distinguish right and wrong and beginning to develop a conscience
Middle and Late Childhood	Learning physical skills necessary for ordinary games
	Building a wholesome attitude toward oneself as a growing organism
	Learning to get along with age-mates
	Beginning to develop appropriate masculine or feminine social roles
	Developing fundamental skills in reading, writing, and calculating
	Developing concepts necessary for everyday living
	Developing a conscience, a sense of morality, and a scale of values
	Developing attitudes toward social groups and institutions
	Achieving personal independence
Adolescence	Achieving new and more mature relations with age-mates of both sexes
	Achieving a masculine or feminine social role
	Accepting one's physique and using one's body effectively
	Desiring, accepting, and achieving socially responsible behavior
	Achieving emotional independence from parents and other adults
	Preparing for an economic career
	Preparing for marriage and family life
	Acquiring a set of values and an ethical system as a guide to behavior—developing an ideology
Early Adulthood	Getting started in an occupation
	Selecting a mate
	Learning to live with a marriage partner
	Starting a family
	Rearing children
	Managing a home
	Taking on civic responsibility
	Finding a congenial social group
Middle Adulthood	Achieving adult civic and social responsibility
	Assisting teenage children to become responsible and happy adults
	Developing adult leisure-time activities
	Relating oneself to one's spouse as a person
	Accepting and adjusting to the physiological changes of middle age
	Reaching and maintaining satisfactory performance in one's occupational career
	Adjusting to aging parents
Late Adulthood	Adjusting to decreasing physical strength and health
	Adjusting to retirement and reduced income
	Adjusting to death of spouse
	Establishing an explicit affiliation with members of one's age group
	Establishing satisfactory physical living arrangements
	Adapting to social roles in a flexible way

Fig. 2.4

Levinson's Stages of Adult Male Development

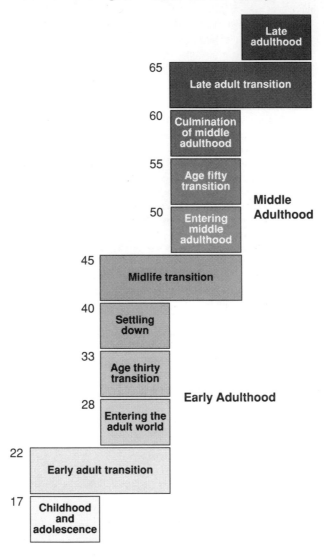

Levinson's, as she includes women in her sample, Sheehy's conclusions replicate Levinson's in terms of developmental progression, identifying similar stages with different labels.

Roger Gould

Psychiatrist Roger Gould, of UCLA, examined the lives of more than 5,000 individuals, both male and female, between the ages of 16 and 60.

The findings are reported in his book, *Transformations*. Gould's description of adult development emphasizes self-awareness, recognition of the gradual transformations that occur throughout one's life span. He theorizes that human development involves the replacement of false childish assumptions from the early years with more adult attitudes and presuppositions. Each stage in Gould's model is characterized by a particular task that facilitates this replacement process. An overview of Gould's theory is presented in figure 2.5.

Fig. 2.5

Gould's Stages of Adult Development

Stage	Approximate Age	Development(s)
1	16–18	Desire to escape parental control
2	19–22	Leaving the family; peer group orientation
3	23–28	Developing independence; commitment to a career and to children
4	29–34	Questioning self; role confusion; marriage and career vulnerable to dissatisfaction
5	35–43	Period of urgency to attain life's goals; awareness of time limitation; realignment of life's goals
6	44–53	Settling down; acceptance of one's life
7	54–60	More tolerance; acceptance of past; less negativism; general mellowing

Filling the Research Gap

We have concluded that few studies have been conducted using empirically based research methods to examine the developmental issues of *single adults*. The early theorists, including Freud, Jung, Erikson, and Piaget, omitted research on the single adult. Havighurst bases his theory of adult development on the marriage model; five of the eight tasks he assigns to early adulthood require a marriage relationship to grow into a "healthy" young adult. Levinson's model is based on *male* development, omitting at least half of the singles population, and his theories are based on the experiences of men who were married or divorced.

What does this say about the 68 million single adults in America today? Where does the single adult fit on these charts of human development? If there are no adult norms that include single adults, could this mean that their lifestyle is flawed? Has their growth and development been impaired? In other words, does the lack of research and the omission of objective materials on single-adult development suggest that being single is an "abnormal" lifestyle? How will single adults find answers that fit their own "passages" through the cycle of life? More specifically, how does a Christian single—whose family background, value judgments, morals, and general world view differ significantly from those of a nonbeliever—handle his or her singleness?

The research compiled for this book was completed in an attempt to answer some crucial questions from a Christian single-adult perspective. Over the past five years we have conducted an intensive search of computerized data banks, hoping to locate valid developmental studies that recognize the single-adult population. Empirical research is lacking in this area, especially research with a focus on the Christian single.

Our aim, therefore, was to venture into this unexplored territory and discover some truths about Christian singles, hoping that with knowledge will come understanding. We wondered, for example, whether the singles mind-set could be juxtaposed on the traditional models of human development discussed above. How do the "tasks," "crisis situations," and "assumptions" at various stages of life differ for singles from those of their married counterparts? In what ways are they the same? How has Christian doctrine and the organized church influenced their lifestyle and attitudes? We have attempted to answer some of those questions.

3

Isolating
the Facts

Although much has been written about the lifestyle of Christian
singles, there are conflicting reports about what is "ideal," or even
"typical" for this population group. Some of the available material
is highly subjective in that it is based on preconceived ideas or written
from an overly judgmental viewpoint. The reliability of such information
is questionable, since certain findings and generalizations will neither
hold up under close scrutiny nor be applicable to individual situations.

The Approach

What was needed, we believed from the start, was an objective
overview of Christian singles that would draw on data that could be
subjected to statistical analysis. The results of our research project are
hardly inclusive of *every* Christian single in the United States, since
such a study would be neither logistically nor economically possible.
However, by using scientifically standard sampling procedures to gather
the desired information and then applying statistically verifiable analyses to the data, we hoped to achieve a clear picture of the target population. We used a comprehensive questionnaire (see Appendix) to gather
the basic data to be analyzed, but supplemented this material by inter-
viewing some of the subjects, thus obtaining an even clearer view of the
sample group's concerns.

The Measuring Rod

Our starting point was to survey several hundred questions from the
studies conducted by Sheehy, Levinson, and others who have studied the

human developmental process. To these we added questions that specifically zeroed in on single adults. From this broad base we then selected the material to be presented to the subjects of our "Singles in America" survey. This ninety-six-item questionnaire examined singles issues in the areas of demographics and general lifestyle—including housing, social life, religious practices, sexuality, divorce, single parenting, and life satisfaction. It is, we believe, the most comprehensive Christian singles survey.

The Subjects

This survey was distributed to singles throughout the United States, in forty states across six geographical regions. Over twenty-five denominations from a variety of rural and urban locations were represented in the sample. Since we intended to cover as broad a spectrum of Christian singles as possible, we selected churches that had singles groups that differed in many respects. Group size ranged from under fifty to over a thousand. Some groups were long-established and could serve as prototypes. Some were directed by women, some by men, some by singles, some by married couples. A few groups were strongly charismatic in orientation, but others were staunchly conservative. Responses from this diverse sampling comprised our data bank.

There were 1343 responses from 459 males and 884 females. Twenty respondents did not indicate their gender. As to marital status, 703 (285 males, 418 females) had never married; 539 (169 males, 370 females) were divorced. About 80 percent of the questionnaires were distributed via church groups. The remaining 20 percent were given out in singles conferences, Sunday school classes, and retreats.

After the data was collected and entered into the computer, five researchers interpreted the material. This process has taken three years to complete.

Interviews

During the process of developing the survey and collecting the information from respondents, we were also involved in conducting interviews and collecting life stories. Many of the singles we spoke with were eager to share their perceptions of the joys and pains of single living. They expressed how their experiences affected their outlook on life. The majority of these individuals wanted to know if their experience was "normal" or whether they were, as they suspected, isolated in their experience of singleness. There was a genuine searching for answers to our interview questions. Some seemed visibly relieved to learn that they were not alone in their apprehension about the unknowns of single living.

Demographics

Those who responded to our survey ranged in age from eighteen to seventy plus, and we sought to achieve a socioeconomic balance in all the age groups. Our sampling included lawyers, doctors, managers,

Fig. 3.1
Singles in America Survey: *Incomes*

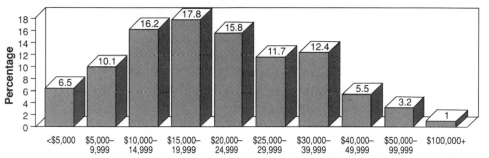

teachers, clerical workers, blue-collar workers, and unskilled laborers. Although 53 percent of the respondents were never married, the remainder included 40 percent divorced, 1 percent separated, and 6 percent widowed. Overall, 35 percent were male and 65 percent were female (see figs. 3.1, 3.2, 3.3.).

Fig. 3.2
Singles in America Survey: *Occupations*

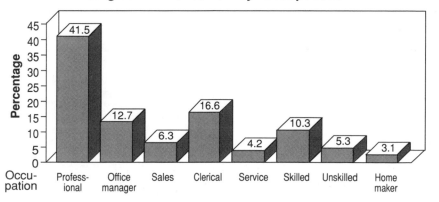

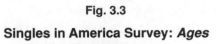

Fig. 3.3

Singles in America Survey: *Ages*

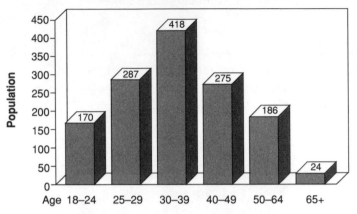

The Implications

To respect the anonymity of our subjects, we have changed the names of individuals cited, but their stories are real and their expressions seem sincere. Some readers may feel threatened by our findings because they contradict some of the accepted views regarding Christian singles. Change is never easy, and it is our hope that this material will challenge Christian single adults to reexamine their own lifestyles and attitudes. More importantly, perhaps, it seems incumbent on the established church and its individual members to accept and facilitate change so that the specific needs of Christian singles may be more effectively met.

We feel confident in exploring this territory because of the value this material can have in assisting those who are single or work with singles. Perhaps we will all better understand ourselves and find answers to some of life's challenging questions. As Gail Sheehy observes in *Passages*, "We all have an aversion to generalities, thinking about ourselves. Yet the older we grow, the more we become aware of the commonality of our lives, as well as our essential aloneness as navigators through the human journey."

4

The Quest
for Identity

For several decades the American culture has focused its energies, attention, and research on children and youth, on the hypothesis that it is during these stages of human development that the greatest changes occur, and thus the most significant learning opportunities exist. Our educational institutions are charged for the most part with nurturing the skills that young people will need to take their place in adult society. Few would question that goal, though many debate the methodology, techniques, curriculum, and even the "skills" an adult must have to survive. By the time an eighteen-year-old graduates from high school, however, he or she will have spent about eleven thousand hours in an academic setting that is ostensibly preparing that young person for adulthood. (Many students continue their formal education for a few years beyond that milestone, adding hundreds of hours to the training period.)

We must question whether *all* growth and change takes place during those childhood and adolescent years. It is as if we expect that everything of importance we will learn about life occurs between birth and the theoretical start of adulthood, roughly around eighteen. That is a ludicrous assumption, of course, but the fact remains that many people act as if the peak of our intellectual, emotional, and spiritual growth is reached at eighteen and we go downhill thereafter. (This may partially explain why so many churches have no Sunday school classes for adults!) Our youth-oriented approach is based on a mistaken notion that concentrating much effort on learning and development during the adult years is mere frosting on the cake and a waste of time and money.

33

Rethinking Developmental Patterns

When scientifically valid research projects, such as Botwinick (1967) and Troll (1982), explored the growth-peak-decay notions of human abilities that had centered attention on childhood/youth growth patterns, it was discovered that the peak in intellectual capacity (as measured by I.Q.) was not eighteen after all, but around the age of fifty-five. This finding has brought about changes in how we see ourselves and how educators see the learning process. No longer must we assume that learning expectations are limited to an arbitrary age period. We can continue to explore new frontiers, refine our skills, and "mature" long into our adult years. This discovery has ushered in the concept of "lifelong learning."

Although there are indeed many developmental changes during the first eighteen years of life, few of those changes are complete. In fact, adjustment in thinking patterns occur over the next several decades of an individual's life span. There may be some realignment of abilities to compensate for decline in certain areas or to respond to specific "crisis" situations. But there can be overall growth and a degree of qualitative improvement on some functioning levels.

The recognition that learning is an ongoing process throughout the entire life cycle has brought about a healthy shift in emphasis in the field of human development. For example, where universities once taught a plethora of courses on childhood and adolescence, many of those institutions are now flooded with requests for an "adult development" curriculum. Some schools are expanding their faculty to meet the need for continued study in this important area of developmental research.

The integration of Christian theology with empirical data about human development can further enhance our understanding. The Bible talks about the Christian life as a dynamic process of continued growth. The new believer is described as a spiritual child, a babe in Christ (1 Peter 2:2). When Paul addressed the church in Corinth, he was dismayed that he could not speak to them as spiritual adults but as "infants in Christ" who were "not yet ready for solid food" (1 Cor. 3:1–2).

Paul's expectation was that they should have grown toward spiritual maturity as believers under the control of the Holy Spirit. Paul provides the goal of spiritual development as "becoming mature, attaining to the whole measure of the fullness of Christ. Then we will no longer be infants. . . . We will in all things grow up into him who is the Head" (Eph. 4:13–15). In addition, the writer of the Book of Hebrews was obviously frustrated by the lack of spiritual development of his adult readers for he writes that "though by this time you ought to be teachers, you need someone to teach you the elementary truths of God all over again. You need milk, not solid food!" (Heb. 5:12).

These biblical writers addressed their messages to adults, with the expectation that their audience still had the capacity to change—to grow, learn, and develop in a multitude of areas. The person you are now is not the same as the person you were five years ago. (At least, you shouldn't be!) You have changed in many ways you may not even recognize. Some of these changes are unavoidable, like those that occur physiologically. But others reflect circumstances and society's influence in your life. Those changes—for better or worse—occur as we let them happen and make choices along the way.

Passage through adulthood is not smooth sailing on an artificial lake where the surface is constant and the climate conditions are regulated and controlled. It is more like a white-water rafting experience. There are times of great stress and turmoil when we must progress from one level of development to another. Then there may be a brief respite as we glide calmly along. The danger comes if we expect the remainder of our trip to be this relaxing, for just around each bend is the potential for another set of rapids.

As mentioned in chapter 2, probably one of the most well-known models of human development was presented by Daniel Levinson, who theorized that all people progress through four major phases of development. He calls each phase an era: Childhood and Adolescence (0–17), Early Adulthood (22–40), Middle Adulthood (45–60), and Late Adulthood (65–death). Each era is presumably preceded by a five-year period of transition, which enables the person to become a more mature individual. Probably the most familiar transition phase is the period between the early-adult and middle years. (This period has been labeled "midlife crisis" by some, "the crazies" by others.) A transition period involves looking back over the recent years, while at the same time anticipating events that may lie ahead. It is a type of border zone that allows one to reflect and to review life up to that point. For some people it is a valuable time of reappraisal, an opportunity to refocus energies and evaluate one's resources. For others it is a time of pain and anxiety, particularly if the early-adult years were characterized by lost opportunities, regret, and failure. If the emphasis is on looking back, the chances are great that negative emotions and nonconstructive thinking patterns will be dominant.

Some degree of self-examination is healthy, for it forces us to question whether or not we are living up to our maximum potential. In essence this means determining if we are being good stewards of the resources that God has temporarily entrusted to us. It is when this evaluation of our progress concentrates on superficialities that many of the extremes associated with "midlife crisis" begin to occur. The most commonly noted example is the man who suddenly announces that he is quitting his job, leaving his wife and family, buying a sports car, and planning to marry a woman half his age. Many of these radical personality changes are temporary, but the consequences of *any* rash behavior can be long term.

As previously noted, many of the popular views of human development are based on the marriage model. That is—if you want to understand adult development—you must observe adults in the context of family life. This is where the traditional explanations of adult development break down for most single adults, since they have a difficult time finding themselves on some of the charts and diagrams espoused by the researchers and popular commentators. Some of the common experiences and concerns of single adults are missing from these schematics and generalizations.

Culture-Induced Singles Anxiety

The lack of empirical data about "singleness" has raised some interesting questions. Is there, for example, a "typical" singles state of mind? Does being single, especially if never married, represent an incomplete, less than optimum, state—a failure to develop normally as a human being? What contribution, if any, can singles make to the overall health and productivity of a culture that is essentially family-oriented? Indeed, does the growing incidence of unmarried people in the general population portend a breakdown of society, a rejection of time-honored values?

For many singles, such valid concerns translate into a culture-induced pressure toward marriage, even an identity crisis of sorts that may elicit self-doubts and varying degrees of anxiety about being unmarried. The level of anxiety tends to fluctuate with age and reflects differences in gender and life experiences, regardless of whether or not the individual has chosen to forego marriage (or remarriage), has not yet found a suitable partner, or has merely delayed making a lifetime commitment for any number of other reasons. (See fig. 4.1).

Because generalizing about complex issues is one way our mental processes deal with reality, we usually set standards of acceptability when dealing with human behavior. Thus, following the lead of traditionalists and (more recently) psychosociologists, we have always tended to judge an individual at least in part according to the position he or she holds on

Fig. 4.1
Anxiety about Marriage

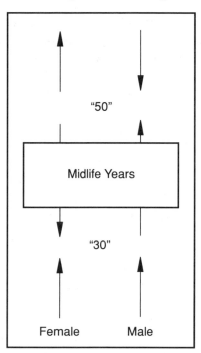

a chart of so-called normal human development. That is to say, for example, a fifteen-year-old is expected to begin going through certain changes associated with adolescent "rites of passage," as perhaps illustrated in the movie *American Graffiti*. Similarly, at nineteen, a "normal" young person is preparing to leave home for college, military service, or a career opportunity. The added implication is that he or she will also be searching for a mate and looking forward to starting a family. Everyone is supposed to be pigeonholed into a role that reflects certain, often arbitrarily defined, cultural directives. Individuals that do not follow those rules are labeled "misfits," if not "social outcasts," as were the beatniks and hippies of recent decades.

According to such standards, there continues to be strong cultural pressure for young Americans to opt for marriage. Especially for females, marriage is usually portrayed as a norm, a desirable goal to be achieved as soon as possible. In colonial times, girls were getting married as early as twelve. By the mid-fifties, more women were entering the workplace and some of the purely economic reasons for marriage had been removed. However, even then, if a girl graduating from high school was not already wearing an engagement ring, people often wondered what was wrong with her. More recently, young women increasingly continue their education beyond high school and have career goals of their own. The pressure for an early marriage may be somewhat reduced—but "finding a husband" is still portrayed as a long-term assignment. For men, too, getting married is a traditional benchmark of our culture. Although this "rule" may be unwritten and unenforceable, it is a behavioral expectation nonetheless.

Never-married single adults who choose to delay marriage fall off the "normal" chart of adult experience. They are often left feeling out of place in society, wondering if they have missed their boat. This is a reaction expressed by many of the young single adults we interviewed.

Our interviews with hundreds of singles revealed an almost unanimous response to specific questions about feelings and reactions to situations described below.

Mary, a college senior at a Christian university said, "The first couple of years of school were fun. I dated quite a bit and had a lot of opportunities to go out with guys, but none of them became serious. Now that I am a senior my parents are putting on the pressure to find a Christian guy who wants to get married. This leaves me wondering if I wasted those earlier years having fun when I should have been trying to find a mate. If I graduate and go home without a fiance, maybe I'm letting my parents down."

Society expects everyone to reach their benchmarks on time. Some choose not to follow the blueprint—the average age for first marriages in America today is twenty-seven. Nevertheless, many young women are anxious about their marriage prospects, especially between the ages of twenty and thirty. By age thirty a woman who is still unmarried will begin to accept the realization that she may never marry. She may say to herself, "There are twelve million more single women than single men, so some of us will have to learn to live without a mate." A significant internal change begins at this point if she can also say, "I better quit spending so much time and energy trying to find a man and start getting on with my life." This may not mean that she wants to remain single, but it does represent a shift in her thinking pattern.

The single adult male faces a similar anxiety pattern, although usually a few years later. Many young men, facing the pressure to go on for advanced academic degrees, want to delay a marriage commitment until they have finished their education and undertaken a few years of career development. This way, they figure, they can provide a good foundation for a stable relationship. Many unattached men in their twenties are simply having fun, "traveling around the world with a backpack," if only in their imaginations. They wish to explore new frontiers before taking on the responsibilities of married life.

Devin, a twenty-five-year-old bank loan officer put it this way, "When I was in college, I realized if I wanted to be successful, I was going to have to concentrate on my education and get the necessary degrees. I kept my dating relationships pretty superficial. When I got out of school and landed this job at the bank, I found that I had some extra money left over each month that I could use for fun. I've been out of school for quite a while now, but I'm still not ready to lose all the freedom that being single gives me."

Our interviews indicate that Devin's attitude will probably change in a few years. (In fact, Devin got married four years after we interviewed him.) A single male may not experience the urgency to marry until his late twenties. Until then, he concentrates on building his career and leaving ample time for play. But, shortly after reaching thirty, a man like Devin will begin to reexamine his commitment to living as a "swinging single." Many of his peers will have married; some are enjoying parenthood. As he begins to ask questions about his lifestyle, a young bachelor typically feels somewhat anxious most noticeably during his thirties. He has done much of what he wanted to do during those unattached years and is now ready to settle down into a meaningful and intimate relationship.

When never-married single adults enter their thirties, they differ in the way they respond to their singleness. Females, now resigned to the realization that they may never get married, often plunge head-on into career development. Some singles may pursue an academic degree, become active volunteers in a church or civic organization, develop a satisfying hobby, or accept a promotion at work that they had turned down earlier. These women often may excel in their jobs, which now become a primary source of their identity. The affirmation they experience in their careers or hobbies gives them a deeper sense of purpose and meaning. This causes a decrease in the "must get married" anxiety they faced in their twenties.

For single males, however, the situation is quite different. The anxiety about singleness continues to build, and they may relentlessly search for the perfect mate. Society says it is all right to be a bachelor in one's twenties, but if a man is still single in his thirties, he is probably irresponsible or unstable. (See chapter 8 for a detailed discussion on some common myths and misconceptions of single living.)

Men who want to get married to avoid certain negative social stereo-types look with increased fervor for a mate. What they find is that many of the women of their age group are no longer so eager for marriage, because they have learned to live quite well without a male partner. In fact, some of these women are now making more money than their male counterparts. The men may want to get married and settle down, but the women may not be interested in a permanent relationship. This con-tributes to a significant identity struggle for men during this period of their lives.

As both genders of never-married adults pass into their forties, each is subject to a diversity of physical changes that parallel those of their mar-ried friends. For the average woman, her degree of singleness-anxiety is usually on the decrease, whereas the male's concern about the matter may continue to rise. When they emerge out of early midlife and approach fifty, both will again face different responses to their unmarried condition.

Our interviews revealed that by the time an unmarried woman reaches her fifties, it is not unusual for her to experience renewed con-cerns, if not anxiety or regrets, about spending the rest of her life as a single. For a few, the very idea may bring on a sense of panic, rather than happy anticipation of carefree retirement years. This woman usually believes (and is probably correct) that she will most likely spend those years alone or, at best, in the company of other unattached females. Even in the case of a previously married single woman, her grown children (if any) have families and concerns of their own that do not necessarily leave room for her in their lives. By the time they are sixty, unmarried women may comment on the lack of available male companionship, even if all they really have in mind is sharing a restaurant meal or theater outing. But many women in these age groups are remarkably happy, resilient, and well-adjusted regardless of whether or not they were previ-ously married.

On the other hand, a single man past fifty, and into the retirement years, usually finds himself in great demand socially and thus less apt to dwell on his unmarried state. The gender-related longevity factors that have caused a higher proportion of women in this age group have worked in his favor. There are plenty of women of all ages to go around, especially for a man who is healthy, financially secure, and unencum-bered by family responsibilities. In fact, such a man may feel better about himself than he has in years! For the never-married, this is often enough to banish any lingering regrets about not marrying, so there is far less urgency to change his status than in the previous decade of his life.

Seemingly this man has successfully challenged one of society's bench-marks. On the more practical level, a never-married man has probably learned to handle all the "homemaking" chores normally assigned to a wife. So why marry? (A widower of this age, however, may urgently seek marriage, if only to duplicate the loving husband-wife sharing that worked so well for him in the past).

Gender Differentiation

Every human being periodically looks in a mirror and asks, "Who am I?" The answers to that question form one's self-image, which may not necessarily be a realistic portrait. Both our true qualities and our perception of them depend on a combination of factors: genetic/physical characteristics, family background, the socioeconomic culture in which we were raised, peer influence, significant life events, and a host of other variables. But even *erroneous* ideas about ourselves have much to do with the way we relate to others and how we plan our lifetime goals. One important concept we learn at an early age is that there are gender differences that go beyond our physical attributes as male or female.

For the members of agricultural societies, gender role assignment was based primarily on physiological realities—the strength advantage of men and the childbearing function of women. Man was to be the hunter or breadwinner; woman, the nurturing keeper-of-the-hearth. In today's technological societies those responsibilities are more divided, but there remains the notion that males and females should follow circumscribed cultural norms. Young girls are still expected to mother their doll families, and boys, after all, are just being boys if they prefer more physical and often "violent" playtime. This gender differentiation solidifies as we grow older, or it may be modified by changing cultural standards, but it is included in our world view—our general expectations, attitudes, and values.

Even in a supposed age of gender equality and individual freedom, children are still taught what it means to be "male" or "female." For the former, this usually focuses on job aspirations. When asked, "What do you want to be when you grow up?" a little boy may answer, "Policeman (or fireman, doctor, sea captain)." If his answer is a traditionally male occupation, he is complimented on his choice. If he fulfills his goal later, his very identity is determined by his profession. Thus, "Who am I?" elicits an "I am an engineer (or whatever)" response. It is in their career roles that most men find their significance as a person.

Fortunately, the image of what is a proper, socially acceptable role is becoming less restricted by gender factors, but there remains considerable resistance to eliminating those barriers completely. Many females still answer the question of "Who am I?" (or "What do you want to be when you grow up?") with "A loving wife and mother." If little girls have been subtly taught that they are weak, frail, in need of protection, they will focus on finding a man they can lean on, someone who will take care of them forever. For them, marriage brings security; it establishes their identity—not as persons in their own right, but as someone's wife. "Just a housewife" may be the only answer they will ever have when questioned about their "career." Of course, that is perfectly fine *if* that is what they really want.

Such male/female norms have long been foundational to the structure and dynamics of American society, especially in the church. Despite ongoing reevaluation and revision of those standards, both genders generally work hard to achieve what their culture expects of them. Traditionally, a young man will busy himself with career building so he can achieve "status" and the wherewithal to establish a stable household for his intended wife. Meanwhile, at least in theory, a young woman is essentially marking time until she finds a supportive arm, that special man with whom she will form a lifetime partnership. A number of changes are taking place in that pattern, but its implications are still reflected in the behavior and attitudes of many singles, including those in our survey.

In mental and emotional makeup, too, society assumes that there are distinct differences between the sexes. Men are expected to be straightforward, direct, uncomplicated—to know where they are going and to get there without being diverted by self-doubts or emotional intrusions. After all, a man must be strong and make it to the top! Probably one of the worst disasters a man can face is job loss. (Remember, his very identity is defined by his profession.) Above all else, most men fear impotence—not necessarily sexual, but loss of strength, power, and effectiveness in the material world.

Women face different kinds of pressures. They are "allowed" to be more quixotic, unfathomable, emotionally bound. Thus, they can make sudden directional changes based on fleeting impulses or hunches that would—in a man—indicate irrational behavior or instability. They, too, have fears, mainly involving interpersonal relationships. Since many women find their sense of stability and security only in a marital commitment, they tend to make every effort to preserve that relationship, even at great personal cost. At the extreme, they will remain with an abusive partner because "otherwise I'd be alone."

Other gender differences are also widely accepted as truisms. For example, when a man is frustrated, when his self-image as a person of strength is threatened, he is expected to vent his emotions in an angry outburst. He may shout, bang on a table, even punch holes in a wall, and get away with it. But he is also expected to get past his emotions rather quickly. Women, according to the common view, respond to frustration with tears (a release considered improper for men). They can cry for hours, sometimes days, to release emotional pressure.

Figure 4.2 summarizes the traditional views about gender differences. Some of these may be entirely culturally determined, rather than genetic givens, and researchers and commentators continue the debate over the matter. Nevertheless, whether flawed generalizations or scientifically verifiable facts, these views continue to affect the lives of every man and woman.

Fig. 4.2
Gender Differences: *The Traditional View*

Central Issues	In Men	In Women
	Significance	Security
Progression	Fairly straightforward, relative consistency, orderly	Mosaic patterns, more options, sudden changes
Identity and self-esteem sources	Achievement	Relationships
Fear	Impotence	Loss
Responses to frustration	Anger	Depression

Self-limiting Preconceptions

Culturally defined gender differentiation partially explains why so many adults feel frustrated with their lives—why "Who am I?" and "Where am I going?" are hard to answer, especially for a woman. When a never-married or newly single woman faces her future, she is forced to make decisions about matters traditionally considered in the male domain. She must choose among educational and career options, allocate her financial resources according to housing, transportation, and other material needs, and make a host of other decisions that depend on sound judgment and conviction. If she is also a single parent, it is even more important that she make wise choices.

Where there is shared decision making, as in a marital partnership, there is at least the opportunity for discussion and feedback between the concerned parties. But a *single* adult bears the entire responsibility for his or her choices and problem solving. For a man, independent decisiveness may not seem a particularly awesome challenge. After all, has not tradition decreed that man is the breadwinner, the household head, the stronger, more rational gender? On the other hand, for a woman today, life demands more than the frailty, dependency, and emotional sentimentality that past generations defined as "femininity." She must learn to live beyond the doubts about her own competency and accept all challenges with courage. Most single women learn these lessons well; a few are unfairly hampered by preconceived notions of gender roles.

Men, too, can be victimized by flawed cultural expectations. For example, is it abnormal for a man to solidify his identity through a personal relationship rather than through his profession? Is a man weak, thus unmanly, if he weeps over a loss? Can a "real man" be a sentimental romantic? Is there a valid prototype for maleness?

It is obvious that society must rewrite some of its personality and cultural norms. Many women have proven their decision-making abilities—their skills as executives, administrators, and negotiators in the home and in the community at large. And some men need relationships to function most efficiently and fulfill their happiness quota. They feel no particular urgency to climb a corporate ladder to establish their personhood.

For a Christian, of course, there is biblical revelation to guide our search for identity. Yes, we were created either male or female, *each* in the image of God. On the basis of Scripture, humanity can best be seen as representing in a yet imperfect way all the qualities of the Creator. But, since each individual is also unique in the degree to which he or she reflects those attributes, even our differences are divinely decreed. There may indeed be inherent gender distinctives in mental abilities, personality characteristics, and role assignments that are truly ordained by God. That is still a matter of theological and scientific debate. Until such issues are resolved (which will not be until eternity), we are fully "human" only as we free ourselves from the questionable, self-limiting restrictions imposed by an imperfect society.

Two

Plotting a Sensible Course

Before proposing some guidelines that will ensure a safe and rewarding singles passage through the mainstreams of contemporary American society, it seems wise to plot a course that reflects what we have already learned about the waterway. Therefore, the first chapter in this section will trace the historical socioeconomic and political factors that have brought singles to their place of influence in today's culture. We will also examine a few theories about why the percentage of singles in the general population continues to increase.

With that as our background, we will examine in chapter 6 some current trends and concerns among singles—the impact of singles on the economy and their spending habits, housing arrangements, social life, sexual practices, and spiritual commitment. Most of our generalizations about this group are drawn from data analyses of responses to our Singles in America survey and our interviews with singles. Some of these conclusions are amplified by other research results and by the popular literature, although those sources do not focus on the Christian single, as our study does. We will also factor out gender differences that seemed to exist in some of the questionnaire responses. Many of the issues touched on in this chapter will be examined in more detail in subsequent sections.

Finally, because the theme of our search was the behavior and attitudes of *Christian* singles, in chapter 7 we present the singles lifestyle from a biblical perspective. The Word of God has much to say about how a single may best realize his or her full potential as an individual without sacrificing spiritual commitment. We trust that "Singles and Scripture" will be helpful to those singles who may question God's purpose for their lives and wish to serve him in ministering to others.

5

The History
of Singles
in America

I n any given society, the incidence and relative importance of singles
usually fluctuates over time according to social, economic, religious,
and political changes within that culture. In many of today's industri-
ally developed nations, especially in the United States, the percentage of
singles in the population is at an all-time high. There has been a corresponding rise in the general public's "acceptance" of the singles lifestyle,
although (as chapter 8 will show) there are misconceptions about that
lifestyle. To predict where singles may be heading in the future, we need
first to understand the historical factors that have brought them to where
they are today.

Chronological Review

In colonial America there was great economic and religious pressure
to be married. Since large families were needed to populate and shape
the new country, it was undesirable and impractical to be single. In
some localities it was considered unlawful or civilly disobedient to
remain single; women who were widowed found town leaders planning
their remarriage before the funeral or bereavement process was over.
For women, the average age at first marriage was about thirteen. There
were fewer women than men, so there was rarely a problem finding a
husband.

As America emerged as an independent nation and expanded its borders, its population and social structure changed. Diverse ethnic groups
comprised the "melting pot" nation, but that nation continued to

endorse marriage and the nuclear family unit as an ideal. Throughout
the nineteenth century, parents of single daughters were always on the
lookout for suitable single men, who were encouraged to make their
choice and settle down as soon as possible. Bachelors were often incor-
porated into these families until they established households of their
own. Once a single woman no longer seemed likely to find a husband,
she was referred to as spinster, or "old maid," derogatory terms that indicated a diminished social status. Unmarried women usually remained in
the family home to provide unpaid services as household helpers, tutors,
or companions. Most females found it impossible to become economically self-sufficient until the late nineteenth century, when increasing
numbers took jobs as "factory girls" in the wake of the Industrial Revolution. Working conditions were poor and pay scales low, even in the traditional "women's professions" of nursing and teaching. Marriage was
indeed a desirable objective for women. For men, too—since in a society
that retained many elements of an agricultural or home-based economy,
being married was a practical necessity and a way of establishing one's
social importance.

Throughout the 1800s, as America moved from infancy to maturity as
a nation, only 3 or 4 percent of its population was single. Religious,
social, and economic institutions continued to endorse marriage-and-
family ideals. Most people married early, the widowed remarried rather
promptly, and divorce was virtually unknown.

The twentieth century would bring lasting changes to the cultural
scene. In the early 1900s, America was a nation of yet-untapped economic and human resources. Before 1920, singles represented a very
small part of the population, but several events would soon affect that
ratio. World War I had called many men into military service; the
women they left behind needed to take on new responsibilities, both at
home and in the workplace. Following the war, there were fewer "available" men, and the single-woman population increased. Although a college education was still beyond the aspirations of most women, there
were many jobs opening up for them in the economic boom of the Roar-
ing Twenties. (The "flappers" of that decade in many ways symbolized
women's new independence.) Some women no longer opted for an
immediate marriage after secondary school. They took jobs in the limited
fields open to them and had brief encounters with breadwinning, even
self-sufficiency. Most women did marry within a few years, and it was
unusual for them to work outside the home unless it was necessary to
supplement the husband's income. Increasingly, "singleness" was a force
to be reckoned with—but marriage was still the norm.

The Great Depression of the 1930s began an economic trend that would affect the averages for marital age and family size. Now it was permissible for young men and women to delay marriage to participate in providing for their younger siblings. Among the already married, birth rates declined in the face of economic instability. During the thirties, about one-third of the population was single.

By the time World War II erupted, men and women alike were "allowed" to be unmarried and even encouraged to stay single. Women, both married and single, were invited to drop their stay-at-home orientation and welcomed into the labor force. As women discovered the satisfaction inherent in a paycheck and a job well done, their aspirations began to change. The men were away, of course, so marriage and birth rates were low during the wartime years of 1941 to 1945.

However, an interesting phenomenon took place after the close of the war. The soldiers returned home from Europe, the Pacific, and—later—Korea, eager to establish family life. Marriages hit an all-time high. By the mid-1950s, couples were entering marriage at the youngest age since record-keeping began. Since women were encouraged to return to the home and remain there, men were to be the chief (if not *only*) providers for their families. These marriages launched the Baby Boom era of the fifties. Marriage and family were once again primary objectives to be actively pursued by everyone. Only about 4 percent of the population was single at this time, roughly equivalent to the colonial period.

By the late fifties, divorce had begun to distort the cultural model of happy marriage and family solidarity. The never-married singles category increasingly included significant numbers of the divorced and separated, a trend that would continue over the next few decades.

The decade of the 1960s saw the children of these broken marriages growing up and challenging the marital ideal. Although it was predicted that all but a small percentage of these young people would eventually marry, as their parents had, by the end of the decade the marriage rate among single persons under forty-five years of age was as low as it had been at the end of the Great Depression.

During the "hippie movement," sexual activity outside of marriage became more common, removing that factor as one answer to "Why get married?" The growing demand for gender equality encouraged women to stand on their own, get in touch with their own strengths, and not rely on marriage and family as their sole source of security and identity. Marriage was still seen as a desirable objective by most men and women, but self-fulfillment and gratification were increasingly important motivations.

The 1970s saw a generation of now-adult baby-boomers who, having enjoyed all the benefits provided by their parents in a relatively affluent era, now sought independence and personal freedom, often apart from the married state. "Singles" became a familiar term in the culture's vocabulary and its use often carried a positive connotation. Independence, sexual freedom, and financial stability, now available outside of marriage, became highly valued goals. By 1977, one-third of the American population was single, including the never-married, divorced or separated, and widowed. The increase in numbers of broken marriages was discouraging many singles from getting married in the first place or at least delaying that decision. Women, especially, were questioning whether marriage was necessary to ensure their happiness. More women than ever before were attending college, pursuing postgraduate degrees, and/or entering professions previously considered suitable only for men. Seemingly, the "good life" was possible outside of marriage. Many of these women had also decided against having children, so—again—"Why get married?"

By 1987 there were 65 million singles in America, with 40 percent of those being men and 60 percent women. The singles phenomenon continues to increase in significance. The average age of first marriages in 1989 was 27.5, partially explaining why there is a greater number of singles than at any other point in our history (see figs. 5.1 and 5.2). Singles have become almost half of the entire population. Predictions suggest that in the early 1990s the married population will be in the minority. Singles have become an accepted segment of the American population, and they are no longer hindered (as they once were) by social stigma and economic disadvantages.

Fig. 5.1
American Households

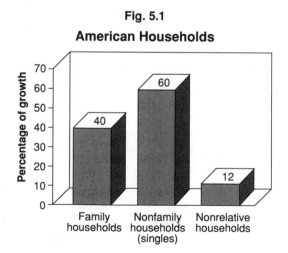

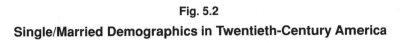

Fig. 5.2

Single/Married Demographics in Twentieth-Century America

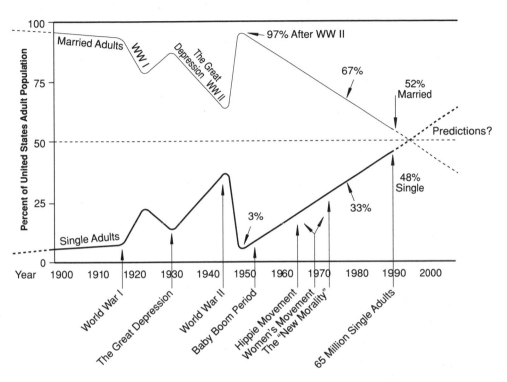

Socioeconomic Explanations

Why are there so many single adults today in America? Or—to put it another way—why does it seem so undesirable or impractical for people to get married and so difficult to *stay* married?

There are nearly as many reasons as there are single adults. Among the theories most often cited to explain the rising singles population are the growing economic independence of women, the high divorce rate, the increase in longevity (which increases the numbers of widows and widowers), more reliable birth control (and thus sexual freedom), the social acceptance of cohabitation without a marriage commitment, and the emphasis on career achievement.

Perhaps the reason heard most often relates to simple economics. As women have been the recipients of more education, moved into the workplace, and become capable of supporting themselves in far greater numbers than ever before, they have felt much less pressure to get married to achieve financial security.

Elaine Tyler May, who explored the marriage and divorce rates from 1880 to 1930 in *Great Expectations: Marriage and Divorce in Post Victorian America*, attributes the growing preference for the singles lifestyle to the women's movement, the political activism of the 1960s, and the spirit of social reform as demonstrated in the civil rights movement. These cultural trends have played a large part in some individuals' desire to remain single so they could channel their energy into more altruistic, society-oriented, and/or lasting enterprises.

Another theory is presented by Warren Farrell, author of *Why Men Are the Way They Are*. He believes men are increasingly reluctant to marry because of what they perceive as numerous inequalities in modern marriage: "Men are finding more incentive to be single because they feel commitment creates an unequal promise." He goes on to say, "Let's say a successful woman meets a successful man. From his perspective, the successful woman is saying, 'I would like three options before we commit: to continue my success as a career woman, to be involved full time with my family, or some combination of the two.' He sees he has only one option: work full time, work full time, or work full time."

Another popular view regarding a purpose for delaying marriage comes from Paul Glick, Census Bureau veteran and noted demographic scientist who is now adjunct professor of sociology at Arizona State University. He believes postponing marriage is due in part to the huge number of options available to adults today that in essence "replace marriage." One such option is cohabitation. Glick writes, "People are going to school longer, they're becoming more independent in their thinking, they are less likely to be tradition minded. They are likely to accommodate the [marital status] situation to their own interests and preferences. There's more tolerance of variation from the norm, and this is one demonstration of that."

Cohabitation is a popular alternative for many people before they rush into a marriage that statistics show has a limited chance of survival. According to Larry Bumpass, a demographer for the University of Wisconsin, "In virtually half of all marriages, people have lived together before they were married and about half of all people in their thirties have lived with someone outside of marriage." Bumpass also discovered that only 60 percent of those who cohabited before marriage with the intent of eventually getting married ever followed through with the ceremony.

One of America's most noted researchers of single-adult development,

Peter Stein, a professor of sociology at William Paterson College, believes that the existence of multiple sources of support is the key reason for not getting married. Says Stein, "Marriage may be No. 6 on their agenda, but not No. 1." He elaborates on his theory by commenting, "I see people who choose singlehood as developing a viable alternative lifestyle where the focus may be on career, education, relationships, political activities, community involvements—a number of issues." In other words, instead of having only a marriage partner for emotional support, sexual fulfillment, recreational outings, intellectual stimulation, and companionship, a single adult may have a different person for each support need.

One prominent theory about the falling marriage rate involves "relationship burnout." The idea is that single adults go through a series of intimate relationships that fail, ending up with the feeling that love can never be trusted. Single adults need to learn how to enjoy intimate relationships without the fear of failure or rejection. And, if the relationship should end, they must learn to see the positive elements for growth and personal development instead of the more damaging and negative attitudes that often result.

Whatever the reasons for remaining single these days, the unmarried population is apparently viewed with less suspicion than in previous eras. In record numbers adults across America are choosing to remain single. This, in turn, has had a profound effect on the culture distinctives of the current generation. In the remaining chapters of this book we will explore some of these changes and determine how this knowledge can help us reach out and minister most effectively to single adults.

6

Variables
in the
Singles Lifestyle

The "singles lifestyle" is a popular descriptive phrase in America today. It is certainly obvious that there have been some major changes in the makeup of our contemporary society. The United States Census Bureau confirms this. According to Steve Rawlings, a Census Bureau family demographer, about 41 percent of all adults of marriageable age (15 and older) are now single (Krier, 1988). Our culture is indeed changing, and most people have come a long way in their acceptance of the singles lifestyle as a valid exception from the norm of society. Although our society was founded on the concept of the nuclear family, "The numbers [of singles] are so high that we've begun to accept the idea of non-traditional households as being normal," says Susan Hayward of the Yankelovich Clancy Shulman market-research company.

But what exactly is the "singles lifestyle"? What are the characteristics of these non-traditional households? There are, of course, many variables, but there are also enough similarities that describe how singles tend to organize their lives and habits that we can make several generalizations about the group as a whole.

Singles and the General Economy

Even back in 1974, *U.S. News and World Report* stated that "millions of unmarried Americans are creating a new lifestyle that is affecting every part of the country and the effects are widening. Singles, including those raising children, now make up over one of every three households in the U.S. Changes resulting from these trends are showing up in a variety of

54

ways. Already, potential slums are being revitalized by affluent singles seeking urban excitement and convenience. Businesses are revising 'family style' products to offer singles everything from more condominiums to single-serving soup cans." Stouffer's alone now makes eighty-six different frozen foods designed to feed one person. Single adults are busy buying everything it took their parents years to be able to afford. Singles are buying more expensive cars than married adults; some of the most expensive cars today are purchased by single men who want to impress their friends with their affluence. Single adults are also the largest purchasers of clothes.

This designed-for-singles trend carries over to kitchen and other household appliances. From coffee makers to microwaves, manufacturers have responded to the demand for products that are convenient for singles living. Even washers and dryers have been reduced enough in size to fit into the smallest of apartment closets. There is no mistaking the impact that singles have had on urban living and thus on what is available in the marketplace.

Singles are demanding (and often getting) an end to policies that favor couples and families in tax payments, insurance plans, bank loans, and air fares. "What this means is that for some time to come, all of us are going to be living in a world comprised to a far greater extent of people living alone and liking it," says Joseph Peritz, a pollster and market analyst in New York City. He further observes, "This is a trend with enormous implications for business, government and everyone else in our society."

Although the figure today no doubt is much higher, *U.S. News and World Report* (October 7, 1974) reported, "Unmarried adults are worth over 200 billion dollars to firms with the right products—and their influence on business is growing fast. More and more businessmen are drawing a bead on a rapidly growing and free-spending group of American consumers—the singles. Single people make up the largest concentrated pool of sales in the country today." This emphasis can make all the difference in whether or not a product line is successful. Market analysts are busily assessing the needs of single adults with the intention of developing products that will appeal to them, whether it is furniture, automobiles, clothes, beer and wine, or insurance.

What makes these single adults especially attractive to manufacturers is their impulsive buying habits. Since many single adults don't hesitate to buy something they are momentarily attracted to, much of their income goes for luxury goods. Comments James C. Arthur, president of

Arthur & Wheeler, a Chicago advertising agency, "Singles would rather have a Rolls-Royce than a Dow Jones."

The economic impact is also seen in the housing industry. The American dream of owning a home is as much of a challenge for the single adult as for his married neighbor and no less a goal. Accordingly, houses are being made smaller and designed around a central-neighborhood theme to accommodate the millions of single adults who are tired of apartment dwelling. The homeowning dream is coming true for singles, who in record numbers are moving into condominiums, townhouses, duplexes, and small single-family homes.

A 1986 *USA Today* front-page article noted that of the 86.8 million households in America, 42 percent were headed by single adults. Our Singles in America survey (Q. 9-11) indicated that 36 percent owned their own home or condominium, 22 percent rented a condominium (or house), and 28 percent rented an apartment. The remainder had a variety of other living arrangements, which included house-sitting or living with parents. (See fig. 6.1.)

Fig. 6.1
Singles in America Survey:
Housing Accommodations

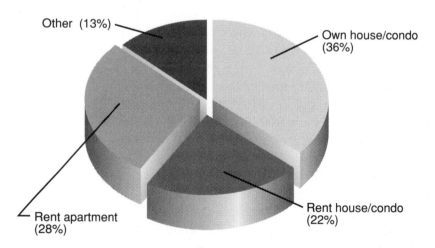

Other (13%)

Own house/condo (36%)

Rent apartment (28%)

Rent house/condo (22%)

Not just the contractors are cashing in on this affluent cross section of modern America. Bankers, brokers, retailers, restauranteurs, publishers, and clothiers are all trying to capitalize on this lucrative market. Travel agents are finding the single adult to be a valued customer, as so many of them are applying the fruits of their labor to such pleasures as an annual winter ski trip to Canada and a summer vacation at Club Med in the Caribbean or European touring.

Publishers find an enthusiastic market for articles and books that will appeal to these avid readers. Contemporary single adults are more educated than their ancestors; with this background comes a thirst for books on every subject—from home repair to health care to relationships. It is not uncommon to see displays of magazines, books, calendars, and how-to guides especially for singles.

Housing Arrangements and Spending Habits

In contemporary society single adults have a variety of relationships and living accommodations. Brown (1980) provides an overview of these arrangements (see fig. 6.2).

Fig. 6.2

Age Factors and General Lifestyle

Age	Proximity to Others	Marital Status	Parental Status
Young	Living alone	Never married	No children
Midlife	Living with roommate	Casual relationships (intimate but not romantic)	A need for children
Older	Living with lover/spouse	Coupled/separated	Full-time parent
Elderly	Living with family, living with community	Married, divorced, widowed	Part-time parent, barred from children, children grown

As previously mentioned, the spending habits of single adults are changing the face of American business. There are significant gender differences in totals spent and on what items. According to *American Demographics*, single women outspend men on apparel in all age groups except for men of ages 55 to 64. (The older men apparently purchase more clothing as gifts. Their higher level of spending made enough of a difference to put men over the top in total clothes spending.) This study, conducted by Stephanie Shipp, head of the analysis branch of Labor Statistics' Division of Consumer Surveys, also found that:

Single women spend a larger percent of their income on groceries for the home, housing, health-care services, and reading materials.

Single men spend a bigger percentage of their income on eating out, alcohol, transportation, entertainment, tobacco, and retirement plans.

Nearly 25 percent of a man's apparel budget goes toward gifts, compared to 14 percent for women.

Single women, when combining all age groups, are more likely to own their own home.

Single men outspend women on cars, car repairs, and other transportation. (Specific findings are included in fig. 6.3.)

Fig. 6.3

Average Annual Spending for Single Americans

All Singles:	Women	Men
Total	$11,102	$15,339
Food	1,587	2,288
Alcohol	131	195
Apparel	657	735
Under Age 25:	**Women**	**Men**
Total	$8,413	$10,172
Food	1,228	1,711
Alcohol	215	482
Apparel	751	558
Age 55–64:	**Women**	**Men**
Total	$12,440	$16,666
Food	1,796	2,554
Alcohol	92	384
Apparel	682	1,128

Source: American Demographics, April 1988

Singles Subgroups

Each "type" of single, as well as each individual, has specific concerns and characteristics that are influenced by such factors as age, gender, and financial condition. Whether an individual has never been married or has only recently entered the single state will affect that person's mindset, planning, and usually many of the practical aspects of his or her lifestyle.

The Never-married Adult

Adults who never marry may be single by choice or by circumstance. In the year 1970, approximately 15 percent of the single adult population had never been married. By the year 1988, that figure had increased to almost 20 percent. Figure 1.1 illustrates the percentage breakdowns for never-married, widowed, and divorced adults for the years 1970 until 1986. In 1989 the U.S. Census Bureau reported the total number of single adults in America (18 years or older) was 68,310,000, not including those who are separated. This is an increase of nearly 2 million over 1988. Of these 68 million singles, 39.9 million (58 percent) have never been married; 14.5 million (21 percent) are divorced; 13.7 million (20 percent) are widowed.

The Divorced Adult

Divorce has been an increasing reality in America and other parts of the world. Today one-half of all currently single women have been previously married. Once they are divorced, statistics show that they tend to be reluctant to remarry. Census figures indicate that the proportion of divorced (and not remarried) continues to be lower among men thirty-five to forty-four than among women of comparable age. Education and profession can be contributing factors. Women who have the most education and highest income may be less likely to marry or to continue in an unsatisfactory marriage. According to the research of Ihinger-Tallman and Pasley (*Remarriage* 1987), social class differentially affects remarriage for men and women. "Among divorced persons, education and income levels are negatively associated with remarriage for women and positively associated with remarriage for men. That is, women in lower classes remarry more often than women in higher classes" (p. 37). In 1987 the marriage rate fell to 9.9 per thousand, the lowest it has been since 1967. The divorce rate was 4.8 per thousand. As of 1987, demographers estimated that 50 percent of all first marriages would eventually end in divorce. The average length of time between first marriage and divorce is about seven years. While numbers can be interpreted in many ways, the bottom line here seems to be that marriage rates per population are slowing while the divorce rate is increasing. We believe this trend will continue for at least the foreseeable future.

The Separated Adult

Separation is probably the type of so-called singleness that is most difficult to describe or understand. It may be one of the most confusing periods of human existence, because the adult who is separated is caught between two worlds. While still legally married, the person is emotionally divorced and may be carrying painful scars and the burden of issues yet to be resolved. Even if a particular separated individual truly wants to permanently dissolve the marriage, there may be obstacles to divorce—religious objections, financial considerations, or a spouse who is creating roadblocks to finalizing the breakup. Whatever the circumstances, separation is a time of turmoil and ambivalence.

The ambivalence expresses itself in a variety of ways. Either partner (or both) may be caught in vacillating emotions about the marriage and about divorce as a suitable solution. There may still be thoughts about trying to salvage the marriage. Pressures from friends and relatives may further complicate matters. The separated adult is often struggling with feelings of guilt and rejection, general anxiety, worries about finances, questions about legal obligations, a loss of hope about the future, and a host of other concerns, especially if there are children in the marriage.

The Widowed Adult

A special 1974 United States Census Bureau report on marital status and living arrangements showed that almost three times as many women were then widowed (9.8 million) as divorced (3.6 million). In 1987 there were over 11 million widows and over 2 million widowers, a total that represents approximately 5 percent of the population of the United States.

Gender Differences Among Singles

Portrait of a Single Man

George Gilder (1974) analyzed federal studies and other statistical data for his book *The Naked Nomads*, in which he presented an alarming portrait of the single man. According to Census Bureau figures, single men earn far less than married men, are roughly twice as likely to commit crimes and go to jail, and die at a relatively early age. Although single men represented only 13 percent of the population at the time of Gilder's study, they committed 90 percent of the violent crimes. They also led in statistics related to suicide, mental illness, alcoholism, drug addiction, and venereal disease. Of those single men who were employed, only slightly more than 60 percent were on the job full time—a little higher than single women but about 20 percent behind married men. Mainly on the basis of these and other statistics as well as many personal interviews, Gilder describes this unattached man as an unmotivated wanderer, with no long-term sexual identity.

Although interesting (and frightening), Gilder's portrait of a single man has limited reference to our own Singles in America survey. First, we made no attempt to compare answers to our questionnaire with those of a married control group. More importantly, our study dealt specifically with only one segment of the singles population—those affiliated with the Christian church. We have assumed factors about one's lifestyle and value systems. That and other particulars related to our sampling technique undoubtedly explain why Gilder's startling statistics about crime, drug use, sexually related disease, income levels, and mental illness are not reflected in our results, analyses, and conclusions.

The single adult men in our study ranged in age from 18 to over 65, but 75 percent were between 18 and 49 years of age. Roughly 85 percent had some college experience; 60 percent had college degrees. This explains why 50 percent of our sample were termed "professionals" (i.e., doctor, teacher, attorney, engineer, etc.). Classified in another way, 62 percent were never married, 35 percent were divorced, 2 percent were widowers, and 2 percent were currently separated. Of those who were divorced at the time of our survey, 16 percent had been divorced between two to five years; 5 percent had been divorced over ten years.

Approximately 17 percent of our sampled men had an annual income of less than $10,000; 27 percent earned between $10,000 and $19,999; another quarter earned between $20,000 and $29,999. Of the remainder, about 17 percent had incomes between $30,000 and $39,999, about 9 percent earned between $40,000 and $49,999, and 6 percent made over $50,000.

About 33 percent of the men who responded to our questionnaire owned their own house or condominium; 22 percent rented a house; 27 percent rented an apartment; and the remainder indicated "other" housing arrangements (see fig. 6.4). Answers to our questionnaires revealed that almost half of our sampled men lived alone; 20 percent of the men lived with their parents; 25 percent lived with same sex roommate(s); 3 percent were currently living with roommates of the opposite sex; and 3 percent lived in a group home or commune.

The "most unpleasant" household duties of our sample were (1) cleaning the house, (2) managing the finances, (3) doing the laundry, and (4) cooking.

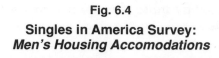

Fig. 6.4

Singles in America Survey:
Men's Housing Accomodations

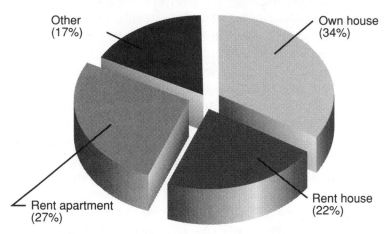

Other
(17%)

Own house
(34%)

Rent apartment
(27%)

Rent house
(22%)

These men agreed with virtually every other national study of singles when asked the question "What is the greatest disadvantage of being single for you?" Their number-one answer was loneliness. Other responses, in ranked order, included restricted sex and social life, a tendency to become self-centered and rigid, and experiencing the dating grind. When asked to respond to what they considered the greatest *advantages* of being single, their responses were (1) freedom and mobility, (2) time to pursue personal interests and hobbies, (3) social life in general, such as eating out, entertaining, and (4) privacy.

Fig. 6.5

Singles in America Survey:
Disadvantages of Singleness
for Men

1. Loneliness

2. Restrictions on sex life

3. Becoming self-centered

4. Having to experience the dating grind

"What is the greatest disadvantage of being single?"

Although a common myth about singles is that they are a mobile group and therefore a poor employment risk, our single-adult men were very stable in their employment history. Over 65 percent of them had remained in the same job or changed only once in the previous five years. They seem committed to their jobs since 50 percent of them devote over eight hours a day to their careers. About 80 percent said they enjoyed their jobs "often" or "most of the time." This is probably one of the factors that contributed to a fairly high level of "life satisfaction" among the men in our survey.

In terms of health, 80 percent of our male subjects exercise at least once or twice a week. Nearly 20 percent spend an hour a day or more in some form of physical activity. These men socialize frequently, although not always with members of the opposite sex. Many are involved in health clubs where they go to stay physically fit and meet with male friends; some say they go to health clubs to meet women. When asked where they meet members of the opposite sex, they responded as follows: (1) church, (2) work, (3) health clubs, (4) school, and (5) singles bars.

When asked what they valued in a woman, the single men in our survey generally agreed on such attributes as sincerity, a good imagination, an interesting personality, a forgiving spirit, and a responsible attitude toward life.

When it came to sexuality, 34 percent of these single men were still virgins, although about an equal percentage had had four or more sexual partners, and 22 percent had lived with a member of the opposite sex. Nearly 10 percent had had 20 or more sexual partners. (See fig. 6.6.)

Fig. 6.6

Singles in America Survey:
Sexual Partners of Men and Women (Total Sample)

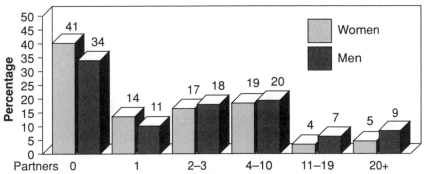

"As a single adult, with how many sexual partners have you had sexual intercourse?"

There was no attempt made to correlate our data on sexual activity with comparable figures for the general population of singles, either as to sexual "inexperience" (virginity), number of sexual partners, or any other measure of sexual practices about which our subjects were questioned. Can one assume that there are significant differences between the values and practices of a Christian versus a non-Christian in this or any other area that involves moral guidelines? Probably yes, but further research would be needed to validate any such hypothesis.

In any event, we did examine the spiritual life of our sampling in some depth. The single men in our study reported a high degree of spiritual commitment—85 percent attended church weekly. Since most took part in other church-related activities several times a week, they can be considered "active" in their church involvement. Many have assumed a leadership role, particularly in (but not limited to) the singles fellowship group. About 40 percent read the Bible on a daily basis; 75 percent pray every day; 35 percent tithe (10%) of their income.

It is interesting to note that—despite our subjects' Christian orientation—most of the men had not been leading the celibate life biblically ordained for an unmarried person. In light of the church's teaching, there may be some degree of guilt experienced by the subjects who reported being sexually active. However, although there were ten questions that examined the group's sexual practices, none focused on these subjects' *attitudes* toward the church's "rules" and their own behavior. (Refer to chapter 12 for a more detailed discussion of singles sexuality, including an elaboration of the many issues involved.)

Portrait of a Single Woman

Cockrum and White (1985) reported that the perils and pains of single adult living are not equally distributed among singles. Studies that they reviewed revealed that loneliness was more often experienced by men than by women. Women were more likely than men to establish systems of support for themselves and were therefore more inclined to experience higher levels of life satisfaction than men.

Sheehy (1976) comments on this gender difference in the "satisfaction" factor: "Between the ages of 25 and 34, there is not a great deal of difference in education, occupation, or income between single men and single women. But by the time they reach middle age, 46 to 54, the distance between them has stretched to a gulf. The single women are more educated, have higher average incomes, and work in more prestigious occupations. And it is not the old maid but the old bachelor who suffers from the poorest showing of psychological distress." The single women in our survey were similar in some ways to those studied by other researchers and characterized in the popular literature. Due to the nature of our sample, however, there were also some unique differences.

The single women we studied were between the ages of 18 and 65 plus. Roughly 70 percent were between the ages of 25 and 49. Most were college educated: 85 percent had college experience of some kind; of those, 52 percent had earned college degrees. When categorized by subgroup, 47 percent were never married, 42 percent were divorced, 8 percent were widows, and 1 percent were currently separated. The length of time currently single women were divorced varied from less than one year (11 percent) to more than ten years (23 percent). Approximately 42 percent had been divorced from four to ten years. Grouped by occupation, 52 percent of our single women were professionals or held managerial positions, 23 percent were clerical workers, and 4 percent were skilled workers. The remaining were in sales, service work, or homemakers.

The data regarding women's income is presented in figure 6.7. It was interesting to note that 38 percent of these single women own their own house or condominium. This was a somewhat higher percentage than among the men, where it was 33 percent. We don't know why this is the case, but it is possible that divorce settlements may have played a part in this finding. Furthermore, 61 percent of our single women lived alone (compared to almost 50 percent of the men). Only 14 percent lived with their parents, and 2 percent were currently living with a member of the opposite sex. The most "unpleasant" household duties cited were (1) car maintenance, (2) cleaning the house, (3) managing the finances, and (4) doing the laundry.

These women agreed with the men in our sample (and most other studies) that the greatest disadvantage of being single is living with loneliness. The next most important negatives for the women were financial insecurities, becoming self-centered, and having restrictions placed on their sex life (fig. 6.8).

Just as there were similarities among our men and women regarding the disadvantages of being a single adult, there were also similar responses regarding the advantages (fig. 6.9).

The women in our sample were about as stable in employment as the men; 70 percent had been in the same job or had moved only once during the previous five-year period. Nearly 20 percent of our women had a second job, compared to 13 percent of the men. Although the financial pressures these women were facing may have forced some into such a position, almost 70 percent of the women said they enjoyed their job all or most of the time.

Fig. 6.7
Singles in America Survey:
Income Levels

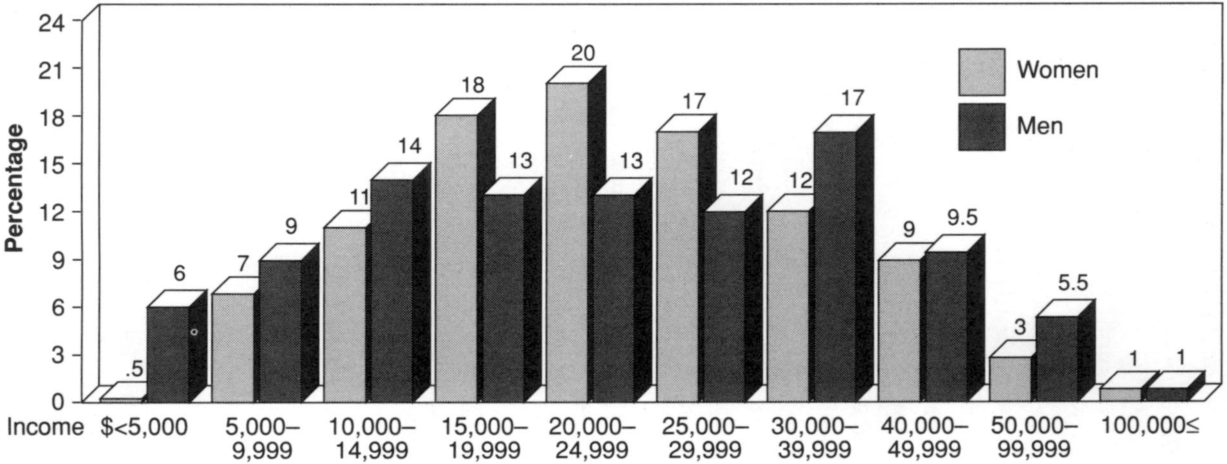

Fig. 6.8

Singles in America Survey:
Disadvantages of Singleness
for Women

1. Loneliness

2. Financial insecurities

3. Becoming self-centered

4. Restrictions on sex life

"What do you consider the greatest
disadvantage of being single?"

There was a significant difference between the perceived health of the women as compared to the men. In response to whether their health had changed over the previous five years, 85 percent of the men said it was the same or had changed for the better. Only 37 percent of the women felt the same way; half of them said that it was the same, and 21 percent that it had gotten worse. One possible reason for this difference may be the relatively higher level of emotional stress experienced by women because of financial insecurity, family pressure, and job discrimination. For the widowed, divorced, or separated single, there may also be parenting concerns that add to the general tension level, since most, though not all, single parents raising young children are women.

It may also be pertinent to the health findings that the women in our study exercised less often per week than their male counterparts. Whereas 18 percent of the men in our study exercised at least one hour a day, only 9 percent of the women had the same commitment to physical fitness. On average, the women got only half as much weekly exercise as the men.

Eleven questions in our study dealt with "social life." We found that

Fig. 6.9

Singles in America Survey: *Advantages of Singleness*

Women	Men
1. Mobility and freedom	1. Mobility and freedom
2. Time for personal interests	2. Time for personal interests
3. Social life in general	3. Privacy
4. Privacy	4. Social life in general

"What do you consider the greatest advantage of being single?"

half of the single women spend one to two hours each day "with friends." When they go out socially it is usually to a restaurant, a friend's house, a movie, or a church activity. As for their dating frequency, 19 percent go out once a week on a date; 25 percent twice a week; 17 percent, three times a week. This is not to say that all the single women we queried date very often. Over 50 percent of our respondents had not gone on a date in the month prior to our survey. See figure 6.10 for the usual places these women go to meet single men.

Fig. 6.10

Singles in America Survey:
Where Single Women Meet Men

1. Church

2. Work

3. Other (i.e. shopping, civic groups, clubs, etc.)

4. School

"Where do you meet members of the opposite sex?"

The sexual partnerings of our single women respondents were as interesting as those of our single men. Although 39 percent of our single women were virgins, 27 percent had had as many as four or more previous sexual partners, and 5 percent had had as many as twenty partners (the corresponding percentage for our male subjects was 10 percent). About 22 percent of these women had cohabited with someone of the opposite sex (about the same percentage as the men). Whereas 14 percent of our women had had sexual relations within the past six months, the comparable figure for the men was 23 percent.

At least some of the "major fears" reported by the women *may* be related to their new-found sexual freedom (see fig. 6.11).

Fig. 6.11

Singles in America Survey:
Single Women's Fears

1. Messing up my personal life

2. Being abandoned

3. Feeling that time is running out

4. No financial security

"At this stage in your life, what are your major fears?"

As we previously observed when reporting on the men's level of sexual practice, we are offering no comparable data for the non-Christian singles population. Without such information, any conclusions drawn about the relative chastity of the two groups or the degree of their sexual activity is purely speculative.

Because in our imperfect world there can be weakenings in even the firmest spiritual resolve. No one who ministers to or works with singles can simply assume that *Christian* singles are a sexually inactive group. Being human, churchgoing adults are subject to the same temptations that face non-Christians (although it is hoped that Christians can more effectively resist those impulses). Despite church teachings against sex outside of marriage, our study shows that single Christians are not necessarily celibate. Since the facts refute certain preconceptions, the church must be willing to examine all the related issues within the context of its theology and—more importantly—help its membership deal with the implications. (More on this topic in chapter 12.)

Paralleling what we learned about the men in our study, the women demonstrated a high degree of spiritual commitment. For example, almost 90 percent attend church on a regular basis. In fact, 60 percent attend two or three times a week. Daily Bible reading is practiced by 36 percent; 84 percent pray on a daily basis. Nearly 70 percent tithe between 1 to 10 percent of their income; 16 percent tithe at a higher rate.

Friendship and the Christian Single

Relationships, social interaction, camaraderie—in short, friendships—are probably no less important to Christian singles than they are

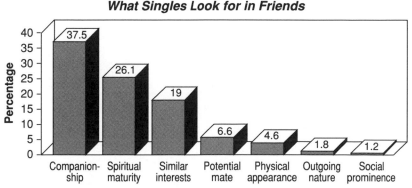

Fig. 6.12
Singles in America Survey:
What Singles Look for in Friends

"What do you look for in a relationship with a friend?"

to their non-Christian counterparts. As might be expected, when we asked our subjects what they looked for in a relationship with a friend, most cited "companionship," "spiritual maturity," or "similar interests," the usual qualities that underlie a friendship (see fig. 6.12). It is possible, of course, that the relative importance of "spiritual maturity" would be less in a nonchurch-oriented sampling.

Now that we have examined (in chapter 5) where singles have been in the past, and (in chapter 6) where they are now in terms of general lifestyle, it seems appropriate to sidetrack somewhat and consider where singleness as such fits into the general teachings of the Christian church. That will be the topic of our next chapter, "Singles and Scripture."

7

Singles
and Scripture

One of the most extraordinary features of Scripture is its amazing ability to transcend geographical and cultural boundaries and the passage of time. God's Word is not an outdated manual of rules written for a select minority living in ancient times. Although it is essentially a record of God's dealings with humankind over a span of several thousand years, its message is just as alive today. The scriptural principles of living are eternal, as binding on us as they were on the people to whom they were first revealed. In some areas the directives are quite specific; in others they provide a general guideline for the decisions we make in the twentieth century.

Hermeneutics, the science of biblical interpretation, is complex by its very nature, which means that a diversity of approaches must be employed to understand the intent of a particular passage. Context, of course, is of great importance. Individual verses must be seen not only with reference to the verses that precede and follow them in close order, but also in light of the entire biblical message. Furthermore, few of us can read the Bible in the language used by its writers, and we are not familiar with the culture of that time. Modern translators have had to weigh the vocabulary and grammatical subtleties of the original Hebrew, Aramaic, and Greek texts—and some of the intent may have been lost in the process. Some words assigned a specific meaning in earlier times have little relevance for later peoples. In addition, since many passages deal in symbolism, allegory, or metaphors, there is further possibility of differing interpretations.

For those and other reasons, the hermeneutics in this chapter may be subject to dialogue and debate, depending on one's theological perspective. With the above qualifications stated, however, it is our intent to review what is recorded about "singleness" in the Bible, making special mention of certain unmarried personalities whose lives were used by God and may therefore serve as examples for us today.

Old Testament Perspectives

The Bible opens with the "first days" scenario, culminating with God's creation of man, who was to live in a beautiful garden. Although God had provided Adam with all the food, shelter, and security he needed to meet his physical needs, he lacked companionship. Perhaps it was *partly* for this reason that God had also created every beast of the field and bird in the sky but apparently that was not enough—so God created Eve to become Adam's helpmate (Gen. 2:18–25).

Although the pronouncement "It is not good for the man to be alone" (Gen. 2:18) confirms the basic need for humans to interact with others of their own kind, this verse is also used by many Christians to support their expectation of marriage for *all*. The passage has been the source of much confusion and pain for singles, who are sometimes told they are "incomplete" without a mate, that it is God's will for all people to marry simply because it is "not good" for them to "be alone." Such a misconception implies that although Adam was created in God's image, he was somehow deficient until Eve was created for him. It might even suggest that Jesus was incomplete, since he was single!

Consistent with other teachings of Scripture, this passage helps us understand our need for interpersonal relations, companionship, and emotional intimacy with others. We do not believe it should be taken as a mandate for marriage, for each of these concerns can be fulfilled without a marriage commitment.

Since the days of Noah, society has been couples-oriented. Some well-meaning Christians find a hidden command to marry in God's requirement that Noah bring *pairs* of animals into the ark, as though God's only concern for life was in the context of twos. "But I will establish my covenant with you, and you will enter the ark—you and your sons and your wife, and your sons' wives with you. You are to bring into the ark two of all living creatures, male and female, to keep them alive with you" (Gen. 6:18–19). God obviously wanted pairs of animals to replenish the population of the world: "—so they can multiply on the earth and be fruitful and increase in number upon it" (Gen. 8:17b). Saying that God cares only for couples stretches the point absurdly.

A "eunuch" in the Old Testament primarily means a "court officer."

The Hebrew *saris* gives an additional meaning, "castrate," often referring to a man who served as a harem official or personal bodyguard. In the Old Testament it is difficult to know which of the two meanings is intended or whether both are implied. For example, Potiphar (Gen. 39:1), who was married (v. 7), is called a *saris,* meaning a court official. There is no reason to assume, as Josephus seems to do (*Ant.* x.10.1), that Daniel and his companions were "castrates," for they were without blemish (Dan. 1:4).

Eunuchs, of course, did not marry. How did God view these individuals whom society looked on as most unfortunate souls? "Neither let the eunuch say, 'Behold, I am a dry tree.' For thus says the LORD, 'To the eunuchs who keep My sabbaths, And choose what pleases Me, And hold fast my covenant, To them I will give in My house and within My walls a memorial, And a name better than that of sons and daughters; I will give them an everlasting name which will not be cut off'" (Isa. 56:3–5). In essence, Judaism knew two kinds of eunuchs: man-made, *saris adam* and natural, *saris hamma.* It is not necessary to assume that all those who were eunuchs were necessarily castrated males. Some may have chosen to remain single as a result of their chosen profession or spiritual calling. If God extends such mercy and promise to the most extreme and unusual example of "unmarrieds," can we not assume that the singles state, per se, is acceptable to him, so long as a single, though without "sons and daughters," chooses "what pleases" God in other respects?

God always relates to people as unique individuals. To say that a single adult is not valuable in God's eyes or is only half a person is to be uninformed about Old Testament teachings.

New Testament Perspectives

The New Testament also provides a background for understanding how God views the unmarried adult. Jesus taught in Matthew 22:30 that marriage was a temporary state of human experience, that marriage would not be part of our condition when we enter eternity.

In the context of an argument with the Pharisees regarding divorce, Jesus' disciples made a statement that amounted to a question about married versus single living. Although Jesus points to God's *ideal* for marriage ("a man will leave his father and mother and be united to his wife. . . . Therefore what God has joined together, let man not separate" [Matt. 19:5–6]), his response helps us understand God's views on this important issue. Jesus clearly teaches in Matthew 19:11–12 that the ability to remain single is a gift from God, implying that those who had not received such a blessing would have to marry and face the pressures that married adults face: "Not everyone can accept this word [i.e., to be married], but only those to whom it has been given. For some are eunuchs because they were born that way; others were made that way by men; and others have renounced marriage because of the kingdom of heaven. The one who can accept this should accept it."

Paul builds on this teaching in his letter to the believers at Corinth, who had apparently written him a letter that included a number of questions about marriage. One such area where they requested clarification was in the "gift" of celibacy. Paul reminds them that one of the purposes of marriage is to avoid sexual immoralities. In fact, he exhorts married believers not to withhold themselves sexually from their mates lest they fall into temptation and commit adultery (1 Cor. 7:1–6).

Paul wishes that all men had the gift of celibacy so they might experience more freedom from the pressures of this life: "I wish that all men were as I am [i.e., unmarried]. But each man has his own gift from God" (1 Cor. 7:7). He acknowledges the tension that exists between trying to please God and mate (vv. 26–35). Individuals who are married must concern themselves with the affairs of the family, which might affect their personal relationship with God. According to Paul, the unmarried adult has greater freedom to develop a relationship with God and be of greater benefit to God's kingdom, since there will be fewer distractions and "undivided devotion to the Lord" (v. 35).

A commitment to celibacy is first of all a free-will decision. It is not a burden or punishment. It is, in fact, identified as a gift from a loving God. Those who are the recipients of this gift will receive greater freedom in at least five areas:

Freedom from Constraints on One's Time. Those who are celibate (and therefore single) have the freedom to come and go as they choose, to set their own priorities, and to establish their own patterns regarding how they use their time.

Freedom to Have a Simple Lifestyle. Those who are married must concern themselves with providing for the diverse needs of a spouse and (usually) children—an entire family. Worldly issues such as what type of car to buy, house to own, community to live in, schools in that community, insurance, and retirement plans all increase in importance when one is married and responsible for others. Being single allows one to maintain a relatively uncomplicated lifestyle that is not restricted by the needs and expectations of a mate, children, and in-laws.

Freedom to Be More Efficient in One's Calling. Without the demands of a family, a person can focus on contributing toward his or her calling in life. Singles are free to work long hours, pursue dreams without being sidetracked, and make an extended commitment in many areas, including avenues of ministry.

Freedom to Develop Deep Friendships. Married people find it difficult to maintain the rich quality of friendships they enjoyed when they were single. Quality relationships take time to develop and nurture. Time that was once given to initiating and building relationships with many friends becomes restricted by the need to focus one's attention on the marital commitment. (This is particularly true when dealing with friends of the opposite sex.) Although marriage does not require one to drop all friendships, there is less time and energy available for them.

Freedom to Serve God. Paul spoke of his desire for others to be single, as he was, because he experienced the spiritual benefits of single living every day. It would not have been possible for Paul to have accomplished all that he did if he were married. Possible proof of that is seen by contrasting the ministries of Peter and Paul. Peter presumably had a wife and family to maintain (Mark 1:30) and traveled far less widely than Paul, who was unencumbered by a family. God was able to use Paul in a unique itinerant ministry focused on church planting, thus fulfilling the Great Commission in an extraordinary way.

Choosing to remain single is no less a gift from God than is choosing a mate. Each condition has its purpose. It is unfortunate that many to whom God has given the *ability* to remain single do not recognize the potential benefits of singleness and, instead, envy their married friends.

Yet we know that not all marriages are "made in heaven" and that many married people are discontented, if not miserable. Perhaps an illustration might make this point clear. Patty was one young woman who chose to marry at an early age because it seemed the proper way to ensure her desire for love, companionship, and security. Patty had not known Dan very long, but he had a steady job, they had fun together, and the engagement ring he bought her was the envy of her friends. She had a few nagging doubts about Dan—mainly about his occasional temper tantrums—but she went ahead with the marriage plans anyway, assuming that she could change him for the better. Besides, Dan was a Christian, and statistics implied that finding a compatible Christian mate was as difficult as winning the state lottery.

Shortly after the honeymoon was over, the beatings started. They were not severe at first, and Patty stuck it out because she had been taught it was always wrong for a Christian to get a divorce. The physical abuse was to continue for years. Finally, after their five children came along, Patty withdrew emotionally from her husband and invested her energies in raising them, but Dan's hostility began to affect the children's well-being. By the time Patty filed for divorce after twenty-two years of marriage, she had suffered mental and physical abuse, and her children, some of whom are still at home, have to face the challenge of growing up in a single-parent family. Even for the grown children, the results of the emotional damage may take years to heal.

Obviously, not all marriages are like that of Patty and Dan. Those that are based on a real commitment, as expressed in the traditional marriage vows, bring a potential of great happiness and fulfillment for both partners. Patty's bad experiences could have been avoided if she had listened to her misgivings and refused to go through with the wedding. With a better self-image, she could have resisted the pressure to marry that was placed on her by her family and friends, many of whom were already married.

Unmarried People in the Bible

Both the Old and New Testaments have examples of single men and women who were used by God for his service. Space does not allow a detailed description of each, but highlighting a few may be helpful.

Ruth

The story of Ruth, a young woman of Moab and an ancestress of David, is a striking example of selfless love and devotion. Ruth was the daughter-in-law of an Israelite widow named Naomi. While Naomi's husband was still alive, there had been a famine in Bethlehem, their home, so they traveled with their two sons to live for a while in Moab. There Naomi's husband died and the sons married Moabite women, Ruth and Orpah.

After several years, the sons, too, died, leaving Naomi a desolate woman empty of all hope. Nevertheless, as she prepared to journey to her native land, she advised her daughters-in-law to return to their own families, where it might be easier for them to find new husbands. Instead of following Naomi's advice, Ruth insisted on accompanying her mother-in-law in the uncertain days that lay ahead: "Where you go I will go, and where you stay I will stay" (Ruth 1:16b).

Logic said that if you wanted to remarry, you should go where there were available men of your cultural heritage. Ruth understood that by following Naomi she might never meet a man with the specific requirements needed for her to remarry, but she was willing to forego such possibilities to pursue what she felt was of greater importance. By so doing, she eventually replaced Naomi's emptiness with peace and fulfillment.

In the course of God's timing, he provided Ruth with a husband, Boaz. She had not closed herself off from the possibility of remarriage but was willing to leave the details and timing of any such relationship in God's hands. In fact, it was the integrity of her lifestyle that caught Boaz's attention. Ruth's testimony in the community was based on her values of faith, honesty, caring for others, and morality. She went about fulfilling her calling in life.

There are many single men and women today who have made the same sort of decision with their lives. Many, as did Ruth, give up the opportunities of marriage to care for a family member. This is an act of love based on a faith in God to provide for their needs. Such a commitment is admirable and deserves a high degree of respect.

Elijah

Another biblical example of an unmarried person's devotion to God's calling is Elijah. Ask an Old Testament scholar which prophets' lives best reflected faithful service to God, even in the face of danger, and Elijah will be at the top of the list. Elijah was a single adult who heard God's calling and was prepared to give the Lord his best, regardless of the cost or consequences. Elijah lived a solitary life characterized by travel, adventure, and hardships. A married man, especially one with children, would not have been as available to God during those adverse days. This is confirmed by the realization that when God chose a successor for Elijah, he selected another single adult with the same level of commitment and faith.

All this is not to say that a married person cannot be significantly used by God. Indeed, many biblical characters were married and had families. The point is that a unique ministry such as that given to Elijah required a person with a single-minded approach to that mission. One of the essential qualities Elijah needed was the freedom to speak his mind without concern for the health and safety of a family. Another was that he be highly mobile—able to travel great distances without prior notice and remain away from home for long periods of time. This could hardly be the job description of a married man with a demanding family life.

Daniel

Little is known of Daniel's later years as to whether or not he married and had a family. It can be said with some degree of certainty, however, that Daniel was most likely single during the period of time recorded in the first two chapters of the Book of Daniel. During this time he is referred to repeatedly as a youth. The life of this single young adult was characterized by discipline, intelligence, and wisdom. Daniel had exceptional knowledge in every branch of literature and the unique ability to interpret dreams and visions. It was due to this latter God-given talent that Daniel was called to serve in the king's court.

Daniel was a man of unusual integrity. He is one of only a handful of men in Scripture who apparently did not possess any character flaws. If ever a single young adult had his life in order, it was Daniel. We can find no sign of emotional imbalance or social maladjustment in the biblical record of his life.

Others

More could be said of other young single adults including Joseph, David, Elisha, and others. Some later went on to marry and have families. The point here is that they served God first and allowed him to control the secondary issues according to his sovereign will and in his perfect timing.

In the New Testament, too, there are a number of single men and women who were used by God. For example, Mary and Martha were single women who lived with their brother Lazarus; they enjoyed an intimate friendship with Christ and showed great devotion to serving him. Mary Magdalene, who also was unmarried, first brought the news of Christ's resurrection to the disciples. She had established a close relationship with Jesus as a result of her cleansing and conversations with him.

Jesus

In his days on earth as God incarnate—the Word made flesh—Jesus is the primary example of a single adult who was totally available for serving his heavenly Father. Little is known of Joseph, Jesus' earthly father, but it is commonly acknowledged that he must have died during Jesus' teenage years, leaving Mary a single parent who raised Jesus and the children born of her marriage to Joseph (see Matt. 13:55–56).

A "Theology of Singleness"

For many people, singleness is a season of life—a particular period of time when God may have given them a specific assignment that they can fulfill best by being single. It may also encompass a time for personal growth and spiritual development. A marriage relationship may or may not come along later.

Any "theology of singleness" must take into consideration certain biblically related principles.

Principle One: God's Unconditional Love. Written across every page of Scripture is the theme of God's unconditional love for humankind and for each unique individual. The focal point of that love is seen in his Son, Jesus, who gave his life on the cross so that we might be redeemed and know what it is to enjoy eternity as a child of God.

Principle Two: The Need for Companionship. The Bible confirms that humans are social beings and have a strong need for companionship with other humans. To desire companionship is a validation of one's humanity and also provides the opportunity to share with others the particular abilities and qualities with which we have been endowed by God. This sharing does not necessarily mandate marriage for all.

Principle Three: God Knows How to Give Gifts. Whether it is the ability to be single or the mutual love found in a happy marriage, both are clearly *gifts* from God. As the infinitely wise Giver, God knows which gift we need and when. His timing is always perfect!

Principle Four: Expediency. This truth is based on the concept suggested in "making the most of every opportunity" (Eph. 5:15–16). Seek God's purpose for your life and pursue it with uncompromising commitment! We are to give God our best and pursue excellence in daily life. He has promised to provide for our every need. The idea running through all Scripture is that God desires our best *because* he has such infinite love and deep compassion. He knows what gifts to give us because he knows our needs, even better than we do. To some he gives singleness and others marriage. To want what you do not have is to question God's love and sovereignty. Desiring a spouse is not a sin unless this objective consumes your thoughts and controls your behavior. Then you will have closed your heart to what God may be saying and attempted to forestall the special purpose he has for your life.

Three

Casting Off
into Uncharted Territories

Life for anyone—but especially for singles—can be approached as an exciting voyage to explore endless possibilities and thereby learn important truths about oneself. In the previous section we plotted a course by surveying some known facts about singles in America, including their history, their general lifestyle as revealed in our questionnaire, and a biblical perspective of the singles lifestyle.

The relative ease of any solo journey is roughly proportional to the degree of preparation made for the hazards that might lie ahead. Providing that kind of forewarning is the aim of this section. We will examine some of the current economic and cultural realities that have special relevance for the unmarried. The particular concerns of singles will vary according to their subgroup, age, gender, personal background, and even where they live. But we will try to generalize about those concerns in light of certain research findings, our interviews with singles, and local church approaches. It is hoped that understanding the issues and potential problems that face singles will reinforce the recommendations we will make in the final section of this book.

8

Passport to Paradise
. . . Myth or Reality?

As we noted in chapter 5, American culture has changed in many ways over the past hundred years because of new technologies, scientific advances, national politics, and economic events of worldwide significance. All these changes have had a profound impact on shaping our values, attitudes, morals, and ethical standards. In particular, civil-rights agendas, especially the demand for gender equality, exemplify recent trends that have influenced our beliefs about certain segments of society. When the cultural mind-set is inaccurate in its assessment of a group's character, misconceptions and unfair generalizations are perpetuated.

Society's attitudes toward unmarried adults cluster around several unfounded notions—myths about the nature of single people, their objectives, and the specifics of their lifestyle. These traditional beliefs tend to present an essentially negative and unfair image of how singles live.

As with all myths, there is an element of truth concealed in them somewhere, but they do a great deal of harm when all singles are assumed to fit these stereotypes and when an individual single uses them to shape his or her self-image. This chapter will explore the development of these stereotypes and discuss some of the myths about today's singles. By sorting through the myths, we hope to find the elements of reality that can help singles orient their lives toward effective behavior patterns in a sometimes hostile world.

Historical Development of the Singles Stereotype

Single adults have been around since the dawn of humankind, but in America they have traditionally comprised only about 3 or 4 percent of the adult population until about the last twenty years. Since the early 1900s, society's awareness of singles has increased dramatically, with that awareness has come some changes in attitude. From around the late nineteenth century through most of the 1920s, single women, no matter their age, were labeled "old maids," a term that is rarely heard today. During the thirties and early forties, mainly the Depression years, single women were usually referred to as "spinsters." It is interesting to note that little cultural attention was focused on single men at that time. In response to the "problem" of single women, there appeared numerous articles in both popular literature and research journals addressing the issue. A survey of these titles by Cargan and Melko in their book *Singles* reveals the following:

Before the Twenties—
    "Why I Am an Old Maid"
    "The Necessary Melancholy of Bachelors"
    "In Defense of Widows and Spinsters"
    "There Is No Place in Heaven for Old Maids"
    "The Compensations of Spinsterhood"

From the Twenties through the Thirties—
    "I'd Rather Be a Spinster"
    "The Dilemma of the Educated Woman"
    "Does It Hurt to Be an Old Maid?"
    "The Sorrowful Mayden and the Jovial Bachelors"
    "Alarming Increase of Old Maids and Bachelors in New England"
    "Family Parasites: The Economic Value of the Unmarried Sister"

The 1950s and 1960s saw an increase in the number of single adults in America as a result of the growing trend to postpone marriage for advanced education or career building and the dramatic rise in the national divorce rate. Reasons given for the upswing in divorces included the too-hasty marriages that took place after World War II, the "Hippie" movement, women's "liberation," and a relaxed morality, especially about sexual behavior. Society as a whole was questioning its values and looking for revised, "how to" approaches to modern living. Articles about single adults carried a new theme during the fifties and sixties, though many still implied that being married was a long-term objective:

"How to Be Human Though Single"
"129 Ways to Get a Husband: Ideas from a Panel of Experts"
"How to Be Marriageable: Results of a Marriage Readiness Course"
"Let's Take a Sane Look at the Hysterical Quest for a Husband"
"Eligible Bachelors for 1965"
"Study Disputes Image of the Happy Bachelor"
"The Blessings of Bachelorhood"
"A Spinster's Lot Can Be a Happy One"
"When Being Single Stops Being Fun"

Fortified by more effective means of birth control, sexual freedom permeated the morality for the 1970s and had a major impact on the development of the "swinging singles" stereotype. In light of television shows and product ads that depicted single men as affluent and sexually active, people began to view single adults as selfish and irresponsible members of society. This unfortunate label created a barrier between married and single adults. Articles began to reflect this pleasure-oriented lifestyle, mingling how-to-find-a-mate advice and warnings about the hazards of single living with suggestions on how to enhance one's life as a single:

"Humanizing the Meat Market"
"Contraceptives and the Single Person"
"Sexual Problems of Women Alone"
"The Pill and the Girl Next Door"
"Celebrate Singleness: Marriage May Be Second Best"
"The Dangers of Being a Single Male"
"Should Doctors Prescribe Contraceptives to Unmarried Ladies?"
"What Women Should Know About Single Men"
"Bazaar's A to Z List on Where to Find a Man"
"Movin On—Alone"
"Women: On Hating and Loving Being Single: A Symposium"
"For Singles, Life Isn't All Swinging"
"Eight Eligible Men"
"49 Million Singles Can't All Be Right"

The eighties had their own unique contribution in formulating the singles stereotype. Words used to describe singles in the most recent literature are: growing, affluent, introspective, hard-working, health-conscious, altruistic, and mobile. Each quality adds a new dimension to our concept of singleness as we enter the nineties. The stereotype will change with each emerging decade, but the challenge facing us today is determining to what degree the stereotype is accurate and to what degree it is an inappropriate collection of myths.

Myths and Misunderstandings of Singleness

Part of the disadvantage of being a subculture within a society is to be misrepresented by fallacious statements and beliefs. Singles will be no exception to this rule so long as myths abound about the "normal" life of a single. Since so little credible research has been done on single adults, a great deal of popular literature merely perpetuates these negative images.

Fig. 8.1

Myths of Singleness

1. The only satisfied woman is a married woman
2. The natural and major fulfillment of every woman is to be a mother
3. Singles are sexually frustrated and are more prone to engage in deviant behavior
4. Finding the right person will solve all your problems
5. Marriage is God's highest calling for *all* men and women
6. All single women want to get married
7. All confirmed bachelors are afraid of responsibility
8. All single adults are very lonely
9. Singles are basically selfish
10. Singles are rich

Myth 1. The Only Satisfied Woman Is a Married Woman

It has long been assumed that women are the weaker sex and thus dependent on the strength and security a man can provide. Without this "protector and provider," the woman has been judged incapable of operating at peak performance. Indeed, from a historical perspective, it was once almost an economic, sociological, and psychological necessity for a woman to marry at an early age. Furthermore, churches have often preached that a person is not fully "complete" until associated with a marriage partner. Women had been reduced to second-class members in a couples-oriented society. These half-persons were destined to live in a kind of limbo until they could finally locate "God's will" for them. For the unmarried women, life became a quest for the "missing piece"—which was usually defined as "husband."

This myth is still supported by the responses of more never-married women than divorced or widowed women, and by the fact that over 94 percent of all women *do* marry by the age of forty-five. It is interesting to note, however, that currently about half of all single women have been married in the past, and that once they have been married they are rather slow to enter another marriage relationship. Many such women vow that they will never remarry.

Nancy, a divorcée, summarized her feelings this way: "I lived with that man for six long years. I had never known such pain and isolation as I did when I was married. I'll think long and hard before I ever get back into a marriage relationship again. Until then, I've got a long road of healing to travel down."

Being married is no more an insurance policy for happiness than singleness is a guarantee of frustration and unhappiness. Many married adults wish they could trade their marital status for the freedom of independent living. Numerous studies indicate that the most contented married persons were those who had not rushed into marriage to escape an unhappy home or loneliness as a single, but had first established a sense of well-being and happiness as an individual.

If society truly believes in the value of lifelong monogamous relationships, what can it do about the decided imbalance in the gender ratio among the adult population? Statistics show that there are approximately 12 million more single women than men. If one adds to this the growing number of adults who will eventually be divorced or widowed, it seems obvious that there will continue to be a sizable difference in the male/female ratio.

The myth that only as a wife can a woman be truly happy is dispelled by the realization that women have far more options, advantages, and career opportunities than ever before—and thus less pressure to get married. It is quite accurate to say that there has never been as much freedom for a woman or reasons for her to remain single.

A viable Christian perspective would be to realize that there are a variety of acceptable lifestyles from which any mature single is free to choose (see chapter 7). Within either of the married versus single alternatives may be found happiness or dissatisfaction. The marital status does not eliminate or increase the potential for one or the other. Like the apostle Paul, both women and men can say that satisfaction and contentment can be found in any condition of life. The true condition for finding peace is not one's marital status but faithfulness and obedience to the revealed will of God.

Myth 2: The Natural and Major Fulfillment of Every Woman Is to Be a Mother

There are a few popular quotes that illustrate this myth: "Behind every great man is a great woman—his mother!" and "The hand that rocks the cradle rules the world." One pastor put it this way: "Mating and mother-hood are God-ordained sources to total fulfillment." Such a mentality feeds the common notion that only through motherhood can a woman find inner peace and fulfillment. This is simply not true.

Sandy, a single parent, put it this way: "I had always grown up with people telling me I would find happiness only if I was married, so I got married. No sooner had I been married than I was told the only way to find happiness was to become a parent. Now that I have three children to take care of, I know better—but it's too late!"

According to many studies, women are more moral, religious, and sensitive than men. However, nowhere has it been shown that life satis-faction is based on the presence of children in the home. In fact, most sociologists agree that shortly after the birth of the first child in a home there is a decrease in marital satisfaction. This decrease tends to continue until shortly after the children become fairly independent young adults. The return of maximum happiness comes after the departure of the last child! This is referred to as the U-shaped curve of marital satisfaction. Some women in their thirties may feel pressure to produce a child because of a theorized biological clock, but many others remain happy, though childless.

Myth 3: Singles Are Sexually Frustrated and Are More Prone to Engage in Deviant Behavior

This common cultural myth is by no means a valid conclusion. According to several national studies of non-Christian singles, questions dealing with "problem areas" and "frustrations" indicate sexuality as fifth in concern. More important issues for singles were: (1) acceptable enter-tainment, (2) managing personal finances, (3) developing rewarding friendships, and (4) raising children as a single parent.

Being single does not make a person more prone to sexual promiscuity. Married people, too, are subject to sexual frustration for one reason or another, and some are promiscuous. Although singles do admit that they face some degree of sexual frustration, they also say that being restricted sexually has tended to make them more creative in other ways.

Myth 4: Finding the Right Person Will Solve All Your Problems

It is easy to confuse a *desire* for a close personal relationship with a *need* for a specific someone to bring you life satisfaction. Finding contentment does not have to be based on having a marriage partner. If you believe this myth, life becomes one long and often frustrating search for Mr. Perfect or Miss Wonderful. It is based on two self-defeating errors. First, there can be only one "right person" for you; and second, finding that person will give your life meaning and total fulfillment.

One of the major problems with this myth is the tendency for single adults to short-circuit their decision-making capabilities. Christians may employ immature decision-making techniques designed mainly to test God's ability to play their games than to determine his will for their lives. An example of this approach is seen in Denny:

"I had been dating Marcy for a few months but was planning to break up with her because I didn't feel good about the direction our relationship was going. I decided to resolve the situation by putting out a fleece to God. One night I told God on the way to pick up Marcy for a date that if she came out wearing a red skirt, a white blouse, a pony tail, and her light blue sweater, I would take it from God that she was the right person for me. I couldn't believe my eyes when she came down the stairs wearing the exact outfit I had described. That convinced me. We were married within six months and divorced a year after that. I now realize that a lifelong commitment to a mate has to be based on something more than an outfit she wears."

It is important to realize that even if you should find that "right person," living with him or her will require a fair amount of adjustment. The first year of marriage is often the most turbulent period of life, since you must learn to communicate, compromise, and adjust to new ways of doing things, as well as new foods, values, priorities, and family members. It is rarely an easy adjustment for anyone. Unfortunately, when people believe they have finally found that perfect mate, they often think life will thereafter be filled with nothing but roses, romantic dinners, and soft music.

Christian singles need to find the balance between leaving it all up to God and taking responsible actions themselves. Many churches where we have gone to speak are filled with single adults who are striving desperately to find that special person who will bring them meaning and purpose. Failing in that search leads to feelings of tension, frustration, and even hopelessness. Our advice is usually to slow down the intensity of their seeking and focus on becoming the person they believe God wants them to become *now*. It is foolish to wait for that person to come along before growing and developing personally in important areas. No one person can guarantee satisfaction, happiness, or self-fulfillment for another.

Single adults need to realize that the more secure they are *as* a single, the better off they will be in terms of their preparation and potential for marriage. Finding a compatible marriage partner will not automatically solve all your problems. In fact, adding another person to your lifestyle usually adds to your problems, at least initially. A marital partner has the potential of making a significant contribution to your happiness, but there is no guarantee of trouble-free living, whatever your circumstances.

Myth 5: Marriage Is God's Highest Calling for All Men and Women

This is a common misconception among many happily married Christians today. They believe the only happy adult is a married adult, and they cannot understand why anyone would not want to have that objective. This myth stems in part from the historical view that a woman was regarded as blessed of the Lord if she were married and fruitful. This view is still being espoused by some authors today, and it can contribute to a state of panic for older singles who see their body clocks ticking away precious potential.

There is no arguing that we still live in a couples-oriented society (although that emphasis is fading). Restaurant seating is geared for couples, food is usually packaged for two or more people, and products for a twosome lifestyle are marketed in our media. Books, magazines, radio, and television continue to sell singles the message that if you want to fit in with the mainstream of society, you need to be paired up.

Singles who are so distressed at not having found a perfect mate that they seek professional help may discover that being single in itself is labeled immature by many so-called experts. According to such counselors, the only solution to the problem lies in ceasing any residual resistance to pairing pressure and revising one's strategies for finding a partner.

One best-selling "authority," David Reuben, in his book *Any Woman Can*, says that any woman can find love and sexual fulfillment—but only if she is married. He describes never-married women as "carefree little girls who don't want to be grown up women" and suggests that they have rejected candidates for marriage "because they don't live up to their unrealistic expectations." He adds, "A divorced woman ought to be married for it is only then that she can have her chance for true happiness and make her second marriage everything her first marriage should have been."

Single men will find the same pro-marriage attitude from Dr. Reuben, since he characterizes them as "professional bachelors who are always charming, always engaging. . . . Everything about them is exciting, flashy and marvelously in, but they are emotional freeloaders. . . . The world's most accomplished time-waster is the perpetual bachelor."

Widows find no sympathy from him either: "A woman over the age of forty is almost certain to deteriorate emotionally (and sexually) if she is out of emotional (and sexual) circulation for too long. Even worse, the older she gets the faster the deterioration proceeds. Human beings are sexual beings and without the constant stimulation of regular and frequent sex they tend to fade and dry up."

Reuben's statements are obviously misguided opinion. To say that there is a relationship between the frequency of sexual intercourse and life satisfaction is to undermine the scriptural teaching of purity for all unmarried adults. Frequency of sexual intercourse is no guarantee of mental health. Rather, life satisfaction depends on obedience and faithfulness to the principles in the Word of God.

Another such "professional" is Allan Fromme, a clinical psychologist, who writes in his book *The Ability to Love* that "it is obvious that many young people who pride themselves on their selectivity are actually demonstrating that they would rather be alone. Indeed, it is better to get married. Even if the marriage turns out to be a mistake, it is more of a mistake not to make this mistake. The longer an individual remains unmarried, the longer he is avoiding a commitment, detaching himself, unrelating himself to other people. And the more he is courting that permanent detachment that we call loneliness."

How many single adults have entered into a marriage that they did not feel was right because of the advice of such "experts"? The pain they may experience in their marriage through emotional, physical, and sexual abuse can be devastating. To say that it is wiser to enter into what you believe might be a poor marriage than to remain single is irresponsible and destructive.

How much better is the advice of the apostle Paul: "I wish that all men [and women] were single like me. But each man has his own gift from God; one has the gift of being single, and another has the gift of being married" (1 Cor. 7:7, paraphrased). Paul refers to being single as a gift or high calling from God, just as being married is a gift. Since both conditions are seen as acceptable, the myth that says only married adults are fulfilling God's highest calling is biblically inaccurate.

Myth 6: All Single Women Want to Get Married

As previously mentioned, more never-married women than divorced or widowed women say they want to be married. In other words, those who have been married before often are in no hurry to get back into a marriage relationship. Indeed, 94 percent of the never-married women do marry by the age of forty-five. But as the divorce figures indicate, a large number of these women will end their marriages by opting for a divorce. According to the Statistical Abstract of the United States 1988 (Bureau of Census, Current Population Reports, Series P-70, No. 423) in 1985 the number of divorced people (nearly 15 million) surpassed widowed persons (14 million). Since the divorce rate for current marriages is hovering around 50 percent, it might be accurate to state that many people who are married wish they were not.

When women had fewer options for their lives in terms of education and employment than they have today, they opted for marriage. Over the years, significant changes in our society have made women the recipients of many benefits. They are therefore postponing marriage to pursue further education and career goals. Some are developing hobbies and traveling before they choose to settle down.

Many of the previously married single women may be hesitant to resume a marriage relationship once they taste their new "freedoms." Alison shared her feelings about remaining single: "Since we were both fairly young when we got married, I had to work to make ends meet financially. In addition to my forty-hour-a-week job I had to manage the family finances, cook the meals, do the laundry, keep the house clean, entertain my husband's clients, and a host of other responsibilities. Now that I'm single again, I have so much freedom to further my hobbies and have fun. Why ruin all that now by getting married again?"

There are many single women who would like to get married one day, but the myth that says *all* single women want to get married is just not accurate, according to the latest research.

Myth 7: All Confirmed Bachelors Are Afraid of Responsibility

At first this myth may seem outdated, but it still appears from time to time in popular literature. Although the media may highlight a particular bachelor who fits this model and hold him up as the norm, the stereotype is simply not true of the majority of single men today. It is based on some of the misguided notions that were quoted under Myth 5—that marriage is God's highest calling for all.

Many of the men we interviewed spoke of the reasons they chose not to marry. Some men wanted to keep their freedom to pursue occupational goals or develop personal interests and hobbies. Others were merely decreasing the intensity of their search and were therefore single longer, so they could learn more about themselves before entering a long-term relationship with another person. Another reason why men in our survey were single was because they had not yet found the woman they would like to marry and were not willing to lower their standards.

It is true that some men may be afraid of the responsibilities of marriage. They probably also feel threatened by intimacy, are unable to share their true feelings with a woman, and believe they are incapable of a lasting commitment. These emotions, however, are hardly characteristic of *all* bachelors.

Myth 8: All Single Adults Are Very Lonely

The studies conducted by Jacqueline Simenauer and David Carroll (1982), Robert Weiss (1973), Leonard Cargan and Matthew Melko (1982), Hugget (1986) and Peter Stein (1978) confirm that loneliness is one of the most critical concerns of single adults. However, as Weiss points out, there are many lonely people in our culture today—and loneliness is by no means restricted to singles. He identifies college students, young wives, prisoners, those who have recently moved, retirees, and the elderly as the groups most susceptible to loneliness.

Loneliness was indeed most frequently cited as the "greatest disadvantage of being single" by both men and women respondents to our Singles in America questionnaire. (See fig. 6.6, 6.9.) But our interviews and everyday experience with singles have led us to conclude that the myth greatly exaggerates the extent and degree of the problem among singles. Many are probably no more lonely than their married counterparts. In fact, singles are generally more able to do something about their feelings of loneliness! With their added independence comes the freedom to explore friendship possibilities at work, school, church, and civic or social organizations. For singles there are few practical reasons to limit personal relationships to their immediate household, as is often the situation with married people. Even if a single shares living accommodations with another person, that arrangement does not carry a long-term commitment, at least in most cases. Roommates may come and go; with each change comes the potential of further friendships. However, because some singles—but not *all*—feel lonely in varying degrees, this topic will be discussed at greater length in chapter 13.

Myth 9: Singles Are Basically Selfish

This myth—amply reinforced by the advertising hucksters—implies that singles who choose not to get married make that decision because they prefer to spend their hard-earned money on themselves rather than sharing it with another person or providing for a family. Having only their own needs and desires to consider, they are free to explore the ends of the earth in carefree vacations, splurge on fancy cars, dine at the best places, and otherwise indulge their fancy for pleasure and excitement. This, too, is a fabrication and is based mainly on certain television soap operas.

There is another perspective of single living, one that is virtually ignored by the media: a lifestyle of giving and sacrificial service to Christ. The mission fields are full of single men and women who have chosen to serve their Master rather than spending empty hours in search of selfish pleasure. It has been our privilege to meet many of them in Asia, Africa, Central and South America, and Europe where we have spoken to singles groups. They have been faithful to the Great Commission of making disciples wherever the need exists. Some choose to live in threatening environments where married couples would not feel free to bring a family. Others serve Christ closer to home by giving of their time, energy, and assets to those less fortunate than themselves. Free from worries about bank balances, retirement accounts, mortgages, and car payments, these men and women give generously to others. They are the silent singles who go about the business of faithful service without care for themselves. Yes, there are some singles who live the flamboyant lifestyle of the rich and famous, but self-indulgence is no more the norm for singles than it is for the population at large, especially among Christians.

Myth 10: Singles Are Rich

Examining *this* misconception provides further fuel for discrediting Myth 9! It takes a great deal of money to finance the exploits of the rich and famous, and that money simply does not exist for the average single adult today.

In theory this myth is based on the premise that since singles do not have a spouse or children to feed, they have more expendable incomes than their married friends. The Internal Revenue Service takes this view when setting their tax brackets, as do supermarkets by setting lower mark-ups for family necessities. In fact, many stores sell such items as diapers and baby food at an insignificant profit margin, knowing they will make up the difference on items that singles will purchase. In 1982 Cargan and Melko examined the income level of singles in their study and found that over 50 percent of single adults between the ages of 30 and 50 make less than $10,000 (the figure was 60 percent for never-marrieds). Under 10 percent of the singles in this age bracket reported incomes over $20,000. This was at a time when the median income for married adults in America was $23,433.

The median family income for a married adult in the United States as of 1986 was $30,809. A chart showing the income levels for single adults in our study appears in chapter 3 (fig. 3.1). The median income level for that group was $15,000 to $19,999, significantly below the national married-adult figures.

Considering the amount of money needed to purchase and maintain a home today, plus the ever-rising, high costs of food, transportation, insurance, and health expenses, most people have a rough time making ends meet, whether single or married. In fact, more and more *couples* are finding it necessary for both partners to work—another break from tradition—whether or not they have children. This alone is enough to refute the idea that a single person has plenty left over from his or her paycheck to either spend recklessly or save for the future.

Single adults are not particularly affluent. Those who do not own a home *may* have more expendable income, but (as we have seen in chapter 6) more and more singles are purchasing homes, which requires budgeting for interest-heavy mortgage payments and other expenses that go along with owning a home. While it is hardly true that "two can live as cheaply as one," singles surely have no easier time balancing a budget than couples do. Divorced singles may have additional financial problems, especially if child and support payments are not realistically assigned. Furthermore, if a recently divorced or widowed woman has never held a job, her lack of marketable skills may limit her to low-paying employment categories. Both male and female single parents, of course, also face the expenses of child care if holding a job is a must, as it usually is.

We have examined several currently popular myths about singles. By no means have we covered them all; there are dozens more. It is easy to create a myth and difficult to refute one. What is needed to dispel the many misconceptions about today's singles is to continue to examine the way singles really live and thus replace fiction with fact.

9

The Monopoly
Maze

I t is difficult to detail the issues that relate to single-adult careers, since
the specific reasons why an individual is single will greatly influence
his or her options and needs. For example, newly graduated college
students who find themselves at the bottom of a career ladder face a different set of circumstances than single-parent women. Widows, too, have
unique concerns about vocational re-entry or even about how to find a
first-time job. As Robert Weiss points out in his popular book *Going It
Alone,* "The financial situation of widows is in general somewhat better
than that of other single mothers, since widows' husbands are likely to
have carried insurance and most widows are also eligible for Social Security. Social Security payments to a widow and her children far exceed the
typical level of child support." This differential is particularly true today,
ten years later, since fewer than half of all divorced women actually
receive any child-support payments! The same complexity of factors
exists between men and women in the area of career choices.

A recent article in *Personnel Administrator* titled "Singles in the Workplace: Myths and Advantages" reported that:

Unmarried American workers spend eight hours of company time per
month on their social lives.

The workplace is the most popular place for single women to meet a
potential lover or husband. [This differed from *our* survey data.]

According to one U.S. study, 55 percent of respondents had been
involved sexually with a co-worker.

In another national survey, 51 percent of all respondents stated they believed that becoming a successful businessperson could help them find a mate.

The divorce rate goes up 2 percent for every $1,000 earned by a woman.

Since 1965, the number of unmarried executives has increased 300 percent.

More than one and one-half million managers/executives have never been married. (Forty percent are female.)

Single Women in the Job Market

Because many single women are delaying marriage to advance their careers and because of the ever-increasing divorce rate, singles comprise a growing percentage of the job market today. There are clearly more job options available to women than ever before. To the degree that our society gradually acknowledges women's professional capabilities, there will be an almost endless array of career options. Women are earning advanced degrees in many fields and are entering careers that were once closed to them. According to Lucia Bequarert, in her book *Single Women Alone and Together,* when a recent survey asked single women what their most important wish was, 45 percent reported that they wanted to find a good man to marry. Interestingly, the same percentage wanted a satisfying career.

It is commonly taught in American universities that women should expect to work after graduation whether or not they get married. Harriet Braiker reports in her book *The Type E Woman* that "American women are still marrying in record substantial numbers and continuing to bear children, but for the first time in history, more American women work than remain at home." They have outside jobs for a variety of reasons, including financial necessity, to supplement the family income and thus improve its quality of life, to pursue a career based on their educational preparation, or to be more personally challenged than they are by their responsibilities at home.

For women who are single parents, these pressures are more acute and at times cause overwhelming conflict. The double-binding commitment of women to family and career has both a negative and positive side. Although our materialistic culture places a great deal of value on almost anyone who is able to secure a moderate degree of possessions, working mothers also face negative feelings of guilt and self-doubt because of their dual roles. With no partner to share her burden, a single mother is especially torn by the need to divide her time and energies between her employer's demands and her family's needs. Juggling priorities can produce a sense of inadequacy and failure. At some point there is a price to be paid for such added strains on a family and an individual. In his book *Educated American Women*, Eli Ginzberg said that "there are exceptional women who can pursue a career and still maintain a normal, healthy family circle, but they are exceptional and should be considered as so."

Most single women work for economic reasons, since they have the same bills and financial responsibilities as any other member of society. In addition to their financial needs, Robert Weiss (*Going It Alone*) reported many single working women also want the nonfinancial benefits that work brings to their lives. In his national survey, Weiss asked working single mothers whether they would continue to work if they had enough money from other sources. In that group, 73 percent said they would work even if they didn't have to. Only 54 percent of working married mothers said that they would continue to work if it were no longer necessary. The reason for the difference seems clear. The single woman experiences a great deal of social contact on the job. Working gives her the opportunity to meet new people and to be challenged by a variety of career-related goals. For many working women, their jobs are form of therapy.

Concerns of Single Working Mothers

Weiss reports that there are several important issues that must be resolved before most single mothers will be satisfied with an employment situation.

1. *The age of their children.* Many single women with preschool children will not even accept a position outside the home because they worry that being separated from their children during the formative years may somehow cause emotional damage to the children. Many mothers hesitate to leave a sick child with a parent or friend and would suffer extreme guilt if they were not always immediately accessible to the child. Single mothers of school-age children may venture out from the home if they are assured of the youngsters' safety and care. But, for the mother of younger children who absolutely *must* work to pay the family's bills, the search for affordable and satisfactory child care is urgent—and usually ongoing.

2. *Commuting Time.* For suburban dwellers today, the highway or public-transit commute is a necessary evil. Most people have come to expect a lengthy and tiring trip to and from work each day. The single working

mother is less likely to accept such a fate. Concern for accessibility to her children may make her take a job that pays relatively little and is otherwise unrewarding *if* it allows her to be within a half-hour distance from them. The chances are slim that she will accept a position requiring much more travel time than that.

3. *Constant Communication.* Single mothers want to know that they can be reached at all times if something were to happen to their children. They are unlikely to work in a job that does not give them the freedom to check on a child or to be contacted by the caregiver in case of emergency.

4. *Flexible Hours.* Jobs that allow a single mother to maintain a flexible schedule are in the greatest demand. This freedom allows a mother to make sure that her children get off to school and come home safely and that she will be able to go to their assistance if the need should arise. It seems obvious that jobs that allow a woman to set her own hours—or, better yet, to work some of her hours at home after the children have gone to bed—will be the most sought-after positions in the future.

5. *Part-time Employment.* This type of work is most popular among widows with some other source of funds. It allows them to get out to meet new people, feel fulfilled, and supplement their income. A single mother may take this option if she can find a part-time job that pays enough for her needs. Besides usually paying far less than comparable full-time positions, these arrangements have relatively little job security and rarely provide fringe benefits such as paid vacations, holidays, or health insurance. Still, many single mothers prefer part-time school hours so they can be with their children. Part-time hours ease doubts about how they are balancing their vocational duties and parental responsibilities.

Singles in America Survey: Single Women

The single women in our study were relatively stable in their employment. About 60 percent were in the same job they had five years before or had changed jobs only once during that time. Over 15 percent of the women we surveyed had more than one job, and half were working more than eight hours a day. In light of those figures, we wondered whether these women enjoyed their careers. Responses revealed that a surprising 72 percent enjoyed their jobs all or most of the time.

Most of the women we interviewed are actively involved in their careers and plan to remain in that occupation indefinitely. Apparently they like working and derive a great deal of personal fulfillment from being in the workplace.

Although *not* explored in our survey, there apparently are other indications that many women are dissatisfied with their career-building opportunities because of what they see as vestiges of gender discrimination. Although much progress has been made in securing women's acceptability in the workplace, their salary averages are still below those of men, even in comparable positions. Most people believe, however, that efforts will continue toward securing pay equality and that women will gradually improve their work status by continuing to advance into managerial positions.

Single Men in the Job Market

Since men have traditionally been viewed as breadwinners, a young man today may have a generally easier time entering the job market than a young woman. The typical never-married single man, because of his limited responsibilities, finds himself able to venture into many new frontiers for employment opportunities. Unlike his married friends, he can take on work-related duties that require long hours, travel, and even risk.

Concerns of Single Working Fathers

A single man who is *also* a custodial father is restricted to a lifestyle far different from his never-married or non-custodial peers. In fact, his concerns more closely resemble those of a single mother, especially in terms of employment options. Married fathers, though they increasingly share in household and day-to-day parental responsibilities, have long been accustomed to organizing their lives around other men who share such "masculine" interests as career, sports, and hobbies. The increased duties that accompany being a single parent change much of that social scenario. In particular, a single father may have to adjust his employment possibilities according to the same issues discussed under "Concerns of Single Working Mothers." A single father, too, must consider the advisability of accepting a lower-paying job so that he can be more available to his children, especially if they are very young. His progress on the corporate ladder may be impeded, at least temporarily, because of his need for shorter commuting time, staggered hours, and work he can do partly at home. Furthermore, he also faces the same search for suitable child care that a single mother does. So far, most of the attention to the needs of single parents has focused on single mothers. There seems an obvious need to develop adequate support systems for their male counterparts.

(See chapter 11 for further discussion of the special concerns of single fathers.)

Singles in America Survey: Single Men

The single men in our study did not seem to match the common stereotypes that are reflected in the myths discussed in chapter 8. The image of the freeloading single man who is irresponsible and careless is more a media distortion than a reality. That is not to say that such men do not exist, but only that they were not represented to any measurable degree in our sample.

Our sampling of Christian single men revealed that they were quite stable in their employment histories. Nearly 70 percent had been in the same job for five years or had moved only once. Fewer men (13%) than women (16%) had more than one job. These Christian single men also work many more hours a day than the national average of eight (over 50% work more than eight hours a day). They also seem self-fulfilled in their employment, since 80 percent said they enjoy their work all or most of the time. This is slightly higher for the men than was reported by the women.

No Certain Future

It is not really clear just how much marital status affects one's employment prospects. Opinions differ about whether or not being single is an advantage in the job market. On the one hand, a single person can usually be relatively flexible and exploratory in his or her career building, at least if there are no dependents to be supported. Nevertheless, married workers may be able to counteract any such advantage, since the fact that they have family responsibilities may make it an economic necessity for them to be steady and reliable in the workplace, which is one way to build job security. One thing certain is that a single *parent* faces a greater challenge than a childless single when it comes to career advancement, economic stability, and sources of emotional support.

10

Is There Life after Divorce?

Stephanie had felt happy and fulfilled in her nearly twenty-year marriage to Matt. Together with their three daughters, they lived in a quiet suburb outside of Boston. Six months ago, Stephanie returned home from an afternoon of shopping and found a note on the kitchen table. As she read its contents, she was shocked to discover that Matt was leaving her for a younger woman. Stephanie had had no idea that Matt had been unhappy in their marriage.

Stephanie and Matt met during their second year of college and married shortly thereafter. Stephanie agreed to drop out of her nursing program to help Matt finish his degree in engineering. She was never able to return to college because of the children that came along in the early years of their marriage. Working part-time as a secretary to help make ends meet was difficult, but she was willing to make the sacrifice because of her love for Matt and their children. She saw it as an investment in their future.

Now Stephanie is faced with the challenge of surviving alone in a world that often requires a college degree for the better-paying positions. She has never established her own credit record and finds it difficult to cope with the trauma of managing the household expenses. The financial and social pressures, however, are not as difficult to reconcile as her internal struggles.

Stephanie wonders how this could have happened to her. She is filled with self-doubt and insecurity as she seeks to determine her own identity. She has always been "Matt's wife." Feeling inadequate and suffering from a shattered self-image, she wonders who she is, what the future holds for her, and even how she will be able to take care of herself.

Matt spoke to us of his disillusionment with life. Shortly after graduation from college, he was fortunate enough to join a small engineering firm and a few years later was offered an opportunity to become a partner in the company. He invested himself fully in the growing firm and became very successful. This over involvement at work led him to neglect his family during those early years. Matt's recent negative experience with middle management and his constant business trips brought on a period of personal instability. When asked why he chose to get married so young, he did not have a clear answer: "I guess it was the thing to do then. All my friends were getting married so I followed along with what they were doing. It was fun for a while, but I just got bored. I felt trapped by it all; the demands of the family finally got to me and I just walked out. This new person in my life gives me the thrills I've been looking for—fewer responsibilities and lots of fun. She's more exciting and less demanding than Stephanie. I feel young again when I am with her."

Matt and Stephanie are hardly alone in their experience. Recent divorce statistics in the United States point to a rise in marital dissolutions. The numbers are overwhelming. Between 1960 and 1978, divorce increased 83% for those aged 45–68. The increase was 296% for those under 30. And now there is a divorce every 27 seconds (*Single Adult Ministries Journal* #77, Vol. 8, No. 1, p. 1). Figure 10.1 summarizes some of the other current divorce trends.

Fig. 10.1
Divorce Trends

1. The number of divorced women at any one time is greater than the number of men because men are more likely to remarry, and to do so more quickly, than women. About five out of six divorced men remarry, compared to about three out of every four divorced women.
2. The median age for divorce (after a first marriage) is twenty-seven for women and twenty-nine for men.
3. The earlier the average age of the partners at marriage, the greater the likelihood of divorce. Most divorces occur at young ages, typically twenty to twenty-four for women and twenty-five to twenty-nine for men.
4. The most typical ages for remarriage after a first divorce are twenty-five to thirty-four for men and twenty to thirty-four for women. For both men and women, thirty-five to forty-four is the most typical age for a second divorce.
5. If present trends continue, about 40 percent of Americans in their late twenties and early thirties who remarry after a divorce may expect their second marriage to also end in divorce.

Divorce Rates

Divorce rates in America have not always been as high as they are today. Due to a variety of factors, these figures have fluctuated over the years. The divorce rates were relatively low during the economic depression of the 1930s, followed by a gradual climb that accelerated to peak levels in the immediate post-World War II period and then succeeded by declines into the 1950s. Meanwhile, the rate of first marriages continued its rather steady decline through the 1960s and into the 1970s; it has now reached a low level similar to that of the latter years of the Great Depression. However, both the divorce rate and the remarriage rate turned upward around 1960 and increased dramatically during the ensuing decade. By 1970, the divorce and remarriage rates were higher than any previously recorded for this country.

The ratio of remarriages to first marriages has increased since 1970. Statistics show that the proportion of marriages that involved a remarriage for the bride, the groom, or both increased from 30 percent in 1970 to 45 percent in 1981, representing an increase of almost one-half. That proportion has changed very little since 1981.

The divorce rate over the past two decades has continued its steep upward movement, while the remarriage rate has declined sharply. Many other factors, including medical advances that have lengthened the life span of the general population, have also dramatically changed the percentages of single adults living in America. But, for the first time in history there are now more divorced than widowed singles. (See fig. 10.2.)

The upsurge of divorce during recent years has probably been stimulated by a growing acceptance of the principle that divorce is a reasonable alternative to an unhappy marriage. While the culturally based negative sanctions have diminished, so, too, have the legal and economic constraints of obtaining a divorce. For example, the reform of divorce laws has generally resulted in a shortening of the

Fig. 10.2

**Population Figures:
*Divorced and Widowed
Americans***

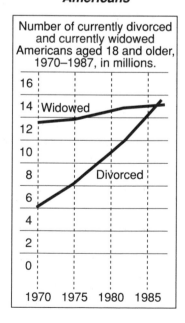

Number of currently divorced and currently widowed Americans aged 18 and older, 1970–1987, in millions.

required period of state residence and the required period of separation before a final decree is awarded by the court. Moreover, all but a few states have adopted some form of no-fault divorce, and most of the remaining state legislatures are attempting to incorporate this feature into their legal codes.

Fig. 10.3
Projected Duration of Marriage Longevity in the United States

Years of Marriage	Percentage of Couples Who Will Divorce in This or Later Years	Average Expected Years of Marriage
1	30.9	23.4
2	49.1	26.3
3	46.7	27.3
4	44.0	29.2
5	41.9	30.4
6	39.0	31.8
7	36.3	33.0
8	34.1	34.2
9	32.2	33.1
10	30.0	36.1
11	23.0	37.0
12	26.2	37.9
13	21.0	40.2
14	22.6	39.3
15	21.0	40.2
20	13.3	43.4
25	7.8	46.3
30	3.3	43.6
35	1.9	50.5
40	0.9	53.1
45	0.4	33.9
50	0.2	58.9
55	0.1	62.7
60	0.1	67.4

NOTE: The above figures are projections based on the average divorce and death rates in 1985.

U.S. News & World Report. *February 27, 1989, p. 75.*

Figure 10.3 illustrates the expected duration of marriages in the United States and projected divorce rates, grouped according to the duration of the marriages as of 1989. (The predictions were based on divorce and death rates in 1985.) Perhaps the most astonishing prediction was that roughly half of the marriages that had existed for one or two years would end in divorce.

There has been a relatively recent and rapid elimination of many barriers that had previously inhibited divorce. Consequently, a reasonable speculation is that at least part of the recent increase in the divorce rate may represent an acceleration in the timing of divorces that, under previous conditions, would have been spread over a greater number of years.

Factors Affecting the Divorce Rate

Divorce transcends all social and economic classes and has little regard to race, age, vocation, or even religious persuasion. In other words, divorce can strike almost anyone! There is no way to predict which couples will end their marriage in a divorce settlement. However, a review of divorce statistics that span a number of years can increase our understanding of the types of people who are most likely to get a divorce:

1. Those who marry young.
2. Those who have had more than one sexual partner prior to marriage.
3. Those with either less than a high-school education or two or more years of graduate school. (Least likely to divorce are four-year college graduates.)
4. Women who earn $50,000 or more annually.
5. Childless couples.
6. Among couples with children, those with daughters are more likely to divorce than those with sons.
7. Those who have been married before (50% divorce, 80% remarry).
8. Those whose parents were divorced.
9. Those who lived together before getting married.

Although divorce can occur at any age, it has generally been more prominent among relatively young adults. The lifestyles of persons born during the Baby Boom years (from the late 1940s through the 1950s) is of particular interest to those interested in studying marriage and divorce. The experience of this very large population subgroup is different from that of any other generation, past or present. As mentioned in chapter 5, many baby-boomers challenged the marital ideal by either delaying marriage (until other objectives had been reached) or foregoing it entirely. Those who did marry were less likely than their parents to regard the union as necessarily a "till death do us part" commitment. (Their parents, too, had begun to dissolve their own marriages at a significant rate.)

Many hypotheses have been proposed to explain the baby-boomer lifestyle and their tendency to question traditional norms. For example, the educational systems during the boomers' growing-up years often reminded parents that young people must be allowed to "think for themselves" rather than blindly accept old truisms. The do-your-own-thing philosophy that evolved from that idea brought confusion as well as fresh air and some healthy change. Ironically, the older generation indirectly contributed to the gradual erosion of tradition. Most of the baby-boomers' parents had been raised in the lean years of the Great Depression and were eager for their children to have better lives than they had experienced. In the relatively affluent few decades following World War II, this translated into materialistic objectives. Even so, as young people discovered that possessions failed to satisfy them, there was disillusionment and frustration. This reinforced their conclusion that society's institutions, including marriage, were flawed in some way.

Meanwhile, the desire for sexual freedom contributed to an increase in extramarital liaisons; some couples even experimented with "open marriages." Overall there was a growing sense of the impermanence of life, especially in light of Cold War politics and the looming threat of nuclear extinction during the years when baby-boomers entered adulthood.

All these trends, coupled with the tensions of living in a competitive, fast-paced culture, undoubtedly contributed to the rise in marital failures. People were looking for quick solutions to complicated problems. For many mates who found themselves in a less-than-satisfactory marriage, the solution lay in a divorce court. Relaxed divorce laws made a marriage package almost as easily disposable as the wrappings that enclosed their fast-food burgers.

A declining fertility rate may also have contributed to the rise in divorce statistics in recent years. Women with few children (or none) are more likely to be in the labor force and are therefore financially independent of their husbands. As family size has declined, so has the proportion of preschool-age children in the family. This additional development tends to provide mothers with more free time to work outside the home. Smaller family size also reduced the pressure to "stay together for the sake of the children," which had traditionally had a stabilizing effect on even an unhappy marriage.

A 1986 study in *USA Today* ("Tracking Tomorrow's Trends") explored some of the factors that can contribute to marital breakup by asking a series of questions about relationship issues. The researchers then compared the responses of married and divorced adults regarding their own experiences with a spouse or ex-spouse. There was a dramatic difference between the two groups as to the relative importance assigned to some—though not all—of the aspects of living compatibly with another person. The results could be headed "Reasons Why People Get a Divorce." Some of those reasons are summarized below:

1. *Lack of Emotional Support.* Divorced people were almost 40 percent more likely than married people to say that their spouses did not give them the emotional support and encouragement they craved. The difference between the two groups was more significant in this area than for any other question asked.

2. *Lack of Common Interests.* Divorced people were 32 percent more likely to cite marital stress caused by lack of common interests and goals. In follow-up interviews they elaborated on this, describing their marriage in such terms as "a fraying fabric." In other words, one doesn't suddenly wake up and decide to get a divorce. Rather, there is a drifting apart over time, and divergence of interests is one benchmark of that growing distance.

3. *Lack of Honesty.* When the subjects were asked if they could talk openly and honestly with their spouses (or ex-spouses), divorced people were 25 percent more likely than marrieds to answer "No." They knew that the lack of open communication caused stress in their lives. Many mentioned that they could not talk openly with a husband or wife without fear of being ridiculed or criticized.

4. *Not Feeling Liked or Appreciated.* Divorced people were 25 percent more likely to say that they didn't feel liked or appreciated by their spouses. (Notice that the word was *liked,* not *loved.*) More than one in four of the divorced subjects said that problems in their marriages led to serious marital stress—and this was especially true for the women.

5. *Financial Problems.* Although this was a distant fifth on the list of stress-producers, it is apparently the issue couples argue about most. Money, though important, seems secondary to building an open and honest relationship.

6. *Use of Free Time*. This was sixth in order of importance, with not much difference between the divorced and married subjects in their responses.

7. *Sexual Incompatibility*—a surprising seventh on the list. This agrees with a nationwide survey of almost a thousand psychiatrists, who ranked sexual problems eighth on a list of reasons why people seek psychiatric help.

One additional factor that can contribute to marital breakup is, of course, having an affair. Since ours is a mobile society that lacks small-town intimacy, we often don't know our neighbors or care about others around us. Many people feel lonely and alienated, even within a marriage. A person whose needs for intimacy are not being met by a marital partner will more readily step into an affair, sometimes without a twinge of conscience. People involved in extramarital experiences are sometimes trying to prove to themselves that they are still attractive and worthwhile. If a husband and wife are getting affirmation from each other, they rarely seek it in other relationships.

Developmental Crises in Marriage

Divorce can impact the life cycle of a marriage at any time, but the divorce rate often rises sharply at a couple of key points on the marriage continuum. Many authorities cite the most difficult and vulnerable times for a marriage as (1) during the first year or two of adjustment and (2) while children of the marriage are in their adolescence.

The first few years of marriage bring changes in lifestyle that require a great deal of adjustment by both partners. If one of the spouses has entered the relationship at too early an age, this transition period can be marked by so much ongoing tension that the marriage will not survive. During the late teens and early twenties, individuals need to establish their independence, the ability to function and think on their own. They also must have learned how to sustain intimacy at a deep level. Anyone who marries before reaching this level of maturity may simply be trading parental security for the emotional support provided by a husband or wife. Later, the longing for a period of independence may be strong enough to cause that person to give up on the marriage.

Tension is also created in the early years of marriage if one partner's developmental rate is ahead of the other's. One may want to start a family; the other is not ready to accept that responsibility. Or one partner may be working at the developmental process of "independence" and "intimacy," while the other is already in the "settling in" phase. If they both understood the normal development cycle, they might stop blaming each other and begin to encourage each other in the growth process.

Another difficult period for a marriage can occur during the midlife years, when people tend to be wrestling with their "significance." They are asking, "Who am I? Does my life matter?" This, too, is a developmental crisis of sorts. A man or woman searching for answers to those questions may have a compulsion to run away, not because of what the spouse has or has not done, but because of his or her own unresolved emotional problems.

By the midlife years, many marriages have also become stale and unfulfilling, usually because the couple has not paid enough attention to their relationship. They may feel that the marriage is unsatisfying and therefore should be ended so each can have a second chance at happiness.

After doing extensive research and dealing with hundreds of Christian middle-aged couples (as part of Anthony's doctoral dissertation), we are convinced that many of the divorces during these years are totally unwarranted. With a little effort on the part of both spouses, they could have become allies, seeking to bring meaning to their lives as individuals and resurrecting their marriage in the process.

Singles in America Survey: Divorced Singles

The general population's attitude toward divorce has changed a great deal over the past few decades. No longer do divorced individuals bear the stigma that once meant being barred from a particular job, political office, or social gathering. The rising population of divorced people has made an impact at all levels of our culture.

The church, however, has not kept pace with the rest of society in its attitudes toward divorced people. Throughout the history of the church, the divorced have been treated as second-class citizens and have often been eliminated from leadership roles. Many of the divorced Christians we interviewed expressed frustration and disappointment over the way they had been treated in their churches. This is one of the factors that may cause a Christian divorced person to lead a lifestyle marked by transience and mobility in his or her church commitment.

Of the Christian adults represented in our Singles in America survey, 40 percent were divorced (28 percent had been divorced less than two years, 25 percent between three and five years, 27 percent between six and ten years, and 19 percent more than ten years). The occupations of our divorced Christians are represented in figure 10.4. The percentages of divorced singles in the various job categories were not significantly different from those for our study group as a whole (see also fig. 3.2).

Fig. 10.4

Singles in America Survey:
Occupations of Divorced Singles

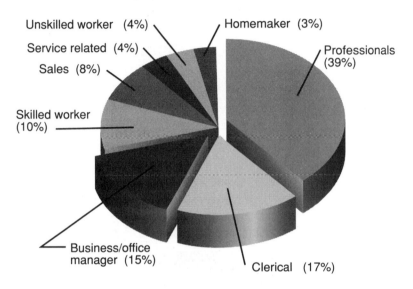

Figure 10.5 represents the income levels of these divorced singles. Here, too, the findings parallel those for the total sample of singles in our study (see also fig. 3.1).

These divorced singles were as active in their job efforts as were the other singles in our study. About 50 percent of each group said they worked over eight hours a day. Our survey indicated that over 11 percent of divorced singles and 12 percent of other singles work between eleven and sixteen hours a day, and 2 percent of divorced singles and 1.8 percent of other singles work over seventeen hours a day.

According to national and other opinion-makers, the most popular meeting place for singles is the singles bar or, more recently, a local health spa. When Simenauer and Carroll explored this issue for their 1982 book, *Singles: The New Americans,* they concluded that one-third of the single-adult population meet other singles through friends. Almost another third meet them at bars and social gatherings. Only 10 percent said they meet other singles at work.

The divorced singles in our study had quite a different approach for

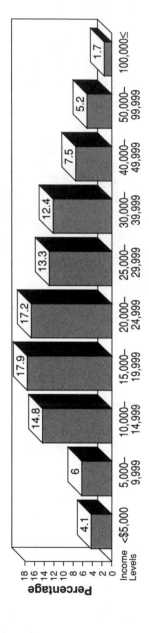

Fig. 10.5

Singles in America Survey:
Income of Divorced Singles

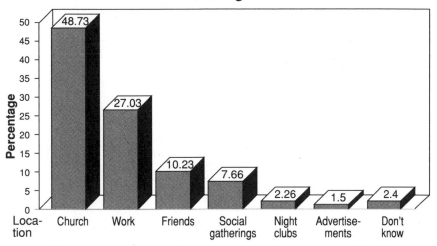

Fig. 10.6
Singles in America Survey:
Where Divorced Singles Socialize

"Where do you meet most of the men/women with whom you socialize?"

meeting other singles. Nearly 50 percent chose to socialize at a church activity, presumably so their new friends would have similar interests and spiritual conviction. Nearly 30 percent met other singles in the context of their work (see fig. 10.6 for a detailed breakdown).

The divorced singles in our survey actively expressed their sexuality (see fig. 10.7), which supports what most leaders of singles groups assume about them. Most of the divorced singles we studied had been

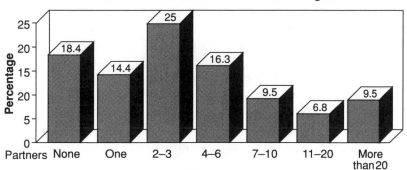

Fig. 10.7
Singles in America Survey:
Number of Sex Partners for Divorced Singles

"As a single adult, with how many sexual partners have you had sexual intercourse?"

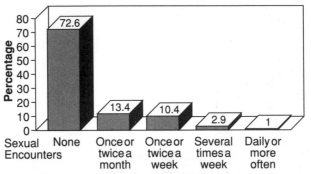

Fig. 10.8

Singles in America Survey:
Sexual Intercourse in the Previous Six Months
(Divorced Singles)

"During the past six months, how often have you had sexual intercourse?"

involved in sexual relations on a fairly regular basis. Nearly 82 percent had had intercourse while single; 10 percent had had intercourse with more than twenty partners (contrasting slightly with 6 percent for the group as a whole). The most significant difference (though not a particularly surprising one) between these divorced Christians and the group as a whole was in the percentages reporting that as singles they had had no sexual partners. For the divorced singles, that percentage was 18, compared to 40 percent for the total group. However, as seen in figure 10.8, the total number of sexual partners does not necessarily indicate the frequency of intercourse. About 72 percent of these divorced singles had not had intercourse during the previous six months (as contrasted with 82 percent for the total sampling).

The Needs of Divorced People

The divorced people we have interviewed tend to speak openly of the pain experienced during and following their divorce, and many are still learning to cope with all the issues involved. Some have been able to discover healing advice, while others are grasping for answers. Jim Smoke, in his book *Growing Through Divorce,* offers some insight into the goals of the recovery process. These "keys to divorce recovery" have been beneficial to divorced singles:

1. Finding and experiencing forgiveness
2. Letting go
3. Getting the ex-spouse in focus

4. Assuming responsibility for myself
5. Assuming responsibility for my children
6. Assuming responsibility for my future

Bill Flanagan, in his book *The Ministry of Divorce Recovery,* identifies some of the special needs of the divorced person. He writes that

. . . people going through this difficult process feel a tremendous sense of alienation, a loss of self-esteem and a monumental sense of guilt, failure and rejection. They also are accustomed to feelings of burnout as they assume added responsibilities in the area of their personal finances, children, and other household disruptions as they seek to assume new responsibilities and take on added burdens. Separated and divorced people most often feel an overwhelming sense of loneliness, as if they are the only persons going through this crisis, with no one else really being able to understand what is happening to them or how they are feeling.

People seek to meet their own needs in three basic ways:

1. *They internalize.* Divorced persons are very good at throwing "pity parties" for themselves. They very often will withdraw into themselves, into their homes, and become reclusive, rejecting all attempts of others to reach out to them in a warm, caring, understanding relationship. It is not uncommon to watch people in the shock of rejection build a wall around themselves, shutting out most of the rest of the world.

2. *They externalize.* People going through this experience of brokenness sometimes enter into the "swinging singles" scene. They succumb to the false option of running away from the issues and problems that surround them. "I can escape my problems if I run fast enough." Many people going through the process of divorce believe that if they move and change their geographic location, they can start out fresh somewhere else and the problems and realities of what is going on in their life will not exist in a new locale. This only compounds the problem, as they soon discover that there really is nowhere to run. Like Jonah in the Old Testament, they soon realize that God's purposes for them know no geographical boundaries, and if they are open and willing to perceive and accept a loving God, they can discover they no longer have to run, but simply trust in the one whose everlasting arms are always there to hold them.

3. *They actualize.* This third possibility is the most difficult and requires a painful acknowledgment of the reality of their situation. To actualize any crisis experience such as divorce, people must come to the place in their own personal journey where they are able to look into the mirror and say, "I am divorced. I am single. I am alone. I don't like it. I don't feel good about it. I wish this was not happening to me, but it is. I

must begin to put the pieces back together. I must understand that I have to start, not where I would like to be, but rather, where I am."

Stages of Divorce Recovery

Three stages in recovering from a divorce have been identified by Jim Smoke in *Growing Through Divorce*. He is the founder and director of the Center for Divorce Recovery, Phoenix, Arizona. Each stage has a particular focus and must be resolved before moving on to the next.

Stage One: Shock

The first stage for many individuals who recognize that divorce seems inevitable is shock at the idea that divorce is part of their personal experience and not just an anonymous statistic. The immediate reaction to the shock is often counterproductive. It may include such "flight patterns" as moving, changing jobs, or retreating from all social interaction. Some individuals go to the other extreme—by telling all the details of the situation to anyone who will listen, and throwing themselves into a frantic whirl of social and professional activity.

Resolution of this stage requires accepting that a vital and intimate relationship has died, but that the parties involved must move on. This requires inner reflection, evaluation of options, and specific planning for what will come next. The biggest challenge here is facing reality rather than holding on to the hope that the marriage might be revitalized. Of course, reconciliation may be possible in some cases, even after a decision for divorce has been announced (most couples have explored this possibility before that time). To that end, Smoke has suggested questions to be asked during this stage to assess the chances for saving the relationship: "Do both parties really want the marriage? Will both parties accept professional help in reconciliation for as long as is necessary? Has a third party become involved with either mate? What have I learned from my past experiences that will shed light on my present situation?" If the answers to those questions imply that, indeed, the hope for renewal is unfounded, each partner can more readily approach the next stage of the recovery process.

Stage Two: Adjustment

Even while a person moves through Stage One, adjustment to the divorce has begun. This is similar to what happens during the grieving process of someone whose spouse has died. Mixed feelings of denial, anger, guilt, and sorrow must be resolved before there can be any real adjustment to the loss. Whereas the first stage involves facing the reality of the divorce, the adjustment stage requires one to decide what to do with that fact!

This is essentially a time when the pieces of a shattered life are put back together, producing a different portrait than before the divorce, or even before the marriage began. Adjustment, which may take months, is experienced according to how well the individual is able to move through the mourning process and come to a firm resolve that life is still worth living, though its characteristics may have changed. It may be helpful to remind a recently divorced person of the adage that "time heals all wounds," but—like most bereaved people—he or she will probably not believe you!

Stage Three: Growth

Smoke writes that each of us can choose to *go* through an experience or *grow* through it. The third stage of recovery involves coming to a point of wanting to learn from the divorce experience and be a stronger and better person because of it. Some ideas that can help you in the growth stage are:

Realizing that time is a healer and that you can walk through life one day at a time

Setting aside time for reflection and focusing on personal growth

Being around healthy people who are *also* growing

Seeking professional counseling if your grief symptoms are severe or prolonged

Accepting that you are now single and must live in the present rather than the past

Committing your new life to God to work for his purpose

Although some people view divorce as an ending to a melodrama of mistakes and failure, the enforced learning experience in the wake of a divorce can be the beginning of an ongoing success story.

11

The Storms
of Single
Parenting

In a July 1985 special issue that focused on single parenting,
Newsweek observed that by "1990 half of all American families may
be headed by only one adult." Although that prediction awaits validation by 1990 Census Bureau statistics, many studies have indicated that
single-parent households have already exceeded this mark in major cities
and that nationally, at least one out of four households with children is
headed by a single parent. This trend has already redefined society's concept of "the all-American family."

There are an estimated 12 million single parents in America. Although

Fig. 11.1

Profile of Single Parents
(1988)

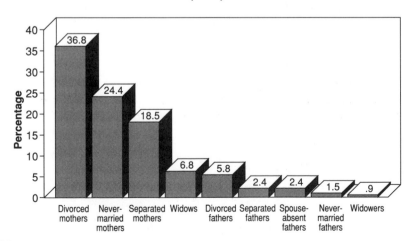

about 85 percent are women, single-parent families are headed by a variety of individuals, as indicated in figure 11.1.

Some additional statistics on single parenting include:

From 1970 to 1983 the number of one-parent families with children increased by 107 percent while two-parent families decreased by 5 percent (U.S. Dept. of Commerce, 1983).

One of every five families with children under eighteen years old in 1984 was a one-parent family, up from one of every ten in 1970 (*Family Relations*, January 1986).

A total of 54 percent of all black children under the age of eighteen now live in a single-parent home (*The Washington Post*, February 16, 1989).

Seventy percent of all children born in 1980 can expect to live with only one parent at some point before they reach age eighteen (*Journal of Marriage and the Family* 47 [1] Feb. 1983).

The number of married-couple households with children will continue to decrease through 1990, while the number of one-parent households will continue to increase by approximately 33 percent (*American Demographics* 6 [1] 1990).

Fig. 11.2
Profile of Households Including Young People

A profile of the households of today's youth show
youngsters 8 to 17 years old live with:

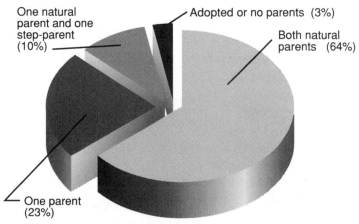

From a study conducted by The Roper Organization for the American Chicle Group of Warner-Lambert Company. Reported in *USA Today*, November 1987.

Thirty-seven percent of women [who were] in their late twenties in
1984 can expect to maintain a one-parent family with children
under eighteen (*Family Relations,* January 1986).

A 1987 study reported that only 64 percent of children aged eight to
seventeen lived with both natural parents (*USA Today,* November
1987). See figure 11.2.

The Structure of Single-Parent Households

Single-parent households are created by a variety of circumstances,
some "unexpected" and others the result of deliberate planning (see fig.
11.3). In the former category are families who have lost one parent
through death or who have been deprived of the presence of one parent
because of divorce, separation, or desertion. Any of these unforeseen situations is, of course, traumatic and will usually be followed by varying
degrees of sorrow, confusion, guilt, and/or anger on the part of both the
children and the remaining spouse (whether widowed or the custodial
parent after a divorce). In addition, a significant number of single-parent
households involve nonmarried mothers who have had an unplanned
pregnancy and decided against either abortion or adoption for the child,
choosing instead to raise the baby alone. A more recent trend is to
become a single parent "deliberately"—that is, for a woman to choose to

Fig. 11.3

**Circumstances Resulting
in Single Parenthood**

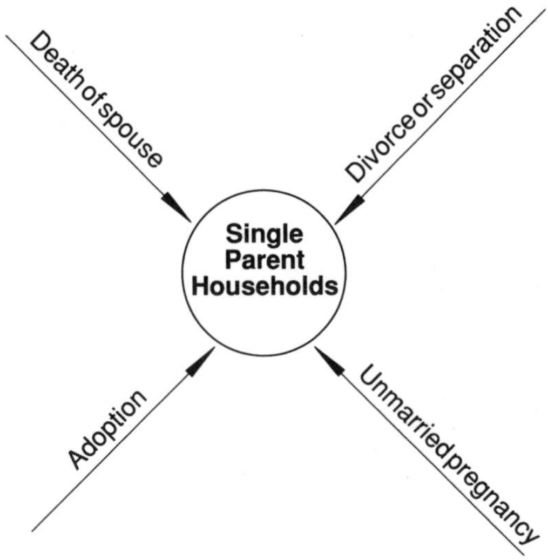

bear a child she wishes to raise as a single mother, or for a single of either sex to become an adoptive parent. Facilitated by the relaxation of laws that once required two parents in any adoptive situation, increasing numbers of healthy, happy, and financially secure singles are providing loving homes for children who have no natural parents or whose natural parents are unable to raise them for one reason or another. Many of these children are past babyhood or are racially mixed, disadvantaged, or physically handicapped—groups that were once considered "unadoptable." Naturally, the particular circumstances that have created a single-parent household will affect the practical needs of the family, the motivations of the parent, and the emotional tone of everyone in that home.

Misconceptions about Children of Single Parents

Most identifiable social groups carry certain negative stereotypes and misconceptions, and single-parent families are not immune to such unfair generalization. For example, it is assumed that families lacking a second parent are inevitably "dysfunctional." It is also commonly believed that most of these families have needs that are unmet, or, at best, are poorly met. To investigate some of these widespread misconceptions, a longitudinal study ("Effects of Marital Disruption on Children's School Aptitude and Achievement" by E. Milling Kinard and Helen Reinherz. *Journal of Marriage and Family* 48 [May 1986]: 285–93.) was launched to compare the development of third- and fourth-grade children in both two-parent and one-parent families. When researchers monitored the children's general emotional and social growth, school performance, and relationships with peers and family members, they found no significant differences between the two groups. In both types of families there were children under tremendous stress, failing in school, and otherwise showing evidence of emotional and social problems because of neglect and poor parental role modeling. The conclusion was that the level of a child's adjustment is related to the *quality* of parenting, rather than whether there was one parent or two.

Current studies of single-parent families tend to indicate that children in healthy single-parent homes may actually excel over children in traditional homes in individual decision making and the ability to work alone on a project or problem. This may be true because practical concerns in a single-family household often make it expedient for these children to acquire a sense of personal accountability and family cooperation at a younger age than children with the ongoing presence of two parents. If the quality of their parenting is high—and so long as they are not required to make decisions inappropriate to their maturity level—children in single-parent families may develop independent thinking patterns at a relatively young age.

It is important to remember that one-parent families cannot be stereotyped. They differ as much in parental skills, motivation, resources, opportunities, and past circumstances as traditional families do. There is mounting evidence that single parents can raise well-adjusted, loving children with a high degree of family bonding and pride.

The Unique Struggles of Single Parents

Any discussion of a particular social group inevitably shifts to focusing on its problems. The basic human needs of a single parent are the same as those of any adult in the general population. However, because of his or her non-traditional parental role, a single parent has unique concerns—challenges that face other parents to a lesser degree, if at all.

The Single Mother

Economic Needs

The most acute problem for female heads of households is their economic condition. The U.S. Bureau of the Census reports that nine out of ten single-parent households are headed by women. (See also "Profile of Single Parents" in fig. 11.1, which indicates that about half of them are single parents as a result of divorce or separation.) It is also reported that child-support payments to white mothers dropped an average of 14 percent between 1983 and 1985 (some women reported a 33 percent decline). Half of the women awarded child support by the courts were receiving the full amount; another 25 percent were receiving none at all. Virtually every survey indicates that black single mothers receive far less in child support payments than white single parents.

Since fathers with custody generally (according to IRS tax services) earn twice as much as single mothers with custody, poverty is the top issue facing the single mother in America today. The 1984 Federal Child Support Enforcement Amendments are making it easier to enforce child-support payments, but many single mothers still find the economic pressures overwhelming.

Over the past few decades, the number of women in the labor force has doubled. By the late 1970s, 77 percent of divorced mothers were employed, as compared to 48 percent of married mothers. Yet, despite this higher degree of participation in the work force, women in general do not have salary levels as high as their male counterparts.

To further illustrate the economic hardships placed on the single mother, it has been reported that "divorced women experience a 73 percent decline in income the first year after a divorce, while a divorced man's income increases by 42 percent" (*Newsweek,* July 15, 1985). If the divorcée had no job outside the home prior to the marital dissolution, she will probably now have to seek employment, yet the years at home may have left her painfully unprepared for today's job market. Widows may fare better financially, depending on pension or insurance benefits, and they are eligible for Social Security allotments if they have minor children. In the case of divorced women, studies indicate that only 13 percent of fathers ordered to support their children were in full compliance ten years after the divorce. Seventy percent were in total noncompliance.

It follows that a divorced mother without adequate financial support from her ex-spouse or marketable job skills will have a difficult time making ends meet. In fact, large numbers of single mothers—whether divorced, separated, widowed, or never married—face a high level of emotional stress because their expenses for such essential items as housing, food, utilities, clothing, and child care are not being met. (See also "Concerns of Single Working Mothers" in chapter 9.)

Child Custody

When divorce destroys a family, it inevitably changes parent-child relationships in many ways. The divorce courts award custody of the children to the mother about 90 percent of the time, on the not necessarily valid assumption that she is better qualified to nurture them, especially in their early years. (But see discussion of "The Single Father" in the next section.) However, the issues surrounding custody and visitation rights pose ongoing problems for all concerned. If parents use their children as pawns in custody battles, the children will be the losers, whatever the outcome, since the emotions surfacing during the struggle usually have a negative effect on the healing process.

Even if a mother has been awarded sole custody and is satisfied with the visitation rights of her ex-husband, these decisions can rarely be considered final. Changing circumstances of either parent, or a belief that a child's best interests are not being served, can result in appeals by the noncustodial parent to amend the original court judgment. Furthermore, when one parent refuses to recognize the court's custody decision or the other parent's visitation rights, he (or she) may resort to such extreme acts as child snatching. According to some studies, this accounts for 85 to 90 percent of all child "disappearances." Despite federal legislation that attempts to address this problem, it is difficult and costly to track down the missing parent and child and to enforce one state's judicial rulings if they have moved to another state.

The traditional tendency to award sole custody to mothers is being changed by such creative approaches as co-parenting, or joint custody. Sharing parental responsibility in this way, especially when both parents want to cooperate with the ruling, recognizes the potential rewards of allowing a child to know each parent on an equal time-share basis. But, even in this apparently fair arrangement, there are side issues. For example, where will the parents live? The logistics can be complicated, especially if they require one parent to adjust his or her career goals to live near the other parent and thereby minimize the disruption of a child's school schedule and lifestyle.

Child Care

As noted previously, a large percentage of single mothers work, many of them because they must. This creates a special dilemma for those with young children (see also chapter 9). In *Being a Single Parent* (1987), A. Bustanoby points out that child-care arrangements are generally limited to three types:

1. Approximately half of all children in day care are cared for in the home of a caregiver who is not a relative. Most states require licensing of these homes, which typically provide care for two or three neighbors plus the caregiver's own children.

2. One-third of the day-care population is cared for by a family member, such as an older sibling, grandparent, aunt, or other relative. Slightly more than half of these relatives baby-sit for free.

3. About 16 percent of the children attend a child-care center. One reason for this low percentage is lack of availability; another is cost.

Placing her children in a day-care arrangement can be stressful for a woman who accepts the cultural view that her rightful place is at home with them. Anything less than that ideal can produce anxiety, fear, and guilt. Recent studies on the effect of day-care programs on child development have yielded conflicting results. More research is needed to determine the possible short- and long-term effects of child care on America's children.

After a child begins school and reaches an age where some degree of self-care is feasible, less formal arrangements are possible. Self-care arrangements have recently become of great interest to child-care providers, policy makers, educators, and the media. By the age of nine, a growing number of children from single-parent homes are in self-care situations after school hours. Many of these "latch-key kids" exhibit an impressive degree of self-reliance; some also take responsibility for younger siblings. Even if the child knows exactly how to handle minor emergencies, and the parent or some other adult is readily accessible, there are obvious dangers inherent in such an arrangement. In some communities, the public schools and religious or private groups have instituted after-school programs for children of working parents. This kind of supervision is usually far superior to self-care, especially for primary-grade youngsters.

Sexuality

Being involved in a marriage allows a woman to explore her sexuality and establish patterns of sexual activity. When this normal function is interrupted by the end of a marriage (whether by divorce or death of the spouse), a considerable degree of personal adjustment must take place. A woman's new status as a single may require her to reevaluate her ethics, moral standards, and values concerning sexual behavior. The sense of isolation felt in the aftermath of the end of a marriage usually compounds the problem.

Robert Weiss (*Going It Alone*, p. 197) reported little evidence of the traditional belief that a man's sexual desire is compelling, while a woman's produces, at most, a state of passive responsiveness to the man's overtures. Women may be more reluctant to take the initiative in expressing this need, but it is just as important. Perhaps mainly because of cultural indoctrination, women seem able to separate themselves from their physical needs; in the sexual realm it is almost as though this drive does not exist. But any repressed need will eventually surface and demand attention.

Weiss observes that formerly-married women have four basic options for addressing their sexuality—physical intimacy with the former spouse, masturbation, short-term partnering (either serially or on a concurrent basis), and/or monogamous partnering on a long-term basis. One avenue of sexual expression may actually increase the overall tension level, while another may be quite satisfying and minimally stressful. These sexual outlets are not mutually exclusive; during any given time period an individual may choose one or more of them concurrently. What options a woman chooses will depend on such factors as her age, her living accommodations, her opportunities to meet a prospective partner and consummate a sexual union, and her value system in regard to the "correctness" of sexual activity outside the bonds of marriage.

It is our opinion that, although well meaning, Weiss has overlooked another viable option for single women (and men). The Bible clearly teaches that abstinence is the best option for those who seek purity in their sexuality. Obedience to such a clear teaching will help singles avoid many of the common pitfalls that are associated with the options presented by Weiss (e.g., guilt; lowering of self-esteem; feeling degraded, used, or manipulated). The biblical ideal of abstinence is not easy to achieve, particularly for those who have been previously married. More will be said on this matter in chapter 12.

Other Concerns

We have noted that women in single-parent roles find that their most difficult adjustment areas are economic stability, custody, child care, and sexual expression. That is not to say that single *fathers* don't have such problems. But, for a single mother, they are more acute. Other needs include finding a support system within the community, learning to live with loneliness, rebuilding trust in people, and handling such practical assignments as home maintenance and auto care. For widows—and divorcées whose ex-spouse is not readily accessible or has been denied regular visitation rights for some reason—there is also the challenge of finding a substitute "father" who can serve as an appropriate role model for the children.

The Single Father

According to the statistics represented in figure 11.1, households headed by single fathers comprise less than 15 percent of the total single-parent living arrangements, but that proportion can be expected to increase in the future. More and more fathers are being awarded sole custody of their children after a divorce. This trend is actually somewhat of a throwback to earlier times in America's history, though for different reasons. Prior to the twentieth century, a father was more likely to be awarded custody of his children than his wife (although there were, of course, far fewer divorces than there are today). This partly reflected the higher mortality rate for women, especially in rural areas. Husbands at that time were also the ones most involved in earning the family's income, and their role as breadwinner brought a higher degree of social recognition and status as a "financially responsible" individual.

However, by the end of the nineteenth century, significant social changes affecting the status of women had begun. As more women sought higher education and entered the workplace, they made their presence felt in society and expressed their desire for gender equality. Even before the highly publicized "women's movement" of the mid-twentieth century, humanitarian organizations, working in a climate of progressivism, were able to secure many benefits for women, including voting and property rights, better health care, and increased job opportunities. All these factors influenced the legal system, which began favoring women in custody suits involving young children.

That trend is shifting today. The growing emphasis within our culture for husbands to participate more fully in the daily hands-on practicalities of running a home and sharing in child-care responsibilities has brought a recognition that men can be highly effective nurturers. As traditional ideas about role assignments are discarded, the courts are beginning to award full or shared custody to increasing numbers of fathers—often with the full agreement of the mothers concerned. Sometimes, the "best interests" of a child are better served if that child lives with his or her father.

As early as 1983, almost 600,000 divorced and separated fathers were raising children under the age of eighteen. This was an increase of 180 percent since 1970 and represents over a million children. (During the same period, the number of divorced and separated single mothers increased by slightly over 105 percent to 4,256,000.)

Research focusing on single fathers is still limited in scope, but there is enough evidence that in many respects their needs and concerns parallel those of a single mother. A few distinctives remain, however.

Housekeeping

When a father starts raising his children alone, an issue requiring immediate attention is the home. His wife had probably handled most of the household chores for the family. Blumstein and Schwartz in their 1983 book, *American Couples,* reported that "working wives do less housework than homemakers, but they still do the vast bulk of what needs to be done. Husbands of women who work help out more than husbands of homemakers, but their contribution is not impressive. Even if a husband is not employed, he does much less housework than a wife who puts in a forty-hour week."

Although fathers may leave much of the housework to their wives during their marriage, they have to assume the responsibilities once they become full-time single parents. In one study of 1,100 fathers reported by G. Greif in his book *Single Fathers* (1985), fathers received the most outside help in the areas of cooking and laundry. But fathers are more likely to handle the shopping and cooking, while their children (eleven years or older) did the cleaning and the laundry. (Few fathers can afford hiring full-time help, although their new responsibilities create a previously not encountered job/home conflict.)

Child Care

Closely related to housekeeping responsibilities is proper day care for the children. In this area, single fathers have the same concerns as single mothers (see previous section), except that the fathers *may* have reached a relatively higher position on a career ladder. It may be necessary for them to leave for work before children are due at school and return home several hours after the children are home. According to Greif, the arrangements that fathers make concerning child care vary according to diverse factors, including age of the children, father's income and work schedule, presence of support systems (families, friends, neighbors), the father's perception of his children's needs, and his feelings about the type of home life they should have. Balancing all those concerns can be difficult, and some compromises may be required.

It has been noted that some children beyond the age of eleven can assume a greater degree of personal and family responsibility. Both fathers and mothers raising children under that age face a dilemma regarding after-school supervision. Many parents pay for extended-care arrangements for children under the age of five, but school-age children are fast becoming part of the "latch-key" generation, which raises all the issues discussed previously under "The Single Mother."

Due to concern for the welfare of their children, some single fathers have had to pass up promotions that might have required relocation. (Even noncustodial fathers may not want to move far from children living with their mother.) Many fathers have to reduce their work hours or choose work assignments that are compatible with the demands of child-care arrangements. The trauma of such adjustments for high-achieving men should not be underestimated. Since many men derive much of their identity from career performance, in this sense the cost of child care can be very high.

Socialization

Most widowed or divorced single fathers see remarriage as a long-term goal, both to achieve loving companionship for themselves and find a "mother" for their children. Therefore, they face the challenge of resocializing themselves through a series of phases that will eventually put them in a position to remarry. The most difficult phase for many men is the first, that of dating. Once they are single again, many of these men feel out of step with current social norms and patterns. Widowers (and widows, too, of course) may feel somewhat guilty about seeking love again, as if this would imply disloyalty to the deceased spouse. They may also be concerned about how the children might feel if another woman "usurped" the role once played by their mother. On the other hand, men who have gone through a bitter divorce proceeding may simply be hesitant to subject themselves to the possible repetition of what they see as emasculation by an ex-wife and/or a female-biased court system. For some, even the thought of reentering the dating scene evokes all the insecurities, hesitations, and posturing experienced years before.

Once a new relationship is started, it may be difficult for the father to bring his friend into the established family structure. A child, especially a young girl, may develop feelings of jealousy and resentment toward both the woman and the father. Although the latter needs to be able to socialize with his female friend in an informal and natural climate, doing so at home may produce turmoil. If the relationship persists, a cohabitation arrangement may result. According to recent U.S. Census figures, about 4 percent of all couples are living together without being married. Almost half of these cohabiting persons have been previously married. (Such an arrangement is often the grounds on which a noncustodial parent may base an appeal for change of custody.)

The socialization process is an essential element in the healing process of divorced and widowed fathers. The need is very real, but the skills to successfully navigate this process may seem elusive.

Other Concerns

In a society that still tends to regard single fatherhood as rather unusual, if not "second-rate"—and that until recently sold child-development manuals mainly to women—there is a great need for support systems attentive to the needs of men who are raising their children alone. Groups such as Parents Without Partners are addressing these concerns quite well, and there are branches in most areas of the country.

On a more personal level, a primary source of support is a female relative—a grandmother, aunt, sister, or sister-in-law. These members of the extended family can assist by serving as ongoing counselors, part-time caregivers, or even live-in housekeepers. (Some single fathers share a home with their own parents or in-laws to be assured of ongoing supervision of their children.) Many men also find helpful support from female neighbors or work associates who have raised children of their own. They can provide advice on questions ranging from how to handle a childhood disease to what type of birthday present is suitable for a child. Neighbors may also offer to care for a child after school or chauffeur him or her to extracurricular activities.

A third source of support can be a woman whom the father is dating on a regular basis. Whether or not marriage is his intention, he may rely on her nurturing abilities, which may be especially important for a preschool-age child or for a young girl entering adolescence. A problem can develop, however, if a child develops a strong emotional bond to the woman that must eventually be severed when the relationship does not lead to marriage.

The Effects of Divorce and Loss on Children

Because divorce is a serious and complicated experience for children as well as their parents, considerable attention is now being paid to the special problems and needs of children of divorced parents. The determining factors in a child's adjustment following the divorce include the environment before, during, and after the crisis, the circumstances causing the divorce, and the emotional tone of the parents. Although most children make healthy adjustments within a few years after the divorce, the time of transition and adjustment is usually traumatic.

Because it has traditionally been assumed that the younger the child, the more damaging the effects of a divorce, some very unhappy couples delay divorce proceedings until their children have left home or at least have reached adolescence. However, as shown in figure 11.4, there are characteristic adverse reactions at any age. Most children after the age of nine have a rather clear understanding of what is happening. Although they may initially react with varying degrees of grief, self-blame, anger, and fear, they usually develop adequate coping mechanisms. Parents contemplating divorce and worrying about the effects on their children might be somewhat encouraged to learn that most school-age children are operating fairly well within a year of a divorce—but preschoolers often continue to be confused and emotionally debilitated well after that time period.

Problem Areas

The predominant problem areas for children of divorce are as follows:
Confusion/Self-Blame. The number-one problem for children of divorce is that they are confused about what is going on; they are often kept uninformed about an impending divorce until one parent actually leaves. Because they may have been punished or caught in the middle of parental arguments, they may feel that the divorce is somehow their

Fig. 11.4

Effects of Divorce on Children

	2 1/2–6 Preschool	7–8 Early Latency	9–12 Later Latency	13–18 Adolescents
Feelings	Irritable, acute separate anxieties, aggression.	Sadness, grief, fear, deprivation, loss and anger.	Loss and rejection, helplessness and loneliness, shame, worry, and hurt.	Disappointment.
Expression	Young kids regress in behavior; aggressive behavior and tantrums; fantasy.	Crying and sobbing, fantasizing, increment in possessiveness and no sharing.	Object-directed toward mother, father, or both; tantrums, demands, and dictatorial attitudes; increase in petty stealing; somatic symptoms; strained relations with parents.	Openness about their situation, involved in social activities.
Coping Mechanism	No coping mechanisms which pushes them toward aggression.	No health mechanism to avoid pain.	Views divorce with soberness and clarity and masks feelings with various available devices. Engages in play.	More self-reliant.
School Achievement	Not applicable.	No difference from other children.	Noticeable decline in school performance.	No difference from other children.
Reason for Divorce	Self-accusations.	Majority concerned with causing the divorce.	Only a few were concerned with their causing the divorce.	They did not see themselves as the reason for divorce.
Cognitive	Confusion about what is happening.	Confusion about what is happening.	Clear understanding of what is happening.	Clear understanding of what is happening.
Visitation	High frequency—once a week	Peak visiting—up to three times a week.	Infrequent and erratic visiting.	Few contacts but more than the 9–12.
One Year Following Divorce	Majority in worse condition.	65% either improved or accepted the divorce—about 23% deterioration.	25% worried about being forgotten or abandoned by both parents. 75% resumed educational and social achievements. Those isolated worsened.	Majority of children operating again as before with some cognitive questions.

fault. It is vital that parents sit down and explain the situation to each child, emphasizing that the responsibility for the dissolution of the relationship is theirs alone, not the child's.

Grief. Divorce brings depression and a sense of loss—a time of grief will follow, as if a death had occurred. It is often expected that only the parents will go through this mourning cycle, but it is important to recognize that the children will need to go through a similar process before recovery can occur. They usually need assistance to work through their grief.

Anger. Resentment or anger is a normal and painful part of the divorce process. Children may feel cheated. They believe they deserve a normal life, and somehow this has been taken away from them. They are often angry at both the parent who left and the one who stayed. And they may show anger toward God for not keeping their family together.

Fear and Insecurity. After one parent has left, the children may wonder if they are loved and worry that the other parent will also leave. They are afraid, and that sets off a chain of insecurities and internal questions. Who will protect me? Who will take care of me? More than ever the child needs continual assurance that someone will continue to care for him or her.

Feelings of Powerlessness. As children watch the divorce play out before them, they realize they have no control over the situation. They feel powerless and may experience a deep sense of helplessness. Children who try to get their parents to reconcile usually learn that there is really nothing they can do about the situation.

Poor Decision-Making Abilities. To the degree that children are hurt, confused, and frustrated by the divorce, decisions and simple choices become difficult for them. It will be hard for them just to choose what clothes to wear on a given day. Until they have made some adjustment to the initial shock, they should not be pressured to choose between parents or where to live.

Sense of Rootlessness. Divorce brings change, not only to the makeup of the family, but also to all areas that impact the overall stability and well-being of the children. They wonder where they will live, what schools they will attend, whether they will have to make new friends. Economic changes—reduced family income, sale of the family home, or a new job for one or both parents—may cause concern about how their lifestyle will be affected, especially in older children. Recovery cannot begin until some of those questions are answered.

Help for Children of Divorce

1. *Talk through their concerns.* The best therapy for children of divorce is open and honest two-way conversation. Getting them to talk will release some of their internal tensions and uncover their specific areas of concern.
2. *Encourage supportive relationships.* Create a sense of security by building on existing relationships within the extended family, among close friends, and in the local church.
3. *Extend comfort.* Give comfort as your children grieve for their loss of the other parent's presence. To the best of your ability, answer their questions about what will happen to their lives.
4. *Admit your own struggles.* No single parent has all the answers. Let your children know that you, too, have struggles. Share your concerns at a level appropriate to the age of each child.
5. *Express your love.* More than ever before, your children need to know that you—*and* the missing parent—love them. Be sure they know they have no reason to blame themselves for the marital breakup.

How the Church Can Help the Single Parent

The church is called on to minister to the unique needs of the single-parent family. Attempts to reach out to this segment of the general population must not only draw on sound biblical principles of love and understanding of human frailties, but must also provide some practical ways to address their needs.

The church must first reconsider its attitude toward fragmented families, especially those who are victims of divorce. It can no longer take the traditional approach of turning its back on these people and hoping they can solve their own problems. What is needed is a change in mindset. The members of the body of Christ must be ready to bind up the wounds of the brokenhearted, comfort the lonely and grieving, and restore to spiritual wholeness those whose lives have fallen apart in the breakup of a marriage.

Part of this realignment of attitude is to educate its members about the unique needs of single parents. We are quick to provide tangible acts of love and kindness to the recently widowed mother, but what about the needs of the family in the following months? Many church members would be happy to lend a hand if they only knew how. The church's example can teach its members to be more aware of compassionate responses to specific needs.

Before it can minister to single-parent families, a church must first examine the kind of single parents who are in the congregation and the local community. It is obvious that the needs of a particular single parent are closely related to the conditions that brought him or her into that role. It therefore becomes imperative to determine the profile of the single parent in the community. What percentage is divorced, widowed, never married? Based on this information, a local church can develop a strategy for its outreach. Figure 11.5 illustrates how a local church might develop a program for single parents. Whereas widowed parents are usually welcomed wholeheartedly and compassionately into congregational fellowship, a certain degree of hesitation or even intolerance sometimes characterizes a local church's attitude toward never-married parents (especially "unwed mothers") and those who are separated or divorced. Too often these groups meet with rejection and faultfinding on the part of family, friends, and society in general. It is important that the church be prepared to provide them with a nonjudgmental and caring climate of acceptance. If pastoral staff members and lay leaders model Christian qualities of love and forgiveness, others in the congregation will be encouraged to follow suit.

Besides inviting single parents to participate in all its regular programs, a local church can help by developing specific support groups that will enrich their lives and strengthen them for meeting their unique challenges. This support can take a variety of forms: a Sunday school class for singles, a divorce/widowed recovery program, home-based fellowships and prayer groups, recreational outings, a newsletter advertising such practical items as job openings, baby-sitters, garage sales, legal advice, and more. Perhaps the church could sponsor a local chapter of Parents Without Partners. The method and range of support will vary according to the makeup and concerns of single-parent families in the community.

One very helpful resource the church can provide is a counseling service. Whether it be individual or small-group counseling, seminars, or large conferences, the church should be prepared to offer single parents guidance and advice. Issues that could be addressed include handling grief, divorce recovery, child development and family discipline, managing finances on a single income, legal and tax ramifications of single parenting, child-care options, and job counseling.

A final requirement for the church is to provide economic assistance to the best of its ability. The early church was known for its generosity toward those in financial need. Although the universal church can hardly eliminate the need for all state and federally funded programs, a local congregation can assist single-parent families in practical ways such as:

1. Sponsoring a child in a summer-camp program
2. Providing a single parent with funds for private counseling or job training or to attend a workshop
3. Subsidizing housing or grocery needs
4. Supplying "nonessential" resources (video and audio tapes, movie tickets, etc.) that the family could not otherwise afford
5. Helping with child care by sponsoring a preschool program or calling on individual members to join a network of informal caregivers

The basis for creating a program and place for single-parent families within the church community requires maintaining an ongoing awareness of their needs and a commitment to use all its human, service-

Fig. 11.5
Developing a Church Program
for Single Parents

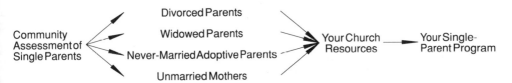

oriented, and financial resources to address those needs. The church must rise to the challenge posed by the increasing numbers of single parents by helping these adults and their children develop their full potential and grow in spiritual maturity. (Many further suggestions are discussed in Part Four.)

12

Sexual
Shipwrecks

In this "sweet land of liberty," where certain individual rights are guaranteed in the Constitution, it is hardly surprising that standards of proper behavior have changed so drastically over the past hundred years, especially in the area of what is "right" and "wrong" sexually. Well into the twentieth century, religious doctrine—as interpreted by the institutional church and transmitted within a family unit—shaped most of society's moral values and forged its legal system. But, as Americans increasingly reaped the benefits of medical and technological "miracles," they gradually placed more emphasis on the pronouncements of the court systems or the behavioral labs than on the biblical absolutes spoken from the pulpit or in the family circle. Even within the body of believers, there was a liberalization of theology—an attitude that seemed to say it was okay to choose which divine guidelines to obey. Sociologists call that "situational ethics," the idea that moral standards depend on time, place, and circumstance rather than rigid definitions of right and wrong.

At the same time, the melting-pot concept of American social history has facilitated an atmosphere of relative tolerance toward others' points of view. This open-ended attitude has been helpful in creating a certain degree of harmony and cooperation; but if the process is stretched to its limits, there will remain few universal standards of conduct. "Do's and don'ts" become obsolete notions if morals are allowed to shift according to the immediate circumstances. When flexible standards are applied to one's sexual decisions, there is a great potential for danger, both practically and spiritually.

Such a liberal approach to sexuality is prevalent among adults in contemporary America, even among Christians. Standards of conduct that were commonly upheld by previous generations have been discarded for a "new morality" characterized by convenience and free expression of feelings. Among many singles, premarital sex is seen as acceptable between consenting adults. There is even circulated the idea that extra-marital affairs are permissible, since they may be "beneficial" to a troubled marriage. Because relaxed sexual standards repudiate much of what Christian singles have been taught was "proper," many of them are confused about how to handle their sexual energy in a world that continues to tell them to "do your own thing."

Perhaps no other cross section of our population is as diversified and difficult to understand as the single adult. In a given singles group will be never-marrieds, divorced singles of all ages, and those going through the pain surrounding a current separation or the death of a spouse. Some of these people are parents; others are not. Discussing sexuality for "Christian singles," therefore, must take into consideration this unique configuration.

The Search for Intimacy

According to Mary Ann Mayo, in her book *A Christian Guide to Sexual Counseling,* many people today (and down through the ages) have confused the search for a male-female *relationship* with the desire for *sexual activity.* As a result, many singles try to fill the God-given need for intimacy with a sexual experience. When one experience brings no lasting pleasure (Scripture teaches that sex can never fully satisfy outside of marriage), a series of sexual liaisons takes place, each time creating more guilt, confusion, and emotional bondage to a battery of hormonal urges.

It is not difficult to understand why such a pattern has gripped the lives of millions of singles today. After all, recreational sex *is* pleasurable for the moment and it can briefly dispel a bout of loneliness. But within a day or two even the memory has faded, leaving a larger emptiness than before. Says Mayo, "Casual sex is like candy: it seems good while one is eating it, but it is nutritionally unhealthful. . . . Scarcely does the person seeking intimacy through sex relate their [sic] emptiness, complications and health problems back to their source: sex with no commitment."

What so many singles today need to realize is that intimacy can exist without sexual expression, that two people can share their thoughts and feelings without sharing their bodies. It is only when such an understanding is acknowledged that true "intimacy"—the bonding of one soul with another—will happen freely. For many singles it is painful not having a special someone to love. But the real pain, the more difficult hurt to heal, is caused by a superficial relationship that went too far physically. Such is the case for couples who choose to live together without making a marital commitment, often as a "trial period" to test their compatibility. These live-in arrangements are not without great risk and in most cases lead eventually to greater emotional pain, since there is then added a sense of failure or abandonment.

Cohabitation

When moral absolutes and the values derived from them no longer remain constant, society's ethical standards become clouded by ambiguity, and decision making becomes difficult and complex. In the light of these shifting messages, many Americans have chosen to reject the traditional bonds of marriage in favor of more flexible living arrangements. During earlier periods, it was rare for a couple to cohabit; such a lifestyle would have been met with scorn and isolation. Today this arrangement is becoming more and more commonplace and is even applauded by some as a sensible "experiment."

Between 1970 and 1980, the number of live-in couples in the United States had more than tripled to 1.6 million. According to 1987 figures, approximately 2.3 million unmarried American couples are currently cohabiting.

Does Living Together Work?

According to a June 1985 article by Joyce Brothers in *New Woman* magazine, many single adults—especially women—are discovering that living together has some major drawbacks. The article (pp. 54–57) listed a number of reasons why such a living arrangement may not be a wise alternative:

Divorce may be more likely later. According to a study conducted by the National Bureau of Economic Research, couples who lived together before getting married had nearly an 80 percent higher divorce rate than couples who did not.

There is a lower level of satisfaction after marriage. A 1983 study by the National Council on Family Relations of 309 recently married couples found that couples who lived together before marriage were less happy in their marriages. Women were especially dissatisfied with the quality of communication with their partners after the wedding.

Men move in primarily for sex. A 1973 survey of Northeastern University students found that the number-one reason women lived with a lover was that they wanted to get married. However, the primary reason for men was "sex—when you want it, where you want it." (Another study showed that 35 percent of the male subjects admitted to having lied to a woman so he could have sex with her. The most common lies were that a man cared for her more than he really did or that he had fewer previous sexual partners than was the case.)

Few marriages actually result from cohabitation. The real truth about live-in relationships is that they do not last. In the heat of tension and turmoil, since neither partner has a binding reason to stay, one can simply walk out. According to a 1985 Columbia University study, only 26 percent of the women surveyed (and a scant 19 percent of the men) ended up marrying the person with whom they had cohabited.

There is a higher risk of sexual disease. A 1973 study cited in the *Journal of Marriage and the Family* reported that live-in males "sleep around" more than married men do. Since that survey there has been some evidence (Srully Blotnick Survey, 1986) indicating a cooling of casual sex among singles in America, perhaps due to the fear of catching an STD.

Sexual hostility is symptomatic. In the 1986 *New Woman* sex survey, 40 percent of cohabiting women said they had endured a kind of sex they didn't want or enjoy. "The main problem," according to California sociologist Dr. Jack Balswick, is "there is no commitment in a live-in relationship. It's all for immediate pay off, immediate gratification. . . . A falsehood many people who buy into temporary relationships believe is the notion that they can build a meaningful relationship without full commitment."

Cohabiting women feel less secure. Women who share their living quarters with a lover feel more insecure about the future of their relationship than women who live alone.

Breaking up is just as painful. The generalization that there are "no strings" and that either party is free to leave any time is simply not true. Since a great deal of emotional bonding takes place during cohabitation, a lover's departure can be every bit as painful as a marital breakup.

The Demographics of Cohabitation

The media-generated portrait of a single adult who cohabits is a college student or a young urban professional. But, according to one study conducted at the University of Wisconsin, this stereotype is simply not accurate. The researchers discovered that financial considerations were the most significant factor in an unmarried couple's decision to live together. Here was a way to test the old adage that "two can live as cheaply as one"! Below are some of the other conclusions of the study:

People who have not completed high school have a 30 percent higher rate of cohabitation than those who go on to college. (Those with lower incomes are considerably more likely to live together without getting married.) The relatively affluent are more likely to be married or live alone. Money allows people the luxury of privacy or the ability to afford marriage if they wish it.

Between one-half and two-thirds of the decline in marriage among young people can be accounted for by the rise in cohabitation.

For those under the age of twenty, the proportion of those married declined from 27 percent in 1970 to 14 percent in 1985. But the number involved in *some* type of "union" (marriage or cohabitation) dropped only 6 percent, from 29 percent to 23 percent.

Of all couples who married between 1970 and 1985, 40 percent had lived together first.

Although the Wisconsin report did not single out religious affiliation as a possible factor, this issue was examined in a Canadian study, which summarized the cohabitation rate according to church involvement (see fig. 12.1).

Fig. 12.1

**Cohabitation Rate
and Church Attendance**

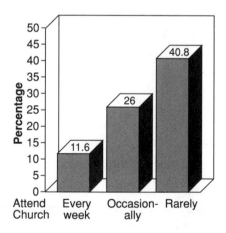

According to Neil Bennett, a professor of sociology at Yale, "people who cohabit premaritally are less committed to the institution, and more inclined to divorce than people who don't live together." The study was based on a 1981 survey of 4,996 Swedish women.

Singles in America Survey: Cohabitation

The Christian singles we sampled in the Singles in America survey were asked whether or not they had "ever lived with a member of the opposite sex in an intimate, unmarried basis." Over 22 percent of our subjects admitted to having chosen this arrangement at one time or another (see fig. 12.2).

Fig. 12.2

Singles in America Survey:
Level of Cohabitation

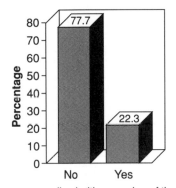

"Have you ever lived with a member of the
opposite sex in an intimate, unmarried basis?"

Christian Celibacy: Fact or Fiction?

Celibacy is rarely mentioned today as a realistic option for single adults. Virginity before marriage is no longer seen as a valued and cherished standard. Some segments consider it strange (if not a liability) to still be a virgin at the age of fifteen. National studies indicate that fewer never-married adults are virgins than ever before. The Alan Guttmacher Institute, a private family-planning research organization based in New York, found that "Despite the concern about AIDS, the percentage of unmarried American women ages 18 to 44 who were sexually active rose to 76 percent last year [1987] from 17 percent in 1982." This data was based on a national survey of more than 10,000 women aged 15 to 44.

A CNN telecast (June 13, 1988) reported on a study conducted in singles bars on the West coast. One-third of the single men surveyed, and one-fourth of the single women, admitted to still being involved in "risky, unsafe sex." According to the *Washington Post* and the *New York Times* (June 5, 1988), federal officials project that at least 450,000 Americans will have been diagnosed with AIDS by the end of the year 1993. This estimate was the first to extend the original Public Health Services figures beyond the 270,000 people expected to have developed the disease by 1991.

The 6th Annual report (1990) of the Centers for Disease Control estimates that 179,000 to 208,000 new cases of AIDS will be reported through the end of 1992. Recent (as of 1/90) estimates of people infected with the virus, with or without symptoms, are 800,000 to 1.3 million. As of November 1990 there have been 57, 525 cases of AIDS *reported* to the CDC; approximately 20 percent of all AIDS victims are in their twenties (which traditionally contains a high number of single adults).Estimates by the CDC for the future are:

> 1990—53,000 to 60,000 new cases
> 1991—60,000 to 68,000 new cases
> 1992—66,000 to 80,000 new cases
> 1993—67,000 to 90,000 new cases

Few published studies have examined the sexual behavior of never-married adults, but a 1983 National Institutes of Health study of the sexual practices of 1,314 never-married women concluded that 80 percent of single American women in their twenties have engaged in sex. One-third of those women had become pregnant at least once, and 40 percent of those pregnant aborted their first pregnancy. According to this governmental study, single American women in their twenties have had sex with an average of four or five men, and one-third of them have lived with a man. (In 1983, 400,000 of the 8.1 million single American women in their twenties gave birth while 660,000 had abortions.)

Singles who were formerly married show even greater sexual activity than the never-married. John Gagnon, in his book *Human Sexualities*, estimates that 90 percent of those who were once married have had sexual intercourse since their divorce or widowhood. Morton Hunt concludes in his book *The Divorce Experience* that only one in twenty men who have been single for one year, and only one in fourteen women, are celibate. In fact, he estimates that two-thirds of the men and over one-half of the women are as sexually active now as when they were married.

Although Christian singles may have a slightly lower level of sexual activity than the national average, few of those responding to our Singles in America survey had chosen a celibate lifestyle. Our study reported that 61 percent of the total sample had engaged in sexual intercourse as a single (52 percent had had intercourse with more than one partner). Over 11 percent of our subjects had experienced sex with more than ten partners, 6 percent with more than twenty! (See fig. 12.3.)

Fig. 12.3

Singles in America Survey:
Number of Sexual Partners (Total Sample)

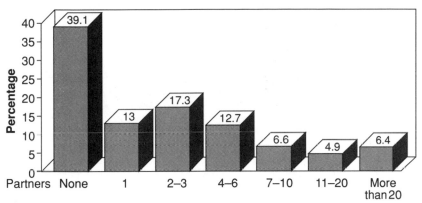

"As a single adult, with how many sexual partners have you had sexual intercourse?"

The data for the divorced singles indicates a higher level of sexual activity, as might be expected. This group had had intercourse as singles. (The phrasing in question 44 was "as a single adult," which could have been taken to mean as a never-married single to some respondents, whereas others thought it meant partners before and after marriage.) Almost 17 percent had experienced sex with more than ten partners and almost 10 percent with twenty partners or more. (See chapter 10 for further details of divorced singles' sexual behavior).

Although the majority of our Christian singles respondents has been sexually active, as measured by the number of partners, over 80 percent had not had intercourse during the six months previous to the survey (73 percent of the divorced singles had not had intercourse during that period). (See fig. 12.4.)

We also asked the Christians participating in our survey to estimate the degree of sexual activity of other singles. When asked, "How many sexual intercourse partners do you think most people your age, marital status, and sex have had?" 97 percent of our respondents apparently believed that "most people" were sexually active (see fig. 12.5). More than half of our subjects said they thought their peers averaged four or more different partners. (In actuality, about 60 percent of our own sam-

Fig. 12.4

Singles in America Survey:
Sexual Intercourse in the Previous Six Months
(Total Sample)

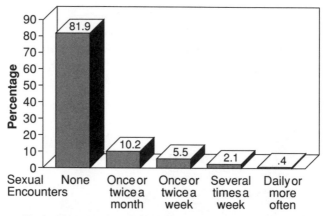

"During the past six months, how often have you had sexual intercourse?"

ple had been sexually active as singles, and 30 percent had had four or more partners. However, our question did not specify that their estimates be based on other *Christians,* so the responses may have referred to the general population.)

Fig. 12.5

Singles in America Survey:
Estimated Number of Sexual Partners
for Peers

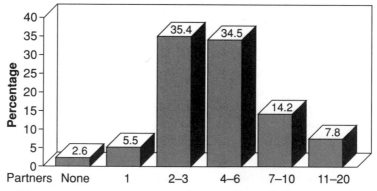

"How many sexual partners do you think most people your age, sex, and marital status have had?"

When asked, "In general, how satisfied are you with your sex life?" over 35 percent said they were either "somewhat dissatisfied" or "very dissatisfied." It is perhaps not surprising that although Christian single adults are fairly active sexually (yet probably not as active as the general population), they are not particularly happy with their non-celibate lifestyle. For some it has produced feelings of emptiness and pain. One woman summarized her feelings this way, "I wanted to be held by a man. Even though I knew he didn't love me enough to marry me, I was still willing to accept the pain for a brief moment of physical comfort."

In Celebration of Celibacy

Clearly, much more should be said and done to uphold the standard of sexual purity and celibacy for today's Christian singles. Such an approach must seek a balance between unequivocally endorsing God's directives regarding sexual behavior and acknowledging his provision of redemption for those who fail to achieve those standards. An overemphasis of either dimension can have severe repercussions. The church should want to neither punish its singles unduly for their lapses nor provide them with a rationalization for their future actions. Even if this balance is maintained, many Christian singles need practical advice on how to overcome the sexual temptation that is a factor in their lives.

Christians have tried a variety of ways to deal with their sexuality. None of these ways has been totally successful, and each has left behind a host of disappointed and discouraged believers. The most popular method of dealing with one's sexual drive is to deny its existence. This approach actually refutes the biblical view that God created sexuality for *all* human beings. It implies that when a person accepts Christ as Savior and Lord, this new believer suddenly loses all sexual desire until the day he or she marries. A second approach (which also argues with Scripture) is to view sexual feelings as dirty and sinful. Therefore, any thought given to this dimension of life proves one unfit for the kingdom of God. Such people go through life as contemporary monastics, trying unsuccessfully to block out all sexual thoughts. A third approach is perhaps most popular in the 30 to 45 age bracket. These people attempt to replace their desire for sexual intimacy with a whirl of activities. Some may throw themselves into their work with such relentless energy that they become burned out on life and emotionally exhausted. Unmarried adults in this category can become so addicted to work that they eventually lose touch with God, family members, friends, and social concerns.

Many unmarried adults pursue hobbies or engage in volunteer work to fill leisure time.

Acceptance. The first step in celebrating celibacy is to accept human sexuality as God created it. It must be seen as a dimension of life that is a gift from God and a reflection of his purpose. Since man and woman were created "in the image of God" and all creation was declared to be "very good," our sexual nature is not to be cursed or despised. God has also given us certain directives as to how we should express this powerful dimension of our humanness. We are able to choose when and where to act on our sexual urges or whether, instead, to set them aside for other concerns. But to deny their existence is unrealistic, nonscriptural, and self-defeating.

Sexual feelings can tell you a lot about yourself if you take the time (and the risk) to listen to them. Hidden within these impulses may simply be the desire to interact on a deep level with a sympathetic fellow human—someone with whom you can share your innermost thoughts and feelings and who cares about what happens to you. Interpreting the messages from your physical nature correctly will remind you of your multifaceted personality. Each part—physical, mental, and spiritual—must be nurtured and respected. It is only as all the dimensions of your life are individually healthy that you can enjoy complete satisfaction.

Stewardship. This Christian principle can give you a new perspective on life! There are several scriptural passages that direct us to replace the world's philosophy of immediate gratification with a focus on more eternal values. This means that our bodies and our spiritual lives are meant to glorify God and be dedicated to serving him. For example:

> Offer your bodies as living sacrifices, holy and pleasing to God—this is your spiritual act of worship. Do not conform any longer to the pattern of this world, but be transformed by the renewing of your mind (Rom. 12:1–2).
>
> For none of us lives to himself alone. . . . If we live, we live to the Lord. . . . So, whether we live or die, we belong to the Lord (Rom. 14:7–8).
>
> The body is not meant for sexual immorality, but for the Lord, and the Lord for the body. . . . Do you not know that your bodies are members of Christ himself?. . . Flee from sexual immorality. . . . Do you not know that your body is a temple of the Holy Spirit, who is in you, whom you have received from God? You are not your own; you were bought at a price. Therefore honor God with your body (1 Cor. 6:13, 15, 18–20).

If Christians—both single and married—could view their sexuality from God's perspective, they would better understand how the principle of stewardship applies to the expression of their sexuality. The apostle Paul saw this clearly when he wrote to the believers in Corinth, who had apparently asked for advice on how to achieve a balance between their physical and spiritual selves:

> Now for the matters you wrote about: It is good for a [person] not to marry. But since there is so much immorality, each man should have his own wife, and each woman her own husband. . . . I wish that all men were [single] as I am. But each man has his own gift from God. . . . Now to the unmarried and the widows I say: It is good for them to stay unmarried, as I am. But if they cannot control themselves, they should marry, for it is better to marry than to burn with passion. . . . I would like you to be free from concern. An unmarried man is concerned about the Lord's affairs—how he can please the Lord. But a married man is concerned about the affairs of this world—how he can please his wife—and his interests are divided. An unmarried woman or virgin is concerned about the Lord's affairs: Her aim is to be devoted to the Lord in both body and spirit. But a married woman is concerned about . . . how she can please her husband. I am saying this for your own good, not to restrict you, but that you may live in a right way in undivided devotion to the Lord (1 Cor. 7:1–2, 7–8, 32–35).

We Christians are called to be stewards of all our gifts—including our sexuality. This involves acknowledging that we have been entrusted with a gift of great value: our sexual nature. We can choose to allow our sexuality to control us or, instead, we can consider it as one more resource available for investment in God's kingdom. Because wise stewards know there will be a day of reckoning, they reject the impulse to splurge on questionable ventures and wait for the right opportunity to make an investment of lasting benefit. How we use our sexuality is no exception to that principle.

Self-discipline. Looking at the creation scenario from a holistic, divinely purposed perspective helps Christians understand that they are sexual beings—and why. The biblical writers who recorded God's revelation did not deny or conceal this fact. They clearly teach that sexuality is an integral part of our nature and that God intended for us to use this gift in certain circumscribed ways. Therefore, spiritually mature believers acknowledge their sexual identities but do not let their sexual urges control their lives.

Self-discipline requires that we postpone gratification of our desires in favor of beneficial long-term goals. It presupposes priorities that supersede our immediate impulses and are thus worthy of our sacrifice. Believers are called on to follow God's direction for their lives, to focus attention on accomplishing his purposes and thus avoid being sidetracked along the way. Because the apostle Paul knew the importance of this principle and applied it to his own life, he said, "I beat [discipline] my body and make it my slave so that after I have preached to others, I myself will not be disqualified for the prize" (1 Cor. 9:27).

Perhaps no other distraction can interrupt a Christian's momentum as surely as his or her sexuality. Undisciplined sexual urges have a way of turning our focus away from what we know is proper Christian behavior; they blur our spiritual vision and distort our judgment. It is fairly easy to discipline ourselves when the goal is specific and clearly defined. For example, if we are overweight, we may be able to diet successfully because we can visualize a trimmer physical appearance. Or smokers quit their habit (although with great difficulty) because they know that cigarettes are ruining their health. It is much harder to sacrifice a personal desire in favor of an *intangible* goal—which is why abstinence for the sake of the rather vague objective of "sexual purity" is difficult for even the most devout Christian.

Yet, being "holy" because God is holy is every Christian's ultimate aim. For a single, that means maintaining chastity except in marriage. It has been that way for twenty centuries, and no one has identified an easier way to achieve that goal than self-discipline. There are no shortcuts and no easy rationalizations.

Controlling one's sexual urges has many rewards. Some of them are practical, since they are based on *avoiding* some of the adverse consequences of sexual freedom: out-of-wedlock pregnancy, sexually transmitted disease, and the loss of self-respect that accompanies promiscuity. The greatest reward, however, is preserving one's right relationship with God and being thereby empowered toward fruitful living in all aspects of life. Sexual purity brings a sense of well-being, the inner peace and contentment that is available only when we have fully accepted God's purposes as our own.

Uncontrolled sexual expression severs a Christian's relationship with the loving God who created us all. It also establishes a shaky foundation for his or her future marriage. One Christian single summarized her feelings on the matter by saying, "If only I had waited a little longer to explore my sexuality. Now I have explored it so often I fail to see its value and worth. It's hard to look in the mirror and see myself as someone created in the image of God. I know God still loves me; but now I have to learn to love myself."

God's Prescription for Reconciliation

God's standards of moral purity and sexual discipline are high, and few attain them in this imperfect world of pleasure-seeking human beings. According to our study and others like it, the majority of Christian singles do not even come close. How does the church come to grips with the realization that most of their Christian singles have been and continue to be sexually active? Following is a biblically based plan of restoration.

Confrontation in Love. People who are experiencing pain often do not think rationally. They act in an emotional manner that denies the reality and consequences of their behavior. It is imperative that leaders of church sponsored singles groups confront any members who are vocal about their sexual exploits and show no desire to cease from their actions. When sexual sin (or any pattern of sin, for that matter) is brought to the surface in a singles ministry, a spiritual leader from the group should arrange to meet separately with the offending party in a location that protects both the privacy and confidentiality of the occasion.

Any such confrontation must take place in an atmosphere of respect and love, yet leave no room for compromise or excuse. To be silent would be to condone a flawed lifestyle. Participating in a known sin without the desire to repent should be seen as a serious offense, and confrontation of the transgressor should be done with a balance of firmness and loving concern. Henri Nouwen, a Catholic author and theologian, suggests that we see ourselves as wounded healers who first acknowledge our own need of healing from the trappings of our humanity and yet at the same time respond to those around us who are also in need of restoration.

Forgiveness and Reconciliation. The answer as to what should be done about known sexual sin in a singles group is obvious to anyone who has read through the pages of Scripture: forgiveness and reconciliation. Such was the response of Jesus to the Samaritan woman at the well (John 4:4–42), the woman caught in adultery (John 8:1–11), and the immoral woman (Luke 7:36–50).

Whenever Christians take a stand on sexuality, it is essential that the message of hope and cleansing be communicated openly and freely. This does not excuse the failure nor does it allow freedom to repeat the offense. Rather, it is a realization of our human condition and fallen nature. This perspective must be communicated first of all by the leadership of singles ministries. Those in such positions must come to grips with their own shortcomings and help unmarried adults address their failures without condescending attitudes that impose additional guilt. Leaders of these ministries must realize that some people find it very difficult to break their patterns of sexual license. Says Mary Ann Mayo in *A Christian Guide to Sexual Counseling,* "There is great danger in underestimating how hard it is for some people to control their erotic desires. A counselor who finds it easy may not be able to sympathize with the person who finds it the supreme challenge."

Most Christian singles who are involved in sexual activity are already experiencing guilt and emotional pain. Their inner lives may be torn by depression, withdrawal, anxiety, and fear. Some find that they are unable to eat, sleep, and enjoy the company of others as they once did, or that their concentration is fragmented and their patience is short. Such reactions need to be dealt with, but it should not be the goal of counseling to deal solely with the symptoms, which are only the outward evidence of the inner battle that any moral compromise can bring to a life. In a context of confidentiality, the counselor should gently encourage the errant single to face his or her failures and accept responsibility for them. A sinner must be reminded of the boundless grace of God and the divine mercy that is continually renewed.

Accountability Groups. Implementing accountability is one of the best approaches that can be used with singles who desire moral purity in their lives. Some church programs for singles require members to join a small support group that involves meeting with five to fifteen other singles once a week in a home or other informal location. Within the context of this nonstructured setting, they are free to share their temptations, pressures and failures. Small groups go a long way toward helping singles resolve some of their feelings of isolation in society. When they develop significant and caring relationships with other people who have similar concerns, their relational void seems less overwhelming. Person-to-person support renews their strength and resolve because it shows that others care for them and want them to succeed.

In the October 1986 issue of the *Single Adult Ministries Journal,* John Splinter, associate pastor and director of singles ministries at Central Presbyterian Church in St. Louis, Missouri, writes, "In my own ministry I am finding that small groups represent a large part of the solution. There are many types of small groups . . . we have more than 20 small groups. The small group is where the real ministry of any church happens. If this is true of the church, it is doubly true of singles ministries, since single adults are frequently so very isolated."

Such groups should provide a climate that encourages open discussion of what it is like to have sexual frustrations, feelings of lust, and urgent sexual drives. Unless these issues are faced in an open atmosphere of mutual support, they will be acted out in private lives. The church has closed its mind for too long to the sexual behavior that has been so clearly demonstrated in contemporary research. Denying the existence of a problem never makes it go away.

Ministry Directions. A variety of programs can be developed by a church to strengthen the resolve of its singles for moral and sexual purity. One possible program element is a panel discussion where single adults have the opportunity to hear from authorities on human sexuality. The moderated panel might include a medical doctor, counselor, minister, and social worker. They could each give a brief presentation on current sexual issues and then open up the meeting for written questions from the audience.

A series of special sermons from the senior pastor of a church might help both the singles who are struggling with their sexuality and any married members who are going through their own inner battles in this area. Addressing the issue of adultery in our society is not popular in our churches, but it is badly needed. Statistics indicate that 40 to 50 percent of all married men say they have had an affair, and most of these married men are having affairs with single women (*Psychology Today*, February 1986).

Above all, the singles director in any congregation must be willing to address this issue in no uncertain terms. It is unfortunate that so many singles leaders do not feel qualified to discuss complex sexual issues with their group members. Others express feelings of inadequacy, intimidation, and embarrassment. The reluctance of many Christian leaders to speak openly about sexuality in light of biblical teachings has undoubtedly contributed to the rise in recreational sex that exists today. Many singles leaders get involved in the situation only after it has reached a complicated crisis stage for a particular individual. How much easier and less confusing it would be to provide sound teaching and guidance before an emergency occurs.

It falls to the single adult to make a choice between celibacy or sexual expression. The choice may seem simple, but—in the heat of passion or the emptiness of a lonely evening—the decision-making process may be clouded. Singles must choose to remain pure and holy in their sexual conduct. In a sense it is their way of demonstrating their faith in God to provide for all their needs—even sexual ones. Singles can choose to view their sexuality as a curse that must be endured until marriage or as a gift from God that helps them understand themselves and their calling as unmarried disciples of Christ. To a large degree it comes down to perspective. If an unmarried adult views life through the lens of this world, sexuality is seen as a wasted potential. However, if one is able to view life from a broader eternal perspective and can see God's sovereign hand in all of human existence, postponing or declining to act on desires for sexual intimacy will be less painful. It becomes a gift that is given back to God as an expression of resolve to be the kind of person we know in our hearts he wants us to be.

13

Life on the Deserted Island

R obinson Crusoe" is a character immortalized by Daniel DeFoe's eighteenth-century novel. Readers have been strangely attracted to this story of a man washed ashore on a deserted island, dealing with daily life as it happened and forced to be creative to survive in an alien environment. Being stranded on a tropical island sounds idyllic, with no phones or other people to bother you, no demands made on your time. While the story is partly based on the real-life experience of the author's friend, Alexander Selkirk, it is still a work of fiction and therefore unreal.

Life as a single adult may also have a certain appeal, since it seems to epitomize adventure and free-spirited independence. This idea is anything but accurate, however, when compared to the realities of living alone. For most single adults it would be more accurate to compare their solitary pilgrimage to the survival experience of Steve Callahan, who survived for forty days on the ocean in a rubber life raft. Each day was a battle for survival against the harsh elements. Eventually he became his own worst enemy and found it difficult to stay calm. Some singles might relate readily to Callahan's experience, since they, too, must search for an attitude of peace and contentment about being alone.

Simenaur and Carroll in *Singles: The New Americans* (1982) rank-ordered the most difficult issues single adults in America face. At the top of the list one might expect to find "sexual expression" or "managing finances." Much to the surprise of the researchers, the most difficult challenge for singles is learning to live with loneliness. A survey by Rubinstein and Shaver reported in *Psychology Today* found the highest rate of loneliness in those between eighteen and twenty-five years of age, traditionally the most prominent single years. They discovered that by the age of seventy, people are more self-sufficient and their lives are simpler. Billy Graham has said that loneliness is the greatest problem facing humanity today. Mother Teresa of Calcutta calls it a heart-hunger and has observed that it is easier to relieve material poverty than what she describes as the "poverty of the heart."

For many singles, learning to cope with loneliness is like the challenge of facing life on a deserted island. But—single or married, whether in an empty room or in a crowd—loneliness descends on every human being at one time or another. No one is immune from the paralyzing sense that there is no other person on earth, at least no one who *cares*.

Misconceptions about Loneliness

Several common misconceptions further complicate how we deal with loneliness. Unraveling these assumptions can help us live more productively on our own "private island."

Christians never get lonely. It is commonly expected that anyone who is a Christian has a personal relationship with God and therefore should never feel lonely. This fallacy can be eliminated by reviewing the first few chapters of Genesis. Adam was created in the image of God and had been placed in the most ideal environment that could be created. He never lacked food, entertainment, or fellowship with his creator. He walked with God through the garden on a regular basis, just as naturally as we would stroll through a park with one of our closest friends. Yet there was something missing. God had provided every imaginable resource, but he knew that Adam needed something more—human companionship. Even though Adam enjoyed a close, intimate relationship with God, he still needed the friendship of another human being. Even before sin entered the world, that need was a fundamental human condition. Loneliness was not a result of the fall, but was derived from an innate characteristic of man.

God created us with a desire for involvement with others. This is part of God's nature as well, for we have been created in his image. It should not surprise us to find godly men and women in need of friendship, not because of spiritual flaws but as a reflection of their humanity.

King David, though highly favored by God, experienced loneliness that gripped him to the depths of his soul. So immense was this feeling at times that he cried out to God in pain. One such time is recorded in Psalm 22:1, when he laments his condition and cries out, "My God, my

God, why have you forsaken me?" David often felt beset by his enemies and abandoned by his friends and helpers. His cry of anguish is an expression of a deep loneliness.

When, as a result of sin, humankind alienated itself from God, human companionship became even more important. Of course, Christ's sacrificial atonement on the cross removed the burden of sin for those who accept him as Lord and Savior and made possible our reconciliation with God. Nevertheless, the need for intimacy with other humans remains.

Loneliness represents rejection, a failure on our part. For many adults their self-image depends principally on how they are viewed or treated by their peers. They live according to what they believe is expected of them instead of being authentic. When such expectations become a prison, escaping from these confines involves emotional pain. If you know you have not attained the goals others have set for you, you may experience feelings of failure, isolation, and rejection, any of which can lead to loneliness. The key that will unlock the door to that prison is self-acceptance. When you accept yourself as the creation of a loving God—an individual with flaws as well as strengths—you are free to become all that God intended for you.

Being with other people will prevent loneliness. A third misconception is that surrounding yourself with other people will make you immune to loneliness. But being part of a crowd is not enough. It may accentuate the problem if there is no interaction—if the presence of others merely reminds you of your own singularity.

Nobody chooses to be lonely. Some people actually choose to avoid intimacy with others. They may get involved in casual relationships and enjoy shared recreational activities, social events, and superficial companionship. If a closeness develops over a period of time, they arrive at a crossroad. Either the relationship will continue to grow or it will be terminated.

Why is that? For some people the threat of intimacy is so overwhelming that they prefer to remain behind the security of known boundaries. Otherwise they feel vulnerable and exposed. Instead of working through their insecurities by sharing them with another, they choose to run from any relationship that invades their private world. By retreating into solitude, they have made a conscious decision to remain lonely.

Changing one's environment will cure loneliness. Many people see their loneliness as a temporary condition brought on by somewhat trivial aspects of their circumstances. They are periodically driven to change jobs, apartment locations, furnishings, or even their automobiles, with the feeble hope that mere change will remove their sense of isolation.

Perhaps this is one reason why so many Christian singles are notorious for church hopping. Rather than trying to understand what is going on inside them, they try to find some form of happiness through externals.

Marriage will remove lonely feelings. Marriage is not an automatic cure! For example, if one partner is a workaholic, the other will feel deprived of marital companionship yet lack the freedom to enjoy the company of others he or she once had as a single.

Robert Weiss, the author of *Going It Alone* and father of loneliness research in this country, writes of this misconception:

> A young wife is confronted with a host of new responsibilities. But having to make both ends meet, often on a shoestring, can be an alarming experience. It is frequently hard enough to make the housekeeping budget stretch to cover the expenses of daily living without having to find money for the endless little things that are needed in a new house or for a new baby. To this is added the responsibility of feeding her husband properly, and the need to make a comfortable, attractive home to which he will want to return. When the first baby arrives the young mother has the anxiety of being entirely responsible for this object which is a human life—and for up to twelve hours in every twenty-four, she may be alone.

Marriage is certainly no cure for loneliness. If it were, there would not be such a high divorce rate. Being "fully human" is not conditional marital status. Its meaning is found in being a whole person in your right.

The Causes of Loneliness

Research has validated what most people know from experience—that loneliness is counterproductive and can have many other adverse effects, ranging from mild discontent or self-doubt (which can manifest itself in a variety of physical symptoms) to overwhelming despair (which may lead to suicidal thoughts). Whatever its consequences in a particular individual, it may be helpful to outline some of the specific situations that trigger loneliness. None of us is immune to occasional feelings of isolation, any more than we can avoid ever feeling angry, fearful, or bereaved. But being prepared for an onset of loneliness brought on by any of the following circumstances can be your first line of defense if you want to prevent this empty feeling from undermining your approach to daily living. (Although these negative experiences are not limited to singles, they may be more immediately painful to someone who has neither spouse, family member, or close friend to provide "tender, loving care.")

1. *Hospitalization and Illness.*The solitude experienced in a hospital room can be overwhelming. Though surrounded by an assortment of competent professionals, a hospitalized patient is essentially severed from all his or her personal connections with relatives and close friends and left to battle the illness alone. Even when the prognosis is hopeful, the loss of personal freedom and removal from everything that symbolizes normalcy cause a deep sense of isolation from the world. Even patients who are not seriously ill and remain at home experience varying degrees of loneliness, simply from being cut off from their usual routine and the people associated with it.

2. *"Students' Syndrome."* Each movement up the educational ladder is a transition that can cause temporary disorientation, since it removes us from the contact of familiar school surroundings, teachers, administrators, and classmates. This sense of being thrust into a strange new world can produce disruptive loneliness, especially for a college student who is away from home for the first time. Some students feel so threatened by this alien environment that they withdraw completely from social events. International students have even more stress thrust on them, since they must adjust to a new culture and language as well as endure homesickness. Says Robert Weiss, "Young people who attend a college distant from their home risk isolation if they cannot quickly fit into the life of the dormitory or other group housing to which they are assigned and have no other basis for developing a congenial social network."

3. *Loss of Friends.* Whether because of geographical relocation, a disagreement, or a gradual erosion because of changing interests, the loss of close, meaningful friendships will cause lonely feelings of regret. Not all old friendships are completely lost, but over the span of years many relationships fade into insignificance because of life's many changes. In time we establish other connections, but there is likely to be a period of social isolation until a new network is formed.

4. *Unemployment.* Particularly for men—who are more apt than women to tie their personal identity and sense of self-worth to their vocation—losing a job can have devastating effects aside from any financial considerations. Being removed from one's familiar workplace, responsibilities, and co-workers creates lonely feelings, which are usually complicated by the frustration of sitting alone while waiting for the phone to ring with a job offer.

5. *Career Changes.* It is estimated that most working people will pass through at least five job changes over the course of a lifetime. Even when a job change is planned or represents a promotion rather than a move to another organization, the employee loses former colleagues, routines,

and surroundings. It is not surprising, therefore, that a new job carries a sense of loss—and therefore some lonely feelings, at least temporarily.

6. *Relocation.* Moving away from known settings, family members, and friendly support systems is always a "crisis situation" of sorts, even if the move is anticipated as a positive change. Relocation is like a North American rite of passage into adulthood, but it can seem like an ending to many treasured experiences, rather than the beginning of a happy new chapter in life.

7. *Birthdays.* Although family and friends consider our birthdays as cause for celebration, counting candles on a cake may evoke bittersweet thoughts for the guest of honor, rather than joyful anticipation of the future. Whether it be thirty, forty, or sixty-five, certain birthdays remind us mainly of our mortality, or missed opportunities, or long-gone companions. And where there are negative feelings and regrets, loneliness is invariably a side effect.

8. *Unfulfilled Dreams.* Most people daydream about how they want their future to unfold, and some of those long-term goals are either unrealistic or derailed by unforeseen circumstances. When we realize that a particular dream will never be attained, the natural consequence is disappointment or despair. Either of those feelings can make us believe we are alone in a hostile world.

9. *Too-Early Achievement.* On the other hand, success can come too early and too easily, leaving one with no sense of purpose, no new worlds to conquer. It was said of Alexander the Great that he sat down and wept once he had conquered India because, though still very young, he had achieved all his goals. If our friends are still seeking what we have already attained, we may lose the sense of camaraderie that once held us together.

10. *Leadership.* Anyone who has ever been in a leadership position knows the truth of the adage "It's lonely at the top." It is never easy to bear the responsibility for making decisions that will affect the welfare of others. Yet the authority from which that responsibility is derived automatically isolates a leader from the rank and file.

11. *Celebrations and Holidays.* The same sense of temporality called up by a birthday surrounds other milestones in life that are automatically assumed to be occasions of joy. Baptisms, confirmations, graduations, weddings, anniversaries, retirement parties—all are reminders of the passage of time, no matter how happily they are observed. These celebrations give us the opportunity to gather with family and friends, but they can be lonely, painful experiences if one dwells on "what might have been."

Holidays, too—especially the period between Thanksgiving and New Year's—can be difficult for people in a mobile society in which one is often separated from loved ones by many miles. For those who cannot join in family festivities, the Christmas season can be a painful ordeal. (Suicides rise dramatically at this time.) Missionaries have told us of the aching loneliness they experience around Christmas, especially if they are living in the southern hemisphere, where some of the familiar holiday observances are not possible.

12. *Death of a Loved One.* Researchers who study the major stress events in human living concede that the most traumatic crisis is the loss of a spouse, parent, or child. Such a devastating event creates immediate turmoil, grief, disorientation, and instability. For some it takes years to recover from the loneliness experienced when a loved one is gone forever.

13. *Divorce.* Emotional isolation and loneliness are the usual scars borne by two people whose marriage has broken down and cannot be repaired. That loneliness may remain long after the painful emotions of guilt, anger, resentment, and grief have been dissipated, especially if the former spouse has found happiness with a new love. Custodial parents who lack the financial and moral support of the ex-spouse often find that the burden of bearing the sole responsibility for the welfare of their children makes them subject to chronic isolation from the world around them.

14. *Aging.* The human body is an amazing phenomenon. Its cells constantly reproduce and renew themselves as our physical beings adapt to the changes that occur over a lifetime. There comes a time when the renewal process diminishes and we realize we are no longer young and vibrant. Receding hairlines, facial wrinkles, slower reaction time, and loss of breath when we exercise are a few of the aging signs we notice when the passing years take their toll on our capabilities and appearance. Being reminded so tangibly of our mortality can create feelings of fear, uncertainty, anger, and regret—and all of those emotions are companions of loneliness.

15. *Retirement.* The good news here is that, at least for some, the retirement years can be a happy time of peace, contentment, travel, and leisure—everything that adds up to a sense of fulfillment and completion. The bad news is that this pretty picture is too often distorted by chronic illness, financial uncertainty, lack of purpose, and personal loss. Even with thorough planning, retirement can be a huge disappointment! Friends and family pass away, grown children move on, and there seem so many empty hours to be filled each day. All those factors, plus relocat-

ing to a "more suitable" but strange new environment, can produce abiding feelings of loneliness in a person who has eagerly anticipated this final period of life.

Prescriptions for Loneliness

Just as there are many immediate causes of loneliness and many different degrees of response, so are there diverse ways of handling it. What may banish lonely feelings for one person may not be equally effective for another. Loneliness is an intensely personal and complex experience that cannot be alleviated by a simple prescription, and curing one bout does not provide permanent immunity. Below are four principles that have been helpful to many in their efforts to locate relief.

Cure #1: Develop Close Friendships

When it comes to friendship, it is the quality of the relationship that counts. As many lonely people have discovered, surrounding oneself with crowds of people merely compounds the problem. In times of emotional stress, when the pain of loneliness is particularly intense, what we may need most is a confidant, someone who understands our needs, shares our values, and really cares that we are suffering. This type of closeness is not easily attained. There are no "instant friendships," simply because it takes a great deal of time and mutual effort to develop the kind of intimacy that will provide ongoing support. The ingredients of such a friendship are many, but—since we must not only like and admire a true friend but also *love* that person—they can be found in the apostle Paul's message to the church in Corinth:

> Love is patient, love is kind. It does not envy, it does not boast, it is not proud. It is not rude, it is not self-seeking, it is not easily angered, it keeps no record of wrongs. Love does not delight in evil but rejoices with the truth. It always protects, always trusts, always hopes, always perseveres (1 Cor. 13:4–7).

Striving for those qualities in a relationship involves respecting boundaries, developing mutual trust by guarding confidences, maintaining realistic expectations, and tolerating each other's differences. This kind of intimacy involves give-and-take: honesty, transparency of motives, and open communication. It requires a degree of risk taking, since one must allow a friend into one's own private world as well as take the time to get below the surface of the other's external image. Such friendships are rare and priceless. No distance will be too great to travel to a friend of this caliber, no resource too valuable to expend on his or her behalf.

If you do not already have such a friend, search diligently for someone who will "always be there for you." Where do you find one? Anywhere—at work, in the next apartment, in a college dorm, or perhaps by renewing an old acquaintanceship you neglected in the past. First impressions are not always accurate, so give yourself the chance to get to know others around you on a deeper level. Make the first overture by inviting for after-dinner coffee or a tennis game someone who seems to share your interests and values. Accept such invitations from others, too. Maybe you won't really like each other after all, but it might be the start of something really great for both of you.

Cure #2: Appreciate Your Times of Solitude

A second constructive approach to loneliness is based on realizing that there is a great difference between loneliness and being alone. The former is to be avoided because of its potential hazards to emotional and physical health. The latter is meant to be appreciated as a stepping-stone on the road to building a healthy self-image. It is important to develop a positive attitude toward "aloneness." Jesus had an obvious appreciation for solitude as an opportunity for renewal and refreshment. The Bible records that he periodically went off alone before and after full days of ministry.

Cultivating aloneness does not come naturally for most people, for we are created as social beings. However, periods of solitude give us renewed strength if we take the time to reflect on life, affirm our worth and personal value system, and examine and revise our priorities. There are many tangible things that can be done to achieve those ends. Consider, for example, keeping a journal, writing poetry or a novel, corresponding with friends and relatives, listening to inspirational music, or just going for a walk at the beach, lake, or mountainside. Perhaps there is a hobby or household project you have been planning but never quite found the time to undertake. The possibilities are endless and limited only by your imagination. Aloneness is a unique personal experience, but using your solitude wisely will enable you to cope with lonely feelings and live fully in many dimensions.

Cure #3: Establish a Support Group

A third cure for loneliness is found in establishing a supportive extended family—a network of friends with similar concerns. Such a group is not meant to replace either our God-given natural family or our special more intimate relationships, but interacting within its framework can relieve the pressures of loneliness by reinforcing our sense of belonging in the wider community. (See chapter 14 for a detailed discussion on establishing a support group.)

Cure #4: Get Acquainted with Yourself

Finally, "This above all; to thine own self be true." Only God and you can recognize both your strengths and your weaknesses. Try to understand exactly what might trigger loneliness in your life and plan specific countermeasures. Although many of the causes of lonely feelings are unforeseen and not subject to advance preparation, others are more predictable. For example, if you suspect that an upcoming birthday will be hard to face in the company of your family (for whatever reason), plan a dinner out with friends who will not call up unpleasant emotions. Or, if you are dismayed over a few gray hairs, thank God for your health and the maturity you have developed over the years. Seek purposeful activity—either alone or with others. Plan for the future; if you are about to achieve one personal goal, start thinking about how you will replace it with another. Learn to value both your solitude and the company of others. There is a proper time for each.

Loneliness does not have to rule your life. When it is seen as a normal part of human experience and its causes identified, progress can be made to destroy its destructive potential. We were all created with a desire to socialize with others and not meant to be an island unto ourselves. Sometimes, however, circumstances interfere with that need and loneliness is the side effect. Then we must selectively apply the "cures" if we are to be all that God intended. Without the freedom to choose our remedies, we are destined for an embittered life devoid of peace, joy, and fulfillment.

Four

Anchoring in Safe Harbors

nyone who has ever been at sea understands turbulence. Even on a full-sized ocean liner, enduring a storm causes stress, anxiety, and, for most people, stomach upsets that are rarely equaled on land. The only remedy for this emotional and physical distress is to head for a sheltered harbor and drop anchor. There are times when the Christian life is like this. Sometimes we find ourselves in the midst of one of life's hurricanes. It matters little what has caused the storm: finances, unhealthy emotions, physical disabilities, or relationship problems. They all seem equally disorienting when one is being pitched back and forth and in danger of going under.

Where are the harbors of safety for Christians today? Non-Christians try to find sanctuary in alcohol, sexual relationships, materialism, drugs, and other mind-numbing behaviors. Unfortunately, these escapisms only add to the problem as they stir up their own swirling currents of danger. For the Christian, safe harbor is found in Christ. In him our anchor holds, and we have the assurance that he is able to sustain fully those who come to him for help (Heb. 7:25). And the church he founded was designed to be the earthly source of strength and courage for believers.

The purpose of this final unit is to examine a few of the safe harbors available for Christian singles today. Each affords a degree of protection from life's storms and tempests.

14

The Security of a Support Group

F ew people care to travel alone across miles of open country. If anything should happen to the car, they would face danger and risk
alone. It is even more hazardous to sail across miles of open water
with no companions. The possibilities of all that could go wrong are so
frightening and the consequences so great that those who have dared to
sail solo around the world are rare individuals with a tremendous
amount of courage and stamina.

God never intended the Christian life to be a solo experience. The
church is described by Paul as being a lot like the human body:

> For even as the body is one and yet has many members, and all the
> members of the body, though they be many, are one body, so also is
> Christ. . . . For the body is not one member, but many. . . . God has
> placed the members, each one of them, in the body just as He desired.
> And if they were all one member, where would the body be? (1 Cor.
> 12:12, 14, 18–19 NASB).

One of the safe harbors that offers sanctuary to Christian singles (and
others in need) is the small support group. There are diverse support systems available in most churches, and many extend a welcome to others
in the broader community as well. Some are rather general in nature and
provide informal fellowship in a home setting, extended families,
discipleship, and shepherding. Others have a focused purpose, such as
divorce recovery, grief counseling, weight loss, or relationship problems;

165

or they address a targeted membership, such as single parents, adult children of alcoholics, substance abusers, or victims of sexual abuse. These groups are a source of security and stability as one navigates around the danger areas of life and develops maturity as a Christian.

For many single adults today, the need for intimacy can be partially fulfilled by same- and opposite-sex friendships in the context of a support group of some kind. In the absence of marriage, networks of human relationships offer meaningful social connections, sharing, and continuity. These groups can be helpful in legitimizing the roles and objectives of singles and supportive in some of the critical times of adult development and transition. "If one falls down, his friend can help him up. . . . A cord of three strands is not quickly broken" (Eccles. 4:10, 12).

Abraham Maslow, a leading educational psychologist, has identified a hierarchy of needs for adults. Knowing these needs is the key to understanding motivation, since one's life is essentially the quest for fulfillment of each of them. Primary on Maslow's list is the need for a sense of belonging. We usually answer the question of "Who Am I?" with reference to another individual or to a group or later point of reference. Answers such as "I am Jane's mother," or "I am an American," or "I am a teacher" reveal our willingness to be identified with a person or group outside ourselves. We want to "belong" to someone or fit in a certain category. Some people choose to announce that affiliation to the rest of the world—a woman traditionally changes her surname when she marries, a patriot may wear a tiny flag as a lapel pin, or a college grad may purchase a school ring.

By definition singles are "unmarried," but society lumps together the many different forms of singleness. There is a simplistic distinction made—one is either "married" or "single," regardless of whether the single is never-married, divorced, separated, or widowed. A single who might prefer being primarily affiliated with a particular subgroup is categorized as simply "an unmarried adult." This contributes to ambiguity about exactly *who* that person is, because it is based on the idea that human identity is affirmed only in the context of relationships formed on the basis of shared concerns and interdependence. In fact, that is exactly what "belongingness" implies.

Different Groups for Different Needs

Generalization helps us deal with the people around us more easily, but—if it goes too far—it oversimplifies the issues. When appraising the needs of "singles," and therefore the kinds of support groups that would be helpful to them, we must first clarify what kind of single is being discussed.

For example, some studies suggest that never-married adults form different kinds of support groups than do their divorced, widowed, and separated peers. The latter three are generally more apt to include family members in their support systems than the never-marrieds. This has been interpreted to mean that never-married singles are less willing to be linked with family members, perhaps because they wish to create a distinction or separateness to their lifestyle. Never-married adults are usually members of support groups that are relatively active, transient, and temporal. Developing long-term intimacy may pose more of a challenge for the never-marrieds, since the obligatory blood ties have diminished influence.

Although singles may recognize their need for supportive relationships, finding the time to develop them may be a problem! Through our Singles in America survey, we discovered that the majority of our Christian singles invested less than two hours each working day in maintaining relationships with friends. The pressures of work, managing a home, and a variety of other issues obviously demanded most of their time. A related finding was that 47 percent of the singles we surveyed spent over nine hours daily on job-related activities. Clearly a high priority for them was the advancement of their careers, and this can be expected to affect both the quantity and quality of the friendships they will be able to maintain. It also helps explain why they had listed living with loneliness as one of the greatest "disadvantages" of being single.

Where did these Christian singles go for social interaction (general social outing, with same-sex or opposite-sex friends—not a date per se)? In studies of non-Christian singles, nightclubs and singles bars are usually the top-ranked choices. Since such environments are not consistent with Christian values, it is not surprising that 31.7 percent of the singles in our study mentioned church activities as an opportunity for socializing. ("Nightclub" was considered an option by less than 4 percent of our sample.) Restaurants were also a popular choice (21.9 percent), as were movies (11.5 percent). On the average, 51.2 percent of our subjects went out socially once or twice a week.

Regarding where these Christian singles went specifically to meet members of the opposite sex, a variety of options were presented. The responses are summarized in figure 14.1.

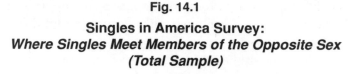

Fig. 14.1

Singles in America Survey:
Where Singles Meet Members of the Opposite Sex
(Total Sample)

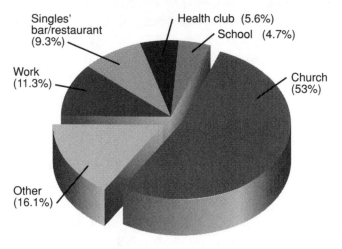

Singles' bar/restaurant (9.3%)

Health club (5.6%)

School (4.7%)

Work (11.3%)

Church (53%)

Other (16.1%)

The Never-Married

From my observations as a singles pastor and a college professor, I have noticed some common patterns emerging in singles who have never married. Such singles can be expected to prefer relationships beyond their family context. Some are on a quest for self-identity and therefore want to distance themselves from constant reminders of their earlier dependency. They usually cultivate friendships with other never-marrieds, especially members of the opposite sex. Of course, some enjoy interacting with married people their own age, particularly those with children if they are geographically removed from their own family and miss their younger brothers and sisters. Because of highly dissimilar concerns, few never-marrieds develop particularly close relationships with either single parents or divorced or widowed peers, unless, of course, their underlying motivation is marriage.

Divorced Singles

Those who have been divorced are more likely than the never-marrieds to include family members in their overall support system, perhaps because of the natural tendency to turn to one's immediate family during traumatic periods of emotional stress. (Work colleagues can also play a significant role in providing guidance and understanding.) Other divorced people would probably rank high on the list of confidants. Nobody knows and understands the pain, anger, guilt, and loneliness of divorce better than someone who has already weathered that particular storm. It is logical to suppose that the *least-preferred* members of support groups for the divorced would be widowed singles and people who are happily married—not because the latter groups are reluctant to reach out a helping hand, but because victims of divorce often harbor feelings of failure and rejection and would be somewhat uncomfortable interacting with people who have had a successful marriage.

Fig. 14.2

Singles in America Survey:
Sources of Support
(Divorced Singles)

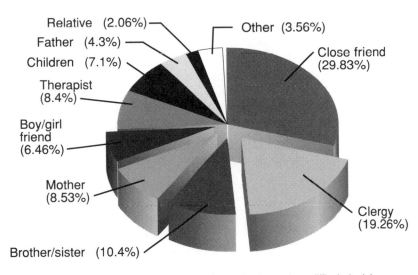

"If you had personal problems, were in trouble, or had to make a difficult decision, on whom could you rely for understanding and support?"

Our Singles in America survey revealed more specific data about the support systems of divorced Christians (see fig 14.2). Going to close friends for understanding in times of trouble received the highest ranking (30 percent). Almost 20 percent would turn to the clergy and about 8 percent to a professional therapist.

Single Parents

It is not surprising that single parents include family members in their support system. When the children are sick, the car is broken, and past-due bills are piling up, the immediate family is generally a source of will-ing assistance (see chapter 11). In an attempt to prove that they can make it alone and that their decision to go through with the divorce was correct, some single parents resist the temptation to ask for such help. Some parents who disapprove of their child's divorce may not be sup-portive. (No adult relishes having to resume the role of dependent child once he or she has been living independently.) Support groups such as Parents Without Partners can be a source of emotional support, coping mechanisms, and practical advice. Furthermore, single parents often receive valuable feedback from their married neighbors, especially in the areas of child development and household management. On the other hand, it would be expected that the never-marrieds have little in com-mon with someone who is struggling to raise a family alone and thus would be the least-preferred members of a single parent's support system.

Widows and Widowers

The challenge of establishing a support system is probably greatest for widowed singles, both male and female, particularly if they are some-what advanced in years and have lost a spouse after many years of mar-riage. Even then, widowers may have a relatively easier period of adjust-ment. As previously mentioned, a widower may find himself in great demand socially, since there are many "extra" women in need of an escort. Of course, unless he can afford to hire a housekeeper, he may need some advice about household chores, but he is probably already established in a career and can fill some of his companionless hours with job-related activities. (However, if he is also a "single parent," a widower has more in common with that group than with childless widowers or those whose children are grown.)

Most widows past middle age face a more difficult recovery process than their male counterparts. For one thing, since many of them have never worked outside the home, they have no career to take up the slack and spark their interest in the outside world. Socially, too, a widow is somewhat at a disadvantage. There are fewer unmarried men of her age available for companionship, much less remarriage (if that is her goal). Older widows discover that most of their friendships had been estab-lished within the married set and—though many still welcome her com-pany—she may feel uncomfortable in her new status as a single. Young widows more readily start new relationships with either the never-mar-rieds or the divorced, but widows of fifty or beyond usually confine their friendships to other widows of their age or renew connections with fam-ily members who live nearby. If she is mentally and physically healthy, a widow's support system can be multidimensional, but it depends on many other factors, too—whether she remains in the same neighborhood as when she was married, the age of her children, her financial situation, and, above all, how willing she is to seek the company and support of others.

Developing Intimacy

There are many reasons why some individuals find it difficult to get involved in a formal support group. A primary concern is that they feel threatened by participating in a group of other adults who will get to know them for who they really are. Many singles try to live according to the standards of material success and carefree independence portrayed by the media. When such a lifestyle is unsatisfying or cannot be maintained, they may hide their feelings behind a facade of superficiality. Many of the singles we have met over the years spoke about their desire to have a "best friend" with whom they could share all their hopes and dreams, one who would keep their secrets and be nonjudgmental about their mistakes.

Developing intimacy is foundational to the establishment of healthy support relationships, whether one-to-one or in a group. The term *intimacy* is often misused and assumed to have only a sexual connotation. But intimacy goes far beyond the images of soap-opera personalities meeting in compromising locations and discussing topics that are "off limits" to children and morally upright adults. Christian singles must develop a more accurate understanding of intimacy if they are to experience the sense of belonging and acceptance that is the natural birthright of every human being. In essence, intimacy refers to the baring of your soul to another person. Therefore, it requires a high degree of openness and vulnerability.

The intimacy we refer to here is *not* a sexual experience. Although intimacy can sometimes be shared in that context, it can also be thoroughly expressed without any physical contact whatsoever. In fact, sexual union between two people can sometimes be a barrier to developing real intimacy.

Kathy is a young single woman who has desperately wanted someone with whom to share her life. She entered relationships with men on a regular basis but stayed in them for only a short time because they quickly became physical and left her feeling used and hurt. When asked why she continued to get involved in sexual relationships that only added to her guilt and pain, she responded: "I get to a point where I can't stand being alone. I want to feel the warmth of someone next to me. I want someone to hold me. So I find somebody who needs that, too, and once the need is met we both move on. The problem is that the need never seems to go away." Kathy believed her need for closeness with another human being could be satisfied by sexual relationships. Not only did these not meet her need for intimacy, but they actually made her feel worse. This left her confused and shaken, unable to trust her feelings and emotions.

Another important point to remember is that true intimacy is not limited to a marriage relationship. It is tragic but true that some married couples have never experienced intimacy, even after years together. Many people have come to enjoy an abiding and deeply personal relationship with someone other than a spouse. This "significant other" can be a colleague at work, a pastor, counselor, or trusted friend. And, since intimacy need not involve sexual expression, that person may be of either the opposite or the same gender. The Bible says that Saul's son Jonathan "became one in spirit with David, and he loved him as himself" (1 Sam. 18:1). Such an expression of oneness between two grown men describes a high level of bonding. The shared commitment of these two men remained for many years and was a source of strength for David in his flight from King Saul.

Intimacy is not a specific destination in a relationship. Intimacy has no stopping point, nor is it an experience one enjoys for only a moment. It is best described as a process of discovery, an ongoing self-revelation that continues to reinforce the bonding between two or more people.

Perhaps the best description of what intimacy is comes from Calderone and Johnson, who suggest that intimacy occurs when two people delight in each other in an atmosphere of security based on mutuality, reciprocity, and total trust. It is then that two people find their lives laid bare before the other: the good and the bad, the successes and failures, the shouts of joy and cries of pain. Such interconnected people even have their own special vocabulary.

Revealing your inner self to another person requires transparency in communication. For many adults, especially men, that is difficult to achieve. H. Norman Wright, prominent marriage counselor, says that men have a much harder time than women sharing their feelings, and that this inability to open up underlies many marital failures today. He refers to open-ended communication as "learning to speak the other person's language."

Honest communication involves the sharing of dreams, goals, ideas, disappointments, and feelings. Because this is a two-way exchange, listening is an essential component of the process. Harold Ivan Smith says in *Single and Feeling Good* that "listening is the invitation to open that long-locked door to a secret corridor within the spirit. It is never a thoroughfare but a path, for few will ever be allowed to enter. Yet in that quiet corridor we discover the potential of a person."

Establishing intimacy also requires courage, for you must risk trusting another person with your innermost secrets. Tim Hansel, the founder and president of Summit Expedition, wrote in his book *Holy Sweat* that "courage is life's great intangible, the invisible determinant, the great multiplying factor." It *is* risky to admit to some past behavior or present feeling of which you are ashamed, or to confide that you are lonely and afraid at times. And expressing your frustrations and regrets might indeed subject you to pity, if not ridicule and disdain. But without the willingness to allow another person to learn those things about you, intimacy will be unreachable.

C. S. Lewis put this so well in *The Four Loves:* "To love at all is to be vulnerable. Love anything, and your heart will certainly be wrung and possibly be broken. If you want to make sure of keeping it intact, you must give your heart to no one, not even to an animal. Wrap it up with hobbies and little luxuries; avoid all entanglements; lock it up safe, dark, motionless, airless. . . . It will not be broken. . . . The only place outside heaven where you can be perfectly safe from all the dangers and perturbances of love is hell."

Achieving closeness also requires a generous investment of time by each person. In a world filled with instant coffee, microwave meals, "one-minute" managers, quick photo developing, and fast-food restaurants it is no wonder that we may expect instant intimacy as well. We sometimes forget that the time-compressed, fast-forward lifestyles seen in television dramas do not tell the truth about human relationships. True intimacy cannot be rushed. It involves late-night talks, long hours of just listening to another person, and a wide variety of time-consuming experiences—but each one will be more revealing than the last and strengthen the intimacy accordingly.

Everyone needs to feel connected to one special "other," and—for happily married people—that soulmate is one's husband or wife. Many singles, on the other hand, live with chronic loneliness simply because they do not realize that such depth of sharing can be theirs, too. They must first learn to reach out in a spirit of total honesty and commitment to someone with whom initial bonding has begun. Ironically, only by making ourselves vulnerable to possible rejection can we achieve the kind of intimacy that will multiply our joys and diminish our sorrows.

15

Church
Ministry Models

There is tremendous diversity of approach and format in the church's ministry to single adults. One congregation's successful design may not work in a different setting, because no model of ministry will be appropriate for all singles. Any outreach must consider the unique needs of its audience, and this has been the overriding theme of the New Testament.

Ministry in the early Christian church was based on the characteristics of people in a specific time and place. Church ministry in Jerusalem just after Pentecost was conducted differently from later ministries in Antioch, Ephesus, or Corinth. The structure of worship, the programs that were developed, and other elements of ministry changed from city to city according to the needs of the people in a local body of believers.

Because the first Christian church in Jerusalem borrowed many ideas from the Judaic tradition, much of the form and theology of this church reflected its Jewish heritage. These new Christians worshiped at the temple, kept the old dietary laws, honored the Sabbath, read from the sacred Scriptures of the Old Testament, and celebrated many of the Jewish ceremonial feasts. Believers in the church in Antioch, however, did not follow the same pattern. Because *their* heritage was Greek, it is not surprising that they chose not to replicate the worship styles being used by the believers in Jerusalem.

Another example of how a ministry must be tailored to meet a congregation's needs is seen in the early church in Corinth. As a seaport and major center of commerce, this city was immersed in immorality and subject to many corrupting influences. Some of those practices crept into the church. Much of what the apostle Paul wrote to the Corinthian church was an attempt to correct its moral laxness and false teachings.

Each new church manifested a form of worship, structure of ministry, and diversity of programming that responded to the unique attitudes and concerns of its membership. There was no distinct plan that could be duplicated from church to church as an ideal model. So it must also be for the church today. Because no pattern of ministry for single adults is

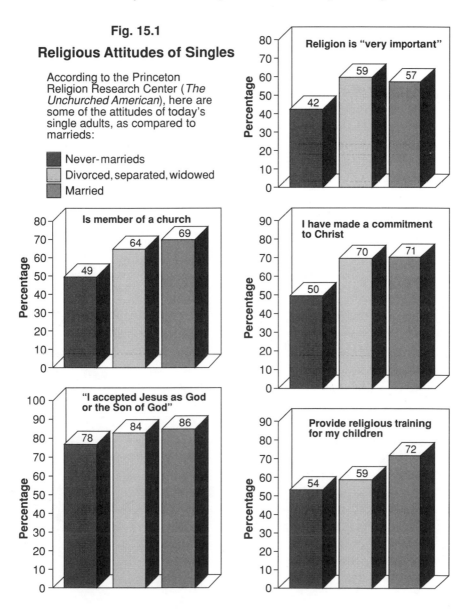

Fig. 15.1

Religious Attitudes of Singles

According to the Princeton Religion Research Center (*The Unchurched American*), here are some of the attitudes of today's single adults, as compared to marrieds:

- Never-marrieds
- Divorced, separated, widowed
- Married

adequate for all congregations, each local church must seek to understand its group's makeup, background, and needs before implementing any design for ministry, even one that has been successful elsewhere.

As we have already seen, the attitudes and needs of "singles" will vary according to their subgrouping and will be different from those of other segments of the general population. According to the Princeton Religion Research Center in a book titled *The Unchurched American*, these differences must be considered before any ministry program is implemented. Figure 15.1 compares the religious attitudes of two major categories of singles with those of married people.

As a result of their study of religious practices, Fred Wilson and Steve Furtosis of Biola University estimated that only 25 percent of single young adults (ages twenty to thirty) in America regularly attend church (two to four times a month. Furthermore, according to their research, the majority of this group attend large churches that have well-established ministry programs. A summary of some of the other analyses is depicted in figure 15.2.

Fig. 15.2

Singles and Church Attendance

"When did you last attend the church or synagogue of your choice?"
(percent)

	Within past 6 months	Within past year	Within past two years	More than two years ago	No opinion
Married	72	79	83	17	—
Never-married	54	63	68	31	1
Divorced/ separated/ Widowed	63	72	77	23	1

"How often did you attend a church in the past six months?"
(Based on those who attended church or synagogue in the past six months.)

	Once a week	Two or three times/ month	Once a month or less	No opinion
Married	51	22	22	5
Never-married	34	26	35	5
Divorced/separated/widowed	47	21	26	6

From *The Unchurched American*, by the Princeton Religion Research Center, 1988.

Traditional Church Programming

Churches have traditionally programmed their adult ministries from a perspective that has essentially been couples- and marriage-oriented. But Sunday school classes that focus on developing a healthy husband/wife relationship, church banquets geared toward couples, and family camping experiences can leave singles feeling neglected or unwanted. If a church has only these kinds of activities, the singles in that church will slowly drift away to other congregations or drop out of religious life altogether. Senior pastors also need to be sensitive to the manner in which they address household matters from the pulpit. Husband-wife jokes, innocent teasing, or stereotyped illustrations may evoke laughter from the audience, but they can also communicate the message that singleness is inappropriate for a Christian. If the preacher's only perspective is the traditional nuclear family, those who do not fit this "ideal" may deduce that they should look elsewhere for a church that is more accepting of their lifestyle.

Many adult ministries have also approached their *social* programming from a couples' point of reference. If many of the nonreligious activities a church sponsors are geared to twosomes, singles are inadvertently rejected. For example, "sweetheart banquets" on Valentine's Day that require a date can leave an unmarried adult feeling alone and isolated from the rest of the congregation. A church can remain family-oriented yet still provide special programs for its singles. The solution is not to eliminate all activities for couples from the church calendar, but to awaken a sensitivity to the need for balanced programs that allow singles to come alone when appropriate and that provide an accepting atmosphere for nontraditional family units.

Another traditional element of church programming is the large group gathering of adults for instructional purposes. It has long been the mode of operation for a church to book an authority on some popular topic and invite the entire congregation to hear this person speak. Although there are times when this approach is appropriate, it should never be the major way to acknowledge the educational needs of the adults in the church. Adult ministries must also consider the unique needs of the subgroupings represented in a congregation. For example, widows have special needs and should be provided with opportunities to learn in informal settings how best to meet these needs. All churches need small-group meetings to zero in on distinct and specific issues.

The church has customarily viewed single adults as the "unfortunate few" who could not find a mate or keep a marriage intact. Such a condescending tone has not been well received by the singles population. It does not take long for visiting singles to realize they are not viewed as important members of the body of Christ. They need only listen to the tone of a pastor's voice when discussing single adults, examine the opportunities for singles meetings posted in the church bulletin, or ask to speak with the "single-adult minister" to get a feel for how a prospective church views unmarried adults. Singles must never be viewed as people to be pitied or prayed for, as though their singleness was a weakness to be overcome. The mind-set in many churches today must be altered if a successful ministry for singles is to take place.

Such ministries must be based on current needs, not traditional approaches. Many single-adult advisors discover this basic principle only when they try to use a flashy-looking curriculum (based on traditional programming) that they had recently discovered at a denominational conference or their local bookstore. Marketing techniques of the nineties can make even outdated ideas look inviting, but if this material does not address the needs of the single adults at a particular church, these resources will be wasted. The end result will be frustrated leaders and decreasing singles attendance.

Assessing the Needs of Singles

Although each church must determine the unique concerns of its single members, there are some basic needs that all singles face and that should be thoroughly understood. These needs form a foundation for ministry design but should not be the only criteria for programming.

Church leaders first need to know what *kinds* of single adults are in the congregation. (Obviously, some of the needs of the never-marrieds are very different from those of divorced single parents.) Designing a ministry to singles at your church should start with a survey to determine the types of singles represented.

Jim Smoke, a noted author and speaker on singles issues, identifies five foundational human needs: relational, social, spiritual, educational, and emotional. Understanding these critical areas will help any church leader design a balanced program that will address the concerns of *each* subgroup (see fig 15.3).

Relational Needs

Because the business community has been quick to realize that single adults have the need to relate to other singles, they know it is profitable to group singles together for certain activities. Many business leaders

Fig. 15.3

Focusing Singles Ministry on Needs

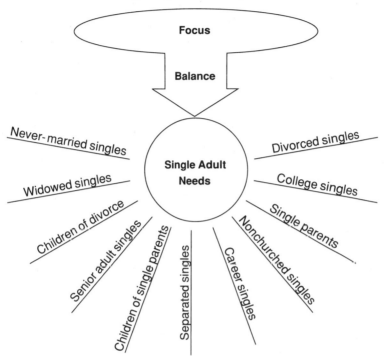

have learned that singles will support programs that address their specific concerns and allow them to meet other singles in the process. The church must also come to this realization. There are many activities that a church can sponsor to enable singles to interact and gain a group identity. Some relational needs can be met by having Sunday school classes specifically geared to singles and special seminars on topics such as divorce, grief recovery, or vocational re-entry. Retreats and weekend campouts for singles also affirm relational, "others"-oriented living.

Most singles are interested in building relationships within the group and should be given the opportunity to do so. Classes should be structured to allow for feedback and discussion. If possible, the available time should allow for small-group dialog. Leaders might stop after a significant point in a message and ask the participants to discuss relevant issues among themselves. (Sitting around tables instead of in rows helps facilitate this teaching method.) Midweek fellowships should center around discussion and interaction rather than merely be another opportunity for content delivery.

Social Needs

Any creative singles program, whether secular or spiritual, will offer a variety of social activities. The Christian singles in our survey were active in their social lives and apparently attended a variety of activities in their community. Many mentioned their search for an alternative to bars and nightclubs. Any outreach that wants to attract a large contingent of single adults will have a diverse calendar of activities that provide for their social needs. This does not mean that every church in a given community *must* have an extensive array of activities. (This should be determined by the group's identity and the church's resources and available time.) What counts is that a congregation attempt to provide a balanced social program for singles. In communities with interfaith councils, it has been particularly effective to plan some singles activities in a spirit of multi-church cooperation and to publicize an extended welcome to all singles in that community.

Spiritual Needs

Because God designed people as spiritual creatures, we all possess a desire to explore and understand the supernatural. Some may deny the need for divine guidance, but few reject it altogether. Many Christian singles who have experienced divorce may drift back to the church, seeking spiritual answers and growth. A sense of inner renewal may take place because they now have more freedom to explore their spiritual nature.

People searching for spiritual direction react more easily to a warm, positive presentation of the gospel than to a cold, judgmental approach. Spiritual teaching and personal counseling must be practical as well as inspirational. Leaders must convey warmth and friendship and be transparent enough in their teaching that listeners feel free to open up and discuss their concerns. The most successful leaders are those who share their own feelings in the process of instruction and counseling.

Teaching spiritual truths must be viewed as more than delivering biblical information. The portrait of Christ in the New Testament shows that he was genuinely concerned about the spiritual growth of his audience. He took into consideration their specific needs and adjusted his methods to meet them. Those who teach single adults should not be afraid to adjust their lesson plan to accommodate a recent teachable moment or current issue.

Educational Needs

Eighty-five percent of the subjects in our Singles in America survey have had some college experience. If this reflects the background of

Christian singles in America, our churches must come to grips with the intellectual curiosity of this group. These singles can be expected to enjoy learning and to thrive on events and activities that cause them to explore the horizons of knowledge and learn new ways of managing their lives.

Churches can meet this important need by offering specialized courses and seminars for singles. The list of these educational opportunities in churches around the country is endless. Some of these include:

The Single-Adult Identity

Divorce-Recovery Workshops

Grief-Recovery Workshops

Managing Your Finances

Sex and the Christian Single

Raising Children in Single-Parent Homes

Entering the Occupational Workforce

Beginning Again

Such courses can be helpful to a single adult who is learning to adjust to the ever-changing conditions of his or her life. Seminars, workshops, Sunday school classes, and periodic singles conferences will be especially beneficial to single adults if those meetings address the need for singles' intellectual growth and emotional development as well as their search for spiritual maturity.

If you are a singles leader, it is important to keep in mind that adults

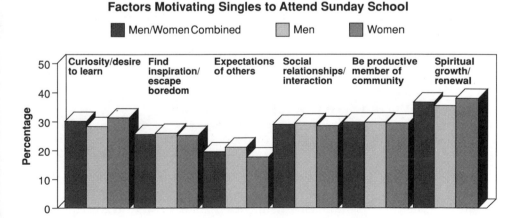

Fig. 15.4

Factors Motivating Singles to Attend Sunday School

learn differently than children. You will want to take into consideration the diversity of background these adults bring to the learning environment. Take advantage of this variety by encouraging discussion, interaction, and involvement. Break into small groups and have all share their feelings about what is being taught. Challenge them to come up with their own ways to apply the day's lesson. If you treat them like dependent learners, you will soon lose them. A class that is dominated by long lecture periods is not taking into consideration a number of key factors that motivate single adults to attend Sunday school (see fig. 15.4).

Emotional Needs

Many single adults are facing difficult decisions about their futures. Some are separated from a spouse and are looking for answers to why the marriage is faltering. Others are adjusting to the pains of divorce or death of a spouse. Single parents are wrestling with a host of difficult issues regarding their living arrangements, parenting, and financial security. Many single adults will face unrest because of such issues, and their emotional needs must never be overlooked or minimized.

Henri Nouwen says in his book *The Wounded Healer* that we who must bear the scars of our humanness are always in the process of healing our wounds. But he admonishes each of us to get involved in the business of helping other people receive healing for *their* emotional hurts, even while we are dealing with our own pain. No Christian is ever free from challenge and struggle, for Christian faith is a battle that is fought each day. Past victories are no guarantee of future success. A productive ministry for singles will acknowledge the wounds associated with certain aspects of single living and provide emotional support for those in need of it.

A thorough understanding of each of these five foundational needs will help leaders design a ministry that will be effective for their particular group of singles. Again, the key is balance. A program based on addressing each of these components will be more successful than one marked by overemphasis of any one element.

Singles in America Survey: Religious Involvement

Since the subjects studied in our Singles in America survey were drawn from church membership rolls, Christian conferences or retreats, we expected to find a higher level of religious involvement than the national average. Indeed, our sample's involvement and attendance at church, their level of tithe, and their participation in spiritual disciplines

Fig. 15.5

Singles in America Survey:
Church Attendance

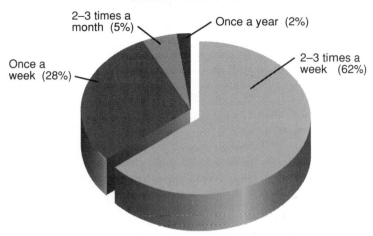

such as Bible reading and prayer were all higher than would be expected in the general population. An overview of these levels of involvement is illustrated in figures 15.5, 15.6, 15.7, and 15.8. Note in particular that 90 percent of our subjects attended church *at least* once a week (62 percent attended two or three times a week). By way of contrast, at least accord-

Fig. 15.6

Singles in America Survey:
Prayer

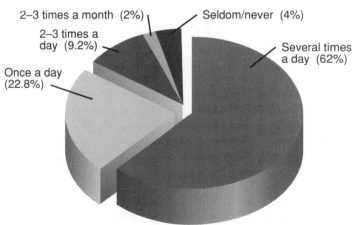

"How often do you pray?"

Fig. 15.7

Singles in America Survey:
Contribution Percentages

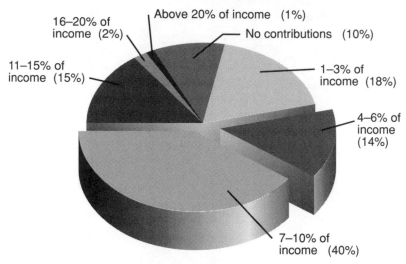

"What percent of your income do you tithe?"

ing to the statistics presented in figure 15.2, the highest frequency of church attendance reported in that study was for the married subjects, (52 percent attended "once a week").

Fig. 15.8

Singles in America Survey:
Bible Reading

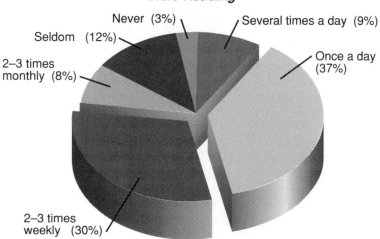

"How often do you read your Bible?"

Guidelines for a Singles Ministry

There are a number of commonly observed realities associated with starting and maintaining a ministry for singles. Unless each of these complications is faced, frustration will result. But there are ways of handling some of these factors so they will have the least detrimental effect on the ministry. Keeping the following goals in view will increase the chances for success:

Expect "Transients"

The number-one reason why unmarried adults remain single, according to national polls, is the freedom and mobility that single living provides. The singles ministry of most churches serves as a revolving door for individuals who are merely looking for something new and exciting to entertain them. Most singles programs have no shortage of curious visitors, but the challenge lies in keeping the regulars from leaving before the newcomers become members. Turnover among unmarried adults is a critical issue for many large churches.

Affirm Church "Ownership"

Because of the considerable mobility of Christian singles, their sense of ownership of a particular church is difficult to establish. Most will stay long enough to observe the full spectrum of singles in the group and determine whether the program will meet their superficial needs, but some quietly move on to new horizons, even if it does. A ministry designed mainly to attract a temporary audience will be characterized by entertainment and flimsy relationships. Single leaders must not get trapped into directing their ministry to this segment of the singles population. Instead of tackling the impossible task of providing something of short-lived appeal to everyone, a church can best instill a sense of belongingness for its community of singles by focusing on their deeper and more permanent concerns.

Recognize What Is Possible and What Is Not

Not all singles groups will be right for everyone. The demographics of a local community will affect the makeup of the congregation and determine its most pressing needs. For example, in a college town or large industrial city the emphasis of a singles ministry might be on reaching students or career-minded never-marrieds. On the other hand, in retirement areas there will be more older people among the membership, so the greatest needs may be for counseling the lonely or the bereaved and advising about job re-entry.

Beyond the simple reality that no one church can provide a perfectly balanced program for all its singles, there are practical considerations as well. There may be space limitations or lack of funds for hiring trained professionals. Each singles ministry will reflect the overall resources and atmosphere of its supporting church body. All will fall short in one way or another, but most are doing the best they can with their available resources.

Strive for Healing within the Group

Among most singles groups are individuals whose primary reason for being there is their spiritual or emotional pain. It takes a great deal of time, patience, and energy to provide the kind of healing these adults need. Although progress may seem slow, singles leaders must never slacken the effort on their behalf. For example, in one group there may be one or more women who are alienated from a parent because of emotional or physical abuse. Someone else may be suffering the pain of a marital breakup or grieving for a lost spouse. Or single parents may be especially stressed by financial problems and their burdensome responsibilities.

Beyond those concerns, there may be singles who are living with guilt and self-recrimination because they have compromised their standards. These people need to see themselves as God does—forgiven and cleansed. Any singles leader must be able to communicate the difference between "holiness" and "wholeness." The former is a goal that all Christians are encouraged to pursue, though it is rarely accomplished in this lifetime. However, it *is* possible to help someone put the fragmented pieces of his or her life back together and restore a sense of wholeness, hope, and purpose to that life.

Secure Total-Member Involvement

New Testament ministry was never meant to be done by only a few select people. God dispersed spiritual gifts to all members of the body of Christ and expects total-member participation in achieving a church's goals. Because a singles ministry also requires that level of involvement, its leaders should encourage input from the members and challenge them to take an active part in implementing those ideas.

Each singles group should periodically elect a leadership council that will be committed to meeting the basic needs previously described in this chapter. From that group should be selected committees that will be responsible for planning and organizing the necessary activities.

Many single adults are capable of assuming leadership roles in our churches. Yet, although they may handle significant responsibilities during the week in their employment, they are often treated like dependent children on the weekend by leaders who are reluctant to allocate responsibility for details of their ministry.

Any successful program requires organization of its participants. There should be opportunities to gather as a large group as well as many chances to meet informally in small discussion panels. The makeup of the smaller units should be somewhat flexible and depend on the topic at hand. Any rigid organization based on age, gender, or category of singleness will limit the free interchange of ideas and may inadvertently encourage the formation of exclusive cliques within the organization.

It is always a good idea to have written job descriptions for those serving on the leadership council. Primary leaders will need to spend considerable time training these "assistants." The leaders should regard themselves as enablers and equippers of others for ministry. The pastor or other group sponsor should meet with the leadership team on a regular basis for planning and evaluation of the program.

Advertise the Ministry

Churches that are able to provide for a singles ministry need to advertise it regularly throughout the local community. To attract younger singles, college and university newspapers are helpful publicity resources; for others, local press releases, flyers, public-service announcements, and other churches can provide a broader outreach. Be certain that the wording and preparation of any printed materials are of high quality; anything less will convey a lackluster concern for the program. To avoid duplication of effort, appoint one member of the leadership corps to be responsible for overall publicity, or ask for a volunteer.

Be Prepared for the Dating Game

Because of the social and relational needs of single adults, there will always be a few singles who attend church activities in search of the perfect mate. Most singles leaders play down this aspect of their ministries, but it is nevertheless a reality to be considered. While leaders should not encourage pairing off, neither should they disapprove of it. After all, what better setting could there be for finding a lifetime partner than the church?

Address Sexual Concerns

One of the most common realities often overlooked is that few Christian singles today are celibate. With this in mind, a singles ministry must deal with the issues that nonmarital sexual activity creates. These singles may be experiencing guilt and emotional pain or have feelings of failure and rejection. Plan programs that will guide group members toward the Christian perspective of sexuality. They need to see that sexuality is a God-given dimension of their humanness, but that it requires a degree of responsibility and self-control.

Maintain the Group's Christian Identity

As soon as singles ministries begin to attract large groups of singles from the broader community, they are faced with the temptation to compromise their Christian message so that they do not "turn off" the non-believers who attend. They may be fearful of losing their momentum and potential members by presenting the gospel and integrating Bible studies into their programming.

There is no need to apologize for being Christian in focus! If participants complain about the religious dimension of the programming, simply state your belief that a solid biblical foundation is the only answer to the needs single adults face today. To undermine that foundation by omitting an emphasis on Christian principles would be to deny the church's mission.

Set Standards of Conduct

Each church has different teachings about the degree of freedom allowed an individual believer. For example, some churches allow their members to consume alcohol at social functions while others do not. Because there are diverse issues that need to be clarified in advance, standards of conduct should be written and distributed among group members. Of course, the senior pastor and board of deacons should be allowed to participate in setting any policies that affect the church's reputation in the community and might undermine its teachings within the general congregation.

A common concern of many singles leaders is the proper attitude toward singles who are living together. Should one condemn them for this arrangement and expect them to separate—thereby removing a positive influence from their lives? Or is it wiser to keep silent and imply that it is not the church's business to set standards for consenting adults—thereby ignoring the scriptural teaching on unmarried sexual behavior? There is no ideal solution, but any opposite-gender singles who are openly living together should be encouraged to attend a couples class and also to reexamine the appropriateness of their lifestyle. As in any area of behavior, Christian leaders must strive to maintain that delicate balance between rejecting an ill-advised act and accepting the person who commits it.

Minimize the Potential for Misunderstandings

Any ministerial leader realizes that there will be occasions when he or she is misunderstood. For example, because the church body is usually not fully aware of the complex needs of singles, it may be suspicious of the "creative," nontraditional approach used in ministering to those needs. On the other hand, the singles themselves may not recognize that their special ministry is only one aspect of the church's overall educational and pastoral mission. Because of differing priorities, resources may not be allocated as evenly as some singles might wish.

In a healthy church body, all the parts work smoothly together because there is open communication between them and a common overall goal. Honesty will remove much of the potential for internal conflict, but occasional misunderstandings will nevertheless arise. A wise singles leader will watch for signs of unrest and make time for the group to discuss the reasons for the unrest. If the misunderstanding is on the part of the larger body, the leader might ask the senior pastor to address the matter in an appropriate congregational setting.

Implementing a Balanced Singles Ministry

Once the church leadership has identified the unique needs of single adults and set long-term goals in line with the "realities" outlined above, it is time to think through the philosophy and design of the program. Any successful ministry requires forethought and preparation. Figure 15.9 illustrates the components of a well-rounded singles ministry and suggests program activities for each component. Few congregations are equipped to fulfill all these elements, but they are presented to assist a church in developing a vision of some general aims.

Outreach Activities

Evangelism. There is a broad variety of activities that allows a congregation to reach out to a lost and needy world. Without neglecting those who walk into the sanctuary on a weekly basis, a healthy church will fulfill the Great Commission by going out into the community and seeking new believers. Opportunities for evangelism can be discovered during

Fig. 15.9
A Well-Rounded Singles Ministry

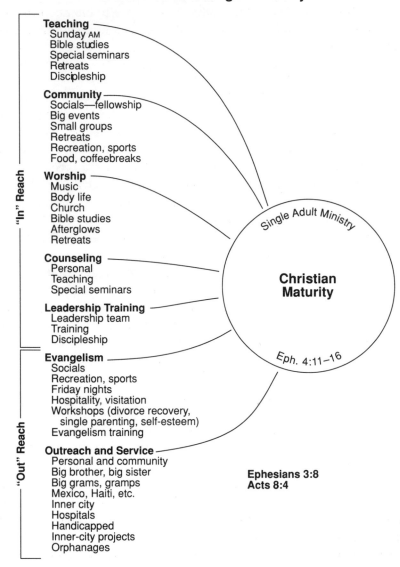

Teaching
  Sunday AM
  Bible studies
  Special seminars
  Retreats
  Discipleship

Community
  Socials—fellowship
  Big events
  Small groups
  Retreats
  Recreation, sports
  Food, coffeebreaks

Worship
  Music
  Body life
  Church
  Bible studies
  Afterglows
  Retreats

Counseling
  Personal
  Teaching
  Special seminars

Leadership Training
  Leadership team
  Training
  Discipleship

Evangelism
  Socials
  Recreation, sports
  Friday nights
  Hospitality, visitation
  Workshops (divorce recovery,
    single parenting, self-esteem)
  Evangelism training

Outreach and Service
  Personal and community
  Big brother, big sister
  Big grams, gramps
  Mexico, Haiti, etc.
  Inner city
  Hospitals
  Handicapped
  Inner-city projects
  Orphanages

"In" Reach

"Out" Reach

Single Adult Ministry

Christian Maturity

Eph. 4:11–16

**Ephesians 3:8
Acts 8:4**

such church-sponsored activities as sports events, socials, Friday-evening outings, and special workshops on singles issues, as well as through a singles visitation team. Although the plan of salvation need not be formally presented each time a singles group gathers, care should be taken not to overlook it completely or to bury it too deeply in discussions of more secular concerns.

Service. The word *minister* means "to serve." No believer can minister in the name of Christ if not actively involved in serving the practical needs of others. Service projects that a singles group might sponsor include visiting a convalescent hospital, being a Big Brother or Big Sister to a child in a one-parent home, supporting a child through an international organization, volunteering at an inner-city rescue mission, implementing a ministry to the handicapped, and identifying and helping on a regular basis needy people within the church (especially the elderly and shut-ins). One need not join the mission field abroad to serve the Lord!

Inreach Activities

Teaching. The educational focus of a singles ministry should be on practical, down-to-earth issues rather than on Bible study per se. Singles respond positively to informal learning opportunities, such as those available in seminars, conferences, small-group fellowships, retreats, and discipleship or prayer groups.

Building Community

Single adults, like all other human beings, need a sense of belonging and group identity. Christian singles want to participate in "owning" their church and will not feel motivated to make a contribution to a church that does not acknowledge their existence or allocates only token resources on their behalf. Building a sense of community within the larger body can be facilitated by publicizing singles events throughout the congregation and by periodic sponsoring of activities that encourage other church members to mingle with singles on a one-on-one basis.

Worship

All believers want to worship their Creator and Lord, but people with common interests often enjoy expressing their praise in innovative ways. For this reason, "afterglow" meetings following a regular churchwide evening service have been popular in the spiritual life of many single adults. Other groups regularly incorporate contemporary music in their worship experience. The type of "creative" worship found at camps and retreats and in the intimacy of small-group fellowships is especially appealing to young singles.

Counseling

Only 20 percent of the Christian singles we surveyed said they would go to either a pastoral counselor or a professional therapist if they needed guidance. Since the majority tended to consult relatives or friends for advice, it would be helpful if singles leaders offered some introductory counseling training. One approach is to have a professional counselor conduct a series of seminars on the basic techniques of counseling. Although lay counselors lack the ability to handle serious emotional and mental disorders, small-group counseling sessions and "hot lines" are often quite successful in presenting coping mechanisms for minor problems.

Leadership Training

As mentioned previously, ministry must be a team effort, especially when working with single adults. Because many in this group prize their independence, they will want some degree of control over their program design. The more input a leader receives from them the better will be the success rate of the programs. The leadership council that is involved in the overall decision making of the group, and others who are responsible for implementation, should receive quality training. This training can take place in a semiannual leadership retreat, special training conferences or seminars, and small-group or one-on-one sessions with the primary leader. (Supplemental resources can be found in the reading list at the end of this book and in Christian bookstores and public libraries.)

The biblical model for designing a ministry is to first identify needs and then plan a strategy to meet those needs through available resources. Some churches have limited resources or are too small to make a formal singles ministry feasible. But in churches that have identified a sizable group of single adults to whom they want to minister, every effort should be taken to ensure quality programming by leaders who are trained to share the responsibilities of the ministry with the singles themselves and with others in the congregation when necessary.

Outreach activities will help these Christian adults focus on their calling to be lights in the world. The in-church activities will fulfill the mandate of Ephesians 4 to build up the body of Christ and equip its members for service according to their gifts: "From him [Christ] the whole body, joined and held together by every supporting ligament, grows and builds itself up in love, as each part does its work" (v. 16).

16

Reaching
Beyond
Our Singleness

Ministering to single adults is always a challenging experience because their needs are diverse and in some cases acute. Jim Smoke has described many aspects of a singles ministry as "emergency room" treatment. He notes that many single adults have lives filled with complex concerns and difficult decisions. For this reason, programs that emphasize service and outreach are often few and far between. Yet, we have observed that churches with ministries designed to get singles involved in service and giving were among the most healthy and vibrant in the country.

Keynoting Christian service shifts your attention from your own needs and onto the needs of others. There is something healthy about focusing your energies on those less fortunate than yourself. It helps put life in a broader perspective. When confronted with those in greater need, suddenly your needs no longer seem so urgent. In fact, serving others enables *you* to experience healing. Henri Nouwen writes in *The Wounded Healer,* "A Christian community is . . . a healing community not because wounds are cured and pains are alleviated, but because wounds and pains become openings or occasions for a new vision. Mutual confession then becomes a mutual deepening of hope, and sharing weakness becomes a reminder to one and all of the coming strength."

Expanding Our World View

In the previous chapter we outlined the rationale and guidelines for a singles ministry. Many churches do quite well in providing for their single adults in such areas as single-parenting support, divorce- and grief-recovery programs, self-help workshops, leadership training, fellowship, worship enrichment, education, and counseling. Where even *these* ministries often fall short is in their ability to reach beyond the limits of their own congregational needs. Too often the church leadership lacks a vision for what can and should be done in the wider community, and outreach has a relatively low priority rating. That short-sightedness ignores a major teaching of Scripture: to seek the lost and minister to our neighbors in the name of Jesus. We have been told to help the sick and visit those in prison (Matt. 25:36), to protect those who are ignored or oppressed (Luke 10:30–37), to "continue to remember the poor" (Gal. 2:10), and to attend to the needs of orphans and widows (James 1:27). Obedience to these directives is required of all disciples of Christ—but it requires a broadened perspective and high-level involvement in the world outside our church buildings.

Frank Tillapaugh, in his popular book *Unleashing Your Potential,* calls on believers to get out of the "fortress mentality" and go into the world to minister in Jesus' name. He writes, "When we consider unleashing the ministry potential of God's people, we need to consider the following question: How can Christians work out their potential if the work of our churches is restricted to the limited programs happening within the walls of the church?" Richard Halverson, chaplain of the U.S. Senate, writes in *The Timelessness of Jesus Christ:* "The work of the church is outside the establishment. Outside the church. In the world. And it takes every member to do it! Nowhere in the Bible is the world exhorted to 'come to the church.' But the church's mandate is clear: She must go to the world."

Perhaps no other segment of the church has better potential for impacting the world for Christ than single adults. Unless they are parents, they are usually unencumbered by family responsibilities; most have somewhat flexible schedules and higher mobility than other groups. Many also have the good health, energy, and enthusiasm of youth. Recognizing the natural compatibility between outreach activities and a singles program, one large church in California gave the title "Minister of Missions and Single Adult Ministries" to one of its pastors. This leader later observed that each year his singles were actively involved in projects all over the world. He commented, "Outreach projects for single adults give them a vision for what Jesus called us to be: World Christians. We try to help Christian singles see the world as God sees it and then enable them to respond by touching the world with God's love." This church has a reputation throughout Southern California for its dynamic outreach programs and creative singles ministries.

For many years our culture has seemed to be telling us to forget others and "look after number one." Such media messages as "You deserve a break today," and "You can have it all" reinforce the worldly attitude that only our personal satisfaction should matter to us. Mike Bellah comments on the side effects of this mind-set in his book, *Baby Boom Believers:*

> Probably no single aspect of the baby boom mentality has done more harm to the cause of Christ than its self-centeredness, its emphasis on individual happiness and success. At the same time, perhaps no single aspect of our mentality has done more to rob us of the very things we seek. Happiness and success seem to come most readily to those who seek them least, to those who instead devote themselves to serving others.

Christian singles and the ministries that serve them must shed their cloistered mentality and develop programs that involve them in service projects in their own communities and overseas. There is no set formula for which projects are most appropriate for a given group. Every community has an inner city with homeless and unemployed people. Even the smallest town has its share of shut-ins who cannot cope with daily concerns, or an elderly population whose limited incomes do not cover their basic nutritional needs. In fact, the neediest people in a community may be within walking distance of the church.

Furthermore, many overseas mission organizations would be pleased to have a singles group come to assist in a specific project. Both of us have been active in service projects that take single adults to all parts of the world. These projects have involved taking singles to Haiti to handle food distribution for malnourished children, going to the Dominican Republic to work at an orphanage, building an airstrip for a remote jungle tribe in Ecuador, conducting a Vacation Bible School for Mayan Indians in Belize, and serving in Mexico in similar ways. We are not alone in recognizing such outreach possibilities. Churches all over the country are catching a vision for expanding the world view of their singles.

Starting an Outreach Ministry in Your Church

Many singles leaders have asked us how to start a ministry of service and outreach. Our customary response is that it takes considerable planning to ensure success. The following steps are recommended:

Step One: Pray Through Your Desire and Search Your Motives

If your primary reason for sponsoring outreach activities is to build a larger group membership or to show everyone in your church what an exemplary servant you are, your efforts will be in vain. You must first search your heart to be sure you are not approaching a ministry for the needy with prideful motives. James 4:3 says, "When you ask, you do not receive, because you ask with wrong motives." You cannot expect God's blessing on your ministry, no matter how noble it may seem to outsiders, if your motives are not genuine and pure.

Step Two: Consult with the Senior Pastor and Governing Boards

Seek the involvement and support of the leadership in your church. Their expectations and goals for the church may be somewhat different from yours, and it is always wise to have the input of others before embarking on a new venture. Remember this: "Without consultation, plans are frustrated, But with many counselors they succeed" (Prov. 15:33 NASB). The general leadership of the church should be asked to endorse the arrangements *before* any service project is announced. If your church has a missions board, consult its members to be sure your idea does not conflict with some other outreach project in progress. This committee may be willing to provide resources that you did not know were available.

Step Three: Involve the Singles Leadership Council in the Entire Preparation Process

Singles who are used to making decisions at work and in their daily lives will resent being left out of your planning. Get your assistants involved in assessing the skills and interests of your singles; ask others in the group for suggestions as you survey available options for service.

Step Four: Determine the Most Appropriate and Timely Project for Your Group

Several factors will have to be examined:

(a) *Short-term vs. ongoing projects.* Each approach has both advantages and disadvantages. Short-term projects entail minimal risk and expense and allow you to "test the waters" to see how your group responds to outreach activities. But taking an ongoing approach allows you to have greater impact in a general area of need; few long-term benefits can be realized in a short-lived experience.

(b) *Local vs. foreign service.* Obviously, localized projects will have greater group participation and be easier to plan and coordinate. They are also less expensive. Serving neighborhood needs allows more people to catch the vision of applied servanthood and to establish a connection with the rest of the community. On the other hand, service abroad may have a deeper and longer-lasting impact. Having multicultural experiences lets us see the world as God does—as a universal brotherhood with common goals and needs.

(c) *Small-group vs. large-scale participation.* There is something very exciting about setting an entire singles group to work on a common service project. Everyone usually enjoys the experience and has the chance to develop a feeling of community and group cohesiveness. This is often not feasible for large groups, and many service projects work best in a small-group environment where intimacy and one-on-one contact can be established. (Participants in special activities should be encouraged to share their experiences later with the larger body.)

Step Five: Plan Details Well in Advance

Details become especially important if the project will take place abroad. Travel documents and immunizations take time to obtain, and airfare is usually cheaper if booked and paid for well in advance. Fundraising plans may be needed. Even if a project is local and requires no out-of-pocket expenses, time is needed to set up a timetable and recruit and train the participants. Poor planning invariably spells failure and will also undermine the success of future opportunities for ministry.

Step Six: Train the Participants for Effective Ministry

People who feel adequate for the task at hand will perform with confidence, enthusiasm, and skill. A training and orientation program should take place far enough in advance to circumvent last-minute problems and avoid forgetting details. Depending on the scope of the undertaking, training sessions might be held on a weekly or bi-monthly basis or in one- or two-day seminars. Be sure that all participants know their specific responsibilities and have the resources necessary for success.

Step Seven: Protect Your Group from the Risk of Injury, Property Damage, or Litigation

Be sure that safe transportation is provided for the group and that drivers have adequate insurance coverage, even if the destination is only a few miles away. Consider whether adequate medical facilities are available in case of injury or illness (especially if the trip is overseas). Any group venturing out on a service activity should have access to a first-aid kit and someone trained to administer emergency treatment.

Plan thoroughly for all contingencies. For example, the church leadership should know how to make contact with you or a group member at all times. (Many single parents will be reluctant to travel great distances to a project if this requirement is not met.)

One very important item is the "liability release agreement." Because of the recent rise in litigation against nonprofit organizations, many churches insist that participants in international service projects (or any other "risky" church-sponsored venture) sign a liability-waiver document. We have had an attorney prepare such a document, which is included at the end of this chapter (see fig. 16.1). We suggest this document be signed by anyone joining a foreign outreach project and that it be left at the church before departure. Although the extent to which such forms can be used in litigation is unclear, they at least indicate a signer's acknowledgment of the possible dangers associated with foreign travel.

Opportunities for Service

Community Projects

Opportunities for service within your local community are found in a variety of settings. The following are only a few of the ideas for projects that are easily implemented in a singles group.

"Special Needs" Children. Chronic-care institutions and their related agencies are always open to having volunteers help with physically or mentally disabled children. You might take one or more of these young people to a zoo or local park, to a lake for duck feeding, or to a theme park or museum. One singles group, for example, planned a Zoo Day for retarded children and brought them by the busload to a nearby zoo for a day of fun and outdoor recreation.

Orphanages. If there is an orphanage nearby, a day spent playing with children who have no parental figures in their lives is a rewarding way to practice servanthood on a very personal level. Some singles groups "adopt" such a child and enjoy an ongoing relationship through regular visits, outings, and birthday and holiday celebrations.

Convalescent Homes. Almost every community has a convalescent or "retirement" home that would welcome regular visits by a group of singles. You might work with the activities director to develop programs of singing, drama, teaching, or concerts, but even informal chats and help with letter writing are usually just as rewarding for the visitors as they are for the residents.

Abused Children. Working through various caregiving agencies, some churches have been able to provide abused children with love and positive role models through their singles organization.

Big Brothers/Big Sisters. Community organizations such as Big Brothers or Big Sisters provide the opportunity for singles to help children who lack adequate family support. Simple activities—a walk in the park, a baseball game, a bike ride—can make a world of difference to an attention-starved child. Other singles might prefer to work with groups of children. For them, there are many opportunities available in Boy- or Girl-Scouts or in sports-oriented groups such as Police Athletic Leagues.

Welfare Agency Programs. First Presbyterian Church of Hollywood, California, has a program that places four or five college-aged singles in an inner-city housing project for one year. These young adults become "good neighbors" by teaching after-school children's clubs, participating in playground activities, tutoring children with learning difficulties, and performing a host of other service-related activities. Todd Bolsinger, director of the program, believes "it is the most effective way to make a difference in the urban areas around many of our churches today."

Latch-key Projects. For singles who have afternoon time available, a program can be developed to provide after-school care for children of working parents. This would be of great benefit to single parents in your own group or in proximity to the church. You may find that older singles with time on their hands would be especially enthusiastic about this idea.

Juvenile Facilities. Many detention facilities welcome concerned adults who are willing to come in during the afternoon and evening to act as role models and friends to these troubled adolescents. Some administrators will provide training and guidance for volunteers, but the main requirement is a willing heart.

Mentally Handicapped Adults. A great opportunity for service exists in group residences for retarded adults. These homes are often located in residential areas, and neighbors may be invited to fellowship with the residents in the evening. Many are capable of communication and in great need of friendship.

Overseas Projects

Service abroad requires extensive planning and preparation. If you have never led such a project, it is vital to secure the advice of individuals and groups who have experience in this area.

There is nothing like the excitement of visiting a Third World culture to extend your world view and make you appreciate the benefits you

Fig. 16.1
Liability Release Agreement

The undersigned (herein the "Individual") wishes to participate in the following activity:

_____

_____

_____

_____

_____

(herein the "Activity") sponsored by _____

_____

a non-profit religious corporation (herein the "Church") _____

Church and the undersigned agree that the activity poses a risk including the following specific risks:_____

_____

_____

_____

_____

_____

as well as similar and dissimilar risks (herein the "Risks")._____

For and in consideration of the Church allowing the Individual to participate in the Activity, and other good and valuable consideration the receipt and sufficiency of which are hereby acknowledged, the undersigned, for himself or herself, assigns, heirs, and next of kin (herein the "Releasors"), release, waive, discharge, and covenant not to sue the Church and its officers, employees and agents (herein the "Releasees"), from all liability to the Releasors, on account of injury to the Individual or death to the Individual or injury to the property of the Individual, *whether caused by the negligence of Releasees or otherwise,* while the Individual is participating in the Activity.

The undersigned is fully aware of the Risks and other hazards inherently in the Activity and is voluntarily participating in the Activity, and voluntarily assumes the Risks and all other risks of loss, damage, or injury that may be sustained by the Individual while participating in the Activity.

The undersigned warrants that he or she has fully read and understands this Liability Release Agreement and voluntarily signs the same, and that no oral representations, statements, or inducements apart from the foregoing written agreement have been made to the undersigned.

CAUTION: READ BEFORE SIGNING

Date: _____   _____

                                               (signed)

                                 _____

                                            (please print name)

enjoy back home. A good place to start is to ask mission organizations if they have a short-term project coordinator. Explain that you would like to bring some single adults on a service project and want to know if they are set up to sponsor such groups. Many missions organizations have facilities and staff specifically designed for these ventures. They can provide you with the kind of project suited to your group's interests, resources, and available time. They may even quote a set price for expenses so that the only other funds needed will be for transportation.

International projects might include:

Building a church, dormitory, camp facility, or low-cost housing

Vacation Bible School

Directing a camp program for children or youth

Food and clothing distribution

Evangelism programs in churches and local communities

Be sure you have a reliable contact person who has experience in handling the details of Third World service projects. Issues such as food, health, transportation, clearing customs, dealing with local police, and adjusting to cultural differences can pose a problem. A group's mission can be undermined or its safety threatened because it is unfamiliar with what is proper behavior in a new country.

Know what kind of project you will be doing before you arrive, but be prepared for changes. Be flexible—nothing ever works according to plan in a developing country. Travel books will be helpful in terms of general preparation. A travel agent can advise you about dress, customs, currency, travel documents, immunization requirements, climate, and many other essential matters. Talk to people who have been in the country, especially anyone from your denomination who has served as a missionary there. You might invite that person to speak to your group prior to your departure.

Community action and foreign service can provide your singles group with a zest for life and renewed spiritual vibrancy. Christians who venture into unfamiliar environments to answer the needs of others always receive far more than they give. Only then can they fully appreciate what Jesus meant when he said,

"Come, you who are blessed of My father. Inherit the kingdom prepared for you from the foundation of the world. For I was hungry, and you gave Me something to eat; I was thirsty, and you gave Me drink; I was a stranger, and you invited Me in; naked, and you clothed Me; I was sick, and you visited Me; I was in prison, and you came to Me. . . . to the extent that you did [these things] to one of these brothers of Mine, even the least of them, you did it to Me" (Matt. 25:34b–36, 40 NASB).

Part

Five

The Future
of Singles in America

Up to this point we have been looking back at the past and evaluating current conditions. We needed to do that so that we can with validity determine our future direction and decide how we are going to proceed. This last section provides a glimpse of what the future of singles ministry can be.

In interviews with Christian singles and in conversations with many single adult leaders, we asked them where they see single adult ministry going in the next decade. Their answers, obviously, were broad and diverse. We began to see some patterns developing for the future direction of our course. The three single adult leaders we present in this next section convey interesting perspectives on an effective singles' ministry.

It is our desire to broaden the ministry vision of many single adult leaders, to challenge them to use new methods, and to develop creative programming which can and will make a difference in ministering to today's singles.

17

The Future
of Singles:
Trends and Patterns

S ince the days of the early church, Christians have been commissioned to reach all lost and needy people with the message of God's love and redemption. Because we are also challenged to apply the eternal truths from the Word of God to an ever-changing world, we must constantly monitor the patterns, norms, and trends of society and look for ways to make our voices heard.

Today's leaders of Christian singles have a proud heritage. Since this specialized field was first recognized as an important ministry in the early 1970s, we have sought to stay on the cutting edge of its methodology and objectives. Most pastors and church boards currently acknowledge that a single-adult ministry is as viable a calling for a church as its programs for children, youth, and families. To implement that reality, the National Association of Single Adult Leaders is now an international network whose purpose is "to encourage and be a resource for equipping lay and professional leaders for ministry."

We still have a long way to go! Three individuals who have been influential spokespersons for single-adult ministry across the nation were interviewed to gain an insight into where we are in singles ministry today and where we are headed. These individuals—Jim Smoke, Bill Flanagan, and Harold I. Smith—have provided some fresh ideas and guiding principles for the singles ministries of tomorrow. As a fitting "conclusion" to our study, we will present their perspectives on what the future holds for Christian singles.

A New Dimension for Singles Ministry

Jim Smoke is the president of Growing Free (a ministry to single adults) and also the founder and director of the Center for Divorce Recovery in Tempe, Arizona. Pioneer, author, speaker, and former singles pastor, Jim is affectionately known as the father of single-adult ministry in America.

Singles ministry has enthusiastically entered the nineties, he says. The kinks are beginning to be worked out, and the concept itself is maturing. As Jim looks ahead after almost twenty years of involvement with singles programs, he sees a number of things that need to take place.

1. The ministry to single adults must receive total church recognition to the point of being *as important as* any other ministry in the church of the nineties. It is no longer an "experiment." It has developed into a full-blown ministry in much the same way that youth ministry reached its current stature.

2. This must always be a ministry born out of the needs of its people. As these needs change and the problems are compounded, the ministry must explore new ways of responding.

3. To exist as a recognized ministry in the church, both physical facilities and budgeted monies must be generously invested. This can no longer be a "broom closet" operation. Real ministries cost real money.

4. The church at large must be educated about the singles culture. Singles are no longer a minority group; in many churches they far outnumber the couples. Understanding single adults and filing away outdated images about them will take time and patience.

5. The church of the 1990s will have to wrestle with new insights about how to present scriptural teaching on divorce and remarriage. Archaic rules that were based on misinterpreting certain biblical passages will have to undergo revision if the church is to minister effectively to its changing population.

6. The ministry of divorce must be expanded and should also include programming for children. No child of a single parent should be put on a shelf while his or her parent is involved in adult programs and events. Since recovery from divorce, for either generation, is usually a two-year process, workshops and counseling must extend over that period of time. (Some of these programs also have relevance for widows, widowers, and their children.)

7. An extended function of any singles ministry is preparing its people for any forthcoming marriage and then helping them establish community with other married people. Divorced and widowed singles should be

educated and equipped for remarriage and step-parenting. The blended family is on the increase in modern society, so it is no longer enough to merely heal the hurts of those whose prior marriage has failed.

8. The religious press must increase its coverage of the growth, complexities, struggles, and successes of single adults in the church. It is unfortunate that so many old negative stereotypes are still alive and well in religious reporting.

9. A church program for unmarried adults will always be a distinct ministry because it is dealing with "a group of men and women in transition who are looking for some stabilization in their lives." Both the ministry's format and its leaders must be flexible—quickly responsive to the changing composition of the group being served and thus to the most pressing needs to be addressed.

10. A singles ministry that wants to be taken seriously will help its single parents confront problems such as low-paying jobs (especially for women), insufficient child-care facilities, overall fatigue, lack of quality parenting times, and the need for affordable housing.

11. The quality singles ministry of the future will offer a continuing syllabus of educational courses that will provide its people with the tools and know-how to improve their lives. A half-day seminar once or twice a year will not get the job done.

12. A singles ministry should not be considered a "baby-sitting service" for a group of adults who are staggering through singleness. It is a constructive program that says, "Tell us your needs and show us how we can help you be a better and growing person."

13. Single adults in the nineties and beyond must be allowed to integrate more effectively into all aspects of church life. For example, single women should be eligible for leadership and singles should be represented on all church boards. The "get married and then you can serve" mentality must be abandoned.

14. A church singles program must reflect the three necessary stages of any caring ministry: "emergency room" treatment, "extended-care" facilities, and "repayment" in leadership of what has been received.

15. Singles ministries of the future, especially in metropolitan areas, must find ways to minister to homosexual singles.

16. If the church does not effectively minister to its singles in the next decade, they will turn to secular programs that cannot answer their spiritual needs.

17. Since the greatest field for evangelism in the next decade will lie within the single-adult population, the church must aggressively extend its spiritual outreach to that group.

18. Any maturing ministry must stay ahead of itself. This is done by looking down the road and assessing needs that reflect cultural trends. If half our population in the 1990s will be comprised of single adults, we can no longer treat them as if they were an insignificant minority.

Where Are We Going?

Bill Flanagan is "Minister with Single Adults" at St. Andrew's Presbyterian Church of Newport Beach, California. Bill has been a pastor for singles since 1971 and a pioneer in this special type of ministry. He believes that single-adult ministry is still primarily a "white" phenomenon and that we therefore "need to take larger steps into various ethnic communities and also reach singles who are part of the more liturgical traditions of the church where we are not well networked." Bill has identified ten specific challenges before the church as we approach the end of the twentieth century.

1. Singles ministries are going to need enlightenment if they are to cope with the threat of the AIDS epidemic. There is no question that this modern plague will become more and more a heterosexual disease, thus affecting all singles across the land.

2. We need to enable single adults to participate in world missions. Many singles today have a tremendous interest in servanthood and want to reach out in their own communities as well as across boundaries of the Third World.

3. At the same time, we need to see networking efforts in our own country cross international borders and relate to singles groups outside the United States, particularly on the continents of Europe, Africa, Asia, and Australia.

4. Single-adult ministers need to contribute fresh theological insights to the issues of AIDS, divorce, remarriage, and sexual relationships from a biblical perspective.

5. Single-adult programs can be an appropriate launching pad for other ministries throughout the church and beyond. In addition to furthering missions, there should be vital spin-off ministries with remarried couples, single parents, co-dependents, and victims of chemical dependencies abuse, or cultural alienation.

6. More single adults need to be involved in the leadership of the total congregation. Not many singles are currently elders, deacons, and members of boards and sessions. These numbers need to increase.

7. Singles leaders should be alert to how they can use their ministry as a stepping-stone to other ministries in the life of the church. More men

and women need to see single-adult ministry not only as a temporary career specialty but as a long-term mission that can be extended to other local congregations and the broader community.

8. In light of the rising divorce rate, the church needs to do better work in the area of premarital counseling, drawing on lessons learned from couples who have already experienced a marital failure.

9. We need to be developing ministries to our senior singles. The *Single Adult Ministry Journal* reports that only 4 percent of all those attending singles groups are over 50 years of age; only 6 percent are between 46 and 50. Yet, there is a steadily increasing number of singles who are well past middle age. The church must respond by addressing their special needs in innovative ways.

10. Single-adult pastors and specialists should be teaching more courses in theological seminaries to train those who will follow them in specific areas of singles ministries. Groups such as the National Association of Single Adult Leaders must continue to develop ways to bring new talent into this field and equip leaders for the challenge.

A Sociological Overview of Ministering to Singles

Harold Ivan Smith, executive director of Tear-Catchers (a ministry to single adults that focuses on recovery and reconciliation), Kansas City, Missouri, is a lecturer, conference speaker, and prolific author of books about singles. His observations provide a sociological approach to what he believes are some of the contemporary issues of singleness.

Harold has observed that much of the writing, programming, and speaking to singles has focused on doing something *about* one's unmarried state. He feels that the new thrust in singles ministry will be on doing something *with* one's singleness. Several cultural trends have brought him to that conclusion:

The current generation of singles approaches life differently than more "mature" singles do. There is a growing number of young adults who have observed certain cultural stereotypes about singleness and have chosen to refute those myths. These "new" singles are the trailblazers in lobbying for full acceptance in society. They reject the "old maid" labeling that characterizes being unmarried as a tragedy. Instead, they view singleness as an opportunity to realize their potential as human beings. Even those who believe they may someday be married are usually committed to *doing*, rather than *waiting* (which is the way most singles behaved in earlier times). These pioneers have fought for economic equality—they have pursued higher education, explored career options, and established stable credit ratings. They are homeowners, neighbor-hood rejuvenators, and trendsetting consumers, especially in the area of electronic gadgetry.

Of course, some of these young adults are "reluctant" singles who consider themselves "just not married *yet*." In so doing, they have rekin-dled the mentality that everyone must be married to be happy, which implies that all singles should be dating in pursuit of a mate. Certain dif-ficulties arise in trying to blend these two types of singles in one organi-zation. But, so long as their differing attitudes and goals are recognized, they can coexist quite amicably.

The business world will recognize single adults as valuable employees. Many employers have found that it makes good sense to have singles in their organization. (Even though it is a violation of civil rights to base hiring or promotion on marital status alone, charges of discrimination on those grounds would be difficult to prove.) Unless they are custodial par-ents, singles can be quite flexible about adjusting their schedules to job requirements. They are generally available for overtime, late-night meet-ings, and conventions. In fact, corporations are increasingly finding that the "work ethic" and productivity of singles is stronger than that of many married people, at least if measured by the time spent in job-related activities. However, that can pose a potential danger for career-oriented singles, many of whom pour themselves into their jobs and become workaholics.

It is also more "convenient" to transfer a single employee, since there will be no need to consult a spouse who–in this era of two-income households—might have a career track that would be disrupted by a move. And it is certainly less expensive to pay the moving expenses of one person rather than an entire family. For these and other reasons, sin-gles in general adjust well to the idea of a six-week out-of-state seminar, a temporary assignment overseas, or permanent transfer to a branch office.

A growing number of singles will begin to ask, "Is this all there is?" Suc-cessful singles who have been enjoying life in the fast lane are usually in for a jolt when they approach midlife. Some will regret that they never got around to marriage or will find that their affluent lifestyle is no longer fun. Others will look over their shoulder and see a whole gener-ation of younger people scampering up the corporate ladder behind them. Middle-aged singles who are disappointed with the direction may switch jobs or want an entirely different career, although the comfortable security of the present may keep them from trying something new, such as returning to school. For others, however, the urge to be their own boss will challenge them and stimulate a round of entrepreneurship.

The threat of AIDS will become a reality in the singles lifestyle. During the first decade of the AIDS epidemic, most people glanced at the statistics but considered themselves at little risk from the disease unless they were male homosexuals or addicted to drugs. Today and into the future, however, AIDS will affect heterosexuals in increasing numbers. For example, it is predicted that by 1992, women will account for at least 10 percent of the total number of AIDS victims. One's past and present sexual practices therefore become of great concern, especially since HIV-positive indicators may not show up for years after exposure to the disease. Even for singles who are no longer sexually active, a brief period of promiscuity could have left them and their future partners at great risk. It is imperative that all singles and the ministries that serve them acknowledge the physical and emotional dangers of unmarried sexual activity beyond the moral issues involved.

Many singles will find themselves classified as "terminally poor." The theme song of some singles—"Don't worry, be happy"—can later translate into financial insecurity. Unless provision is made for the future, including the retirement years, a single may eventually find that he or she is permanently at a low socioeconomic level. This is especially true for single parents, in light of the economic problems many of them face on a daily basis.

Appendix
Singles in America

A Christian Singles Questionnaire

Carolyn Koons
Michael Anthony

I. General Demographics

1. Age:
   - _____a. 18-24
   - _____b. 25-29
   - _____c. 30-39
   - _____d. 40-49
   - _____e. 50-64
   - _____f. 65 and above

2. Sex:
   - _____a. Female
   - _____b. Male

3. Education:
   - _____a. Less than high school diploma
   - _____b. High school diploma
   - _____c. Some college
   - _____d. College degree
   - _____e. Some graduate school
   - _____f. Graduate or professional degree

4. Marital Status
   - _____a. Never married single
   - _____b. Divorced (once)
   - _____c. Divorced (more than once)
   - _____d. Widowed
   - _____e. Separated

5. How many years have you been divorced (accumulative):
   - _____a. Less than one year
   - _____b. One year
   - _____c. Two years
   - _____d. Three years
   - _____e. 4-5 years
   - _____f. 6-8 years
   - _____g. 9-10 years
   - _____h. 10 years or more

6. Occupation
   - _____a. Professional (doctor, teacher, engineer, etc.)
   - _____b. Business official or manager
   - _____c. Sales person
   - _____d. Clerical worker
   - _____e. Service worker (policeman, fireman, etc.)
   - _____f. Skilled worker (draftsman, machine operator, etc.)
   - _____g. Unskilled worker
   - _____h. Homemaker

7. What is your annual income?
   - _____a. less than $5,000
   - _____b. $5,000 - $9,999
   - _____c. $10,000 - $14,999
   - _____d. $15,000 - $19,999
   - _____e. $20,000 - $24,999
   - _____f. $25,000 - $29,999
   - _____g. $30,000 - $39,999
   - _____h. $40,000 - $49,999
   - _____i. $50,000 - $99,999
   - _____j. $100,000 and above

8. What size city do you live in?
   - _____a. Metropolis (with a population of at least a million)
   - _____b. Large city (with population between 500,000 - 1 million)
   - _____c. Medium sized city (with population between 100,000 - 500,000)
   - _____d. Small city (with population between 25,000 - 100,000)
   - _____e. Suburb
   - _____f. Small town (with population between 10,000 - 25,000)
   - _____g. Rural area (with population less than 10,000)

II. General Lifestyle (Housing, Work, Health)

9. How would you describe your living arrangement?
   - _____a. Temporary location to store your belongings
   - _____b. Convenient with moderate identity
   - _____c. Close expression of your identity (comfortable)

10. Type of accommodation?
    - _____a. House/condominium (own)
    - _____b. House/condominium (rent/lease)
    - _____c. Apartment
    - _____d. Other

11. Living arrangements?
    _____a. Independently alone
    _____b. Living with parents
    _____c. Share with same sex room-
          mate(s)
    _____d. Share with opposite sex
          roommate(s)
    _____e. Commune/group arrangement

12. What is your most unpleasant domestic activity?
    _____a. Shopping
    _____b. Laundry
    _____c. Cooking
    _____d. Cleaning
    _____e. Managing finances (bills,
          banking, insurance, invest-
          ments)
    _____f. Automobile maintenance
    _____g. Yard work
    _____h. Other _____

13. What do you consider the greatest disadvantage of being single?
    _____a. Loneliness
    _____b. Fear due to living alone
    _____c. Economic insecurity
    _____d. Restricted sexual and social
          life
    _____e. A tendency to become rigid,
          self-centered, selfish
    _____f. The social stigma of not being
          married
    _____g. The dating grind
    _____h. Don't know

14. What do you consider the greatest advantage of being single?
    _____a. Mobility and freedom
    _____b. Availability of romantic
          partners
    _____c. Time to pursue personal
          interests
    _____d. Economic security and
          independence
    _____e. Privacy
    _____f. Social life in general: dating,
          entertainment, excitement
    _____g. Don't know

15. Have you ever felt discriminated against because you are single? If so indicate where:
    _____a. Hiring
    _____b. Salary
    _____c. Promotion
    _____d. Invitations to work-related
          activities
    _____e. Church leadership position
    _____f. None of the above

16. Have you ever felt discriminated against regarding the following? If so, indicate where:
    _____a. Bank loans
    _____b. Credit ratings/charge accounts
    _____c. Major purchases (car)
    _____d. Real estate
    _____e. Renting (alone or with a
          group)
    _____f. None of the above

17. In the area of main employment how many different jobs have you had in the past five years?
    _____a. 1
    _____b. 2
    _____c. 3
    _____d. 4
    _____e. 5
    _____f. More than 5

18. How many different jobs do you currently have?
    _____a. 1
    _____b. 2
    _____c. 3
    _____d. More than 3

19. On the average, how many hours in a day do you spend in work related activities:
    _____a. Under 6
    _____b. 6-8
    _____c. 9-10
    _____d. 11-12
    _____e. 13-16
    _____f. 17+

20. How often do you enjoy the work that you do?
    _____a. Almost all the time
    _____b. Most of the time
    _____c. Fairly often
    _____d. Occasionally
    _____e. Rarely

21. If you would like to make a major change in the kind of work you do but feel you can't at this time, what are the reasons? Check as many as apply.
    _____a. Loss of income
    _____b. Loss of prestige
    _____c. Risk of failure
    _____d. Family wouldn't approve
    _____e. Friends and/or colleagues
          wouldn't approve
    _____f. No decent opportunity at my
          age
    _____g. Lacking of training skills
    _____h. Just feel scared
    _____i. Would damage children
    _____j. I don't want to make a career
          change at this time

_____k. Other
_____

22. Which of the following have been true
of you in the last year? Check as many
as apply.
_____a. Frequent headaches
_____b. Digestive problems
_____c. High blood pressure
_____d. Constant worry and anxiety
_____e. Tiring easily
_____f. Feeling that I just can't cope
_____g. Crying spells
_____h. Feelings of worthlessness
_____i. Often feeling irritable or angry
_____j. Feeling sad or depressed

23. In general, how has your health
changed over the last five years?
_____a. It has gotten much better
_____b. It has gotten somewhat better
_____c. It has stayed about the same
_____d. It has gotten somewhat worse
_____e. It has gotten much worse

24. How much time do you spend in
exercise per week?
_____a. None
_____b. 1-2 hours
_____c. 3-5 hours
_____d. 6-10 hours
_____e. 11 and above

III. Social

25. On the average, how many hours each
working day do you spend with
friends?
_____a. 0
_____b. 1
_____c. 2
_____d. 3
_____e. 4
_____f. 5
_____g. 6 or more

26. When you go out socially, you usually
go to (indicate up to three that apply):
_____a. Restaurant
_____b. Nightclub (bar)
_____c. Movie
_____d. Theatre or concert
_____e. Visit friends
_____f. Visit relatives
_____g. Social/health club
_____h. Church activities
_____i. Other (please specify)
_____

27. How often do you go out socially?
_____a. Less than once a week
_____b. Once a week
_____c. Twice a week
_____d. Three times a week

_____e. Four or more times a week

28. Where do you meet most of the
men/women with whom you socialize?
_____a. Through friends
_____b. At social gatherings
_____c. At bars, discos, nightclubs,
etc.
_____d. Church & church singles
functions
_____e. At work
_____f. Through personal ads in
newspapers, magazines
_____g. Don't know

29. On the whole, has single dating been
for you:
_____a. Highly enjoyable
_____b. Frustrating but worthwhile
_____c. Something to be endured until
the right man/woman comes
along
_____d. Fun but nothing too
significant
_____e. A tedious grind
_____f. Less exciting than I'd hoped it
would be
_____g. Don't know

30. On the average, do you find that a
majority of those you date are:
_____a. Sincere, decent, and open
_____b. Interested in a nice evening
but nothing serious
_____c. Anxious only to find marriage
_____d. Looking for men/women with
money, fame, and power
_____e. Superficial, missing that
certain "something"
_____f. Generally undesirable
_____g. Generally desirable
_____h. Don't know

31. What is the most frequent reason you
stop dating a particular person?
_____a. I find him/her dull and
superficial
_____b. She/he refuses to have sex
_____c. She/he is immature or neurotic
_____d. She/he is a poor lover
_____e. It is usually my way to go out
with a woman/man a few
times and then move on
_____f. She/he presses me too quickly
for intimacy and involvement
_____g. She/he loses interest
_____h. Don't know

32. Where do you meet members of the
opposite sex?
_____a. Work
_____b. School
_____c. Church

_____d. Health club
_____e. Singles bar/restaurant
_____f. Other _____

33. How often do you feel bored?
    _____a. Almost never
    _____b. Rarely
    _____c. Occasionally
    _____d. Fairly often
    _____e. Most of the time
    _____f. Almost all the time

34. If you had personal problems, were in trouble, or had to make a difficult decision, on whom could you rely for understanding and support? (Indicate up to three that apply.)
    _____a. Therapist or counselor
    _____b. Boyfriend/girlfriend
    _____c. My children
    _____d. My mother
    _____e. My father
    _____f. One or more of my brothers and sisters
    _____g. Other relatives
    _____h. My close friends
    _____i. Minister/clergy
    _____j. Other _____

35. What do you look for in a relationship with a friend?
    _____a. Similar interests/hobbies
    _____b. Physical appearance
    _____c. Social prominence
    _____d. Spiritual maturity
    _____e. Popular and outgoing
    _____f. Potential mate
    _____g. Companionship
    _____h. Other _____

IV. Sexuality

36. As a single do you ever feel pressures to get married? (Choose as many answers as are appropriate.)
    _____a. Almost never
    _____b. Yes, from my parents
    _____c. Yes, at my job
    _____d. Yes, from my own personal feelings
    _____e. Yes, from the people I date
    _____f. Yes, from my children
    _____g. Yes, from my church
    _____h. Don't know

37. How many close personal friends do you have of the opposite sex?
    _____a. none
    _____b. 1-2
    _____c. 3-4
    _____d. 5-6
    _____e. 7-8
    _____f. 9-10

38. How many close personal friends do you have of the same sex as you?
    _____a. none
    _____b. 1-2
    _____c. 3-4
    _____d. 5-6
    _____e. 7-8
    _____f. 9-10

39. Is there one person you date exclusively or almost exclusively?
    _____a. yes
    _____b. no

40. In the past month, how often have you dated?
    _____a. none
    _____b. 1-2 times
    _____c. 3-5 times
    _____d. 6-7 times
    _____e. 8-10 times
    _____f. 11-15 times
    _____g. 16 or more times

41. Have you ever lived with a member of the opposite sex in an intimate, unmarried basis?
    _____a. Yes
    _____b. No
    _____c. Yes, more than one
    _____d. Yes, more than two

42. In general, how satisfied are you with your sex life?
    _____a. Very satisfied
    _____b. Somewhat satisfied
    _____c. Neutral
    _____d. Somewhat dissatisfied
    _____e. Very dissatisfied

43. How many sexual partners do you think most people your age, sex, and marital status have had?
    _____a. None
    _____b. 1
    _____c. 2 or 3
    _____d. 4 to 6
    _____e. 11 to 20
    _____f. More than 20

44. As a single adult, with how many sexual partners have you had sexual intercourse?
    _____a. None
    _____b. 1
    _____c. 2 or 3
    _____d. 4 to 6
    _____e. 7 to 10
    _____f. 11 to 20
    _____g. More than 20

45. During the last six months, how often have you had sexual intercourse?
    _____a. Never or almost never

_____b. Once or twice a month
_____c. Once or twice a week
_____d. Several times a week
_____e. Daily or more often

V. Developmental

46. Why are you single? (Indicate up to three responses.)
_____a. Marriage entails too much commitment and responsibility
_____b. I haven't found the right person to marry
_____c. I prefer the lifestyle
_____d. I liked being married but my marriage failed; I'll marry again when the chance comes
_____e. I prefer members of my own sex
_____f. Why get married when people can live together
_____g. I don't want to be tied to the same person for life
_____h. Don't know

47. Using the scale, please rate how important each of these circumstances is in making you happy. (3=much, 2=little, 1=none)
_____a. Good health
_____b. Being in love
_____c. Personal growth
_____d. Job or career
_____e. A good sex life
_____f. Financial security
_____g. Social and family life

48. On the whole, has being single been a pleasant or unpleasant experience for you?
_____a. It has been wonderful.
_____b. I've been married and I've been single and I prefer being single.
_____c. I've been married and I've been single and I prefer being married.
_____d. It has been an unpleasant experience.
_____e. Anything would be better than being single.
_____f. It is fine for a while. Then one gets tired of it.
_____g. There have been plenty of problems but basically it is fine.
_____h. Don't know.

49. Do you think that being single will be a permanent status for you?
_____a. Yes
_____b. No

_____c. Don't know

50. Compared to you, how happy are most of your married acquaintances?
_____a. Much happier than I
_____b. Somewhat happier than I
_____c. About as happy as I
_____d. Somewhat less happy than I
_____e. Much less happy than I

51. Why are you not married? (Indicate those that apply.)
_____a. Something is wrong with me
_____b. I never found the right person
_____c. I lost the right person
_____d. I do not want the responsibility of children
_____e. I am having too much fun
_____f. I like my freedom and privacy
_____g. My career prevented this commitment
_____h. It never seemed like a desirable option
_____i. Other (please explain)
_____

52. Is there one person or experience that made you decide to stay single at this time?
_____a. Yes
_____b. No

53. Do you consider that you are single by:
_____a. Deliberate choice
_____b. Chance
_____c. Circumstances beyond your control (describe)
_____

54. How would you describe your current level of life satisfaction (state of well-being, contentment, happiness)?
_____a. This is the dreariest time of my life.
_____b. My life could be happier than it is now.
_____c. I feel old and somewhat tired.
_____d. These are the best years of my life.
_____e. As I look back on my life, I am fairly well satisfied.
_____f. I have made plans for things I will be doing a year from now.
_____g. I've gotten pretty much what I wanted out of life.
_____h. I am just as happy as when I was younger.
_____i. I would not change my past life if I could.
_____j. I feel my age, but it does not bother me.

55. Indicate below the character traits that you value in a member of the opposite sex. (Indicate up to four responses.)
_____a. Ambitious (hardworking, aspiring)
_____b. Capable (competent, knowledgeable)
_____c. Forgiving (willing to pardon others)
_____d. Helpful (working for the welfare of others)
_____e. Honest (sincere, truthful)
_____f. Imaginative (daring, creative)
_____g. Independent (self-reliant, self-sufficient)
_____h. Loving (affectionate, tender)
_____i. Responsible (dependable, reliable)
_____j. Self-controlled (restrained, self-disciplined)

56. How much control do you have over the important events in your life?
_____a. Almost total control
_____b. Mostly under my control
_____c. About half the time I can control the important events
_____d. Mostly not under my control
_____e. Almost no control

57. How easy is it for you to reveal your intimate thoughts and feelings to your friends and relatives?
_____a. Very easy
_____b. Fairly easy
_____c. Fairly difficult
_____d. Very difficult
_____e. Not applicable

58. At this stage in your life, what are your major fears?
_____a. Not advancing fast enough
_____b. Time is running out
_____c. No longer being physically attractive
_____d. Loneliness
_____e. Messing up my personal life
_____f. Being "locked in," unable to freely change my way of life
_____g. Not having enough money
_____h. Being abandoned by spouse or lover
_____i. Declining physical capabilities, illness
_____j. I have no major fear

59. Are you currently involved in a small accountability group?
_____a. No
_____b. Yes, we meet once per week
_____c. Yes, we meet bi-monthly
_____d. Yes, we meet quarterly
_____e. Yes, we meet annually

60. Do you have a mentor—an older, non-parental person who has helped to guide, encourage, and inspire you over a period of years (after age 18)?
_____a. No
_____b. Yes
_____c. Yes, more than one

VI. Religious Practices

61. Religious affiliation
_____a. Assemblies of God/Pentecostal
_____b. Baptist
_____c. Catholic
_____d. Episcopalian
_____e. Methodist
_____f. Lutheran
_____g. Presbyterian
_____h. Independent
_____i. Nazarene
_____j. No religious affiliation
_____k. Other _____

62. Religious attendance
_____a. 2 or 3 times a week
_____b. Once a week
_____c. 2 to 3 times a month
_____d. 4 to 6 times a year
_____e. Once a year
_____f. Less than once a year
_____g. Not at all

63. Indicate your level of involvement at your church:
_____a. Very active involvement
_____b. Active involvement
_____c. Moderate involvement
_____d. Seldom involvement
_____e. No involvement

64. What activities are you actively involved in at your church?
_____a. Sunday school teacher/worker
_____b. Choir/music program
_____c. Leadership role (elder, deacon, trustee)
_____d. Missions activities
_____e. Singles ministry
_____f. Youth sponsor
_____g. Worship services
_____h. Other _____

65. If you are involved in your singles ministry, what activities are you involved in the most?
_____a. Sunday A.M. singles class
_____b. Midweek Bible study
_____c. Special seminars/workshops
_____d. Retreats/camps
_____e. Socials
_____f. Missions/outreach activities

_____g. Singles ministry leadership position

66. How often do you read your Bible?
  _____a. Several times a day
  _____b. Once a day
  _____c. 2-3 times a week
  _____d. 2-3 times a month
  _____e. Seldom
  _____f. Never

67. How often do you pray?
  _____a. Several times a day
  _____b. Once a day
  _____c. 2-3 times a week
  _____d. 2-3 times a month
  _____e. Seldom
  _____f. Never

68. What percent of your income do you tithe?
  _____a. None
  _____b. 1% to 3%
  _____c. 4% to 6%
  _____d. 7% to 10%
  _____e. 11% to 15%
  _____f. 16% to 20%
  _____g. above 20%

VII. Single Parenting (Single parents only please answer these questions.)

69. How do most of the men/women you date feel about the fact that you have a child/children?
  _____a. It frightens them off
  _____b. It has frightened some, others respond positively
  _____c. It is of secondary importance to them
  _____d. It has ruined my romantic life
  _____e. Most men/women like it.
  _____f. Most men/women don't care
  _____g. Don't know

70. How do your children usually react to your dates?
  _____a. They endorse and strongly encourage it
  _____b. They seem to have no hang-ups about it
  _____c. With indifference
  _____d. With reserve
  _____e. With resentment, aggressive anger
  _____f. They try to make each into a substitute parent
  _____g. I rarely bring dates home
  _____h. Don't know

71. What aspects of the single household are the most difficult for your child/children? (Choose as many answers as are appropriate.)

  _____a. My involvements with other women/men
  _____b. My ex-spouse's involvements with other men/women
  _____c. Lowered standard of living
  _____d. My depression, worry, and self-concern
  _____e. My absence during the day due to work
  _____f. Being shunted around home from home
  _____g. Don't know

72. How many children do you have?
  _____a. One
  _____b. Two
  _____c. Three
  _____d. Four
  _____e. Five
  _____f. Six or more

73. I am the (check the appropriate answer)
  _____a. Primary custodial parent
  _____b. Non-primary custodial parent
  _____c. Equal-mutual custody

74. How many days per month do you have custody of your children?
  _____a. 30 days
  _____b. 25-29 days
  _____c. 20-24 days
  _____d. 15-19 days (dual/equal custody)
  _____e. 10-14 days
  _____f. 5-9 days
  _____g. 1-4 days
  _____h. 0 days

75. Under what circumstances are you a single parent?
  _____a. Widowed
  _____b. Divorced
  _____c. Unwed parent
  _____d. Adoption

76. How do you feel about remaining a single parent?
  _____a. Both my child/children and I like it better this way.
  _____b. My child wants me to remarry but I have no desire to do so.
  _____c. I would live with someone but not marry them.
  _____d. I don't want to remarry but probably will for the sake of my children.
  _____e. I'd like to marry again.
  _____f. At first I wanted to remarry quickly. Now that I see I can swing it on my own I'm in no hurry.
  _____g. Don't know.

VIII.Life Satisfaction

Here are some statements about life in general that people feel differently about. Would you read each statement on the list, and if you agree with it put a check mark in the space under **Agree**. If you do not agree with a statement, put a check mark in the space under **Disagree**. If you are not sure one way or the other, put a check mark in the space under **?**. *Please be sure to answer every question on the list.*

	Agree	Disagree	?
77. As I grow older, things seem better than I thought they would be.	____	____	____
78. I have gotten more of the breaks in life than most of the people I know.	____	____	____
79. This is the dreariest time of my life.	____	____	____
80. I am just as happy as when I was younger.	____	____	____
81. My life could be happier than it is now.	____	____	____
82. These are the best years of my life.	____	____	____
83. Most of the things I do are boring or monotonous.	____	____	____
84. I expect some interesting and pleasant things to happen to me in the future.	____	____	____
85. The things I do are as interesting to me as they ever were.	____	____	____
86. I feel old and somewhat tired.	____	____	____
87. I feel my age, but it does not bother me.	____	____	____
88. As I look back on my life, I am fairly well satisfied.	____	____	____
89. I would not change my past life if I could.	____	____	____
90. Compared to other people my age, I've made a lot of foolish decisions in my life.	____	____	____
91. Compared to other people my age, I make a good appearance.	____	____	____
92. I have made plans for things I'll be doing a year from now.	____	____	____
93. When I think back over my life, I didn't get most of the important things I wanted.	____	____	____
94. Compared to other people, I get down in the dumps too often.	____	____	____
95. I've gotten pretty much what I expected out of life.	____	____	____
96. In spite of what people say, the lot of the average man is getting worse, not better.	____	____	____

Bibliography

Adams, P. L., J. R. Milner, and N. A. Schrepf. 1984. *Fatherless children*. New York: John Wiley and Sons.

Amato, P. R. 1987. Family processes in one-parent, step-parent, and intact families: The child's point of view. *Journal of Marriage and the Family* (May): 327-37.

Bellah, M. 1988. *Baby boom believers*. Wheaton, Ill.: Tyndale.

Bernikow, L. 1986. Loneliness as an American epidemic. *U.S. News & World Report* (July 21).

Blomquist, J. M. 1986. Exploring spiritual dimensions: Toward a hermeneutic of divorce. *Pastoral Psychology* 34/3 (Spring): 161-71.

Blumstein, P., and P. Schwartz. 1983. *American couples*. New York: William Morrow.

Botwinick, J. 1977. Intellectual abilities. In *Handbook of psychology of aging*, ed. J. E. Birren and K. W. Schaie. New York: Van Nostrand Reinhold.

Braiker, H. 1987. *The type e woman*. New York: Dodd, Mead.

Brothers, J. 1985. Why you should not move in with your lover. *New Woman* (June): 54-57.

Bustanoby, A. 1987. *Being a single parent*. Grand Rapids: Zondervan.

Cargan, L., and M. Melko. 1982. *Singles: Myths and Realities*. Newberry Park, Calif.: Sage Publications.

Cavanaugh, M. 1986. *God's call to the single adult*. Springdale, Penn.: Whitaker.

Dickinson, H. 1986. Bound or free? *Theology* (Mar.): 102-8.

Duin, J. 1986. We must learn to celebrate celibacy. *Christianity Today* (Mar.): 13.

Eisenstadt, M. 1986. On turning 40. *U. S. News & World Report* (April 21): 75.

Farrell, W. 1988. *Why men are the way they are*. Berkeley: Berkeley Publications.

Fitzgerald, H. E., and M. G. Walraven. 1985. *Human development 85/86*. Guilford, Conn.: Dushkin.

Flanagan, B. 1986. *The ministry of divorce recovery*. Colorado Springs: N. S. L. Publications.

Fromme, A. 1982. *The ability to love*. New York: Wilshire.

Gagnon, J., and B. Smith. 1977. *Human sexualities*. Chicago: Scott, Foresman.

Gilder, G. 1974. *The naked nomads*. New York: New York Times Book Company.

Glen, N. D., and K. B. Kramer. 1987. The marriages and divorces of the children of divorce. *Journal of Marriage and the Family* 497 (Nov.): 811-25.

Glick, P. 1984. Marriage, divorce, and living arrangements. *Journal of Family Issues* 5: 7-26.

Gould, R. L. 1978. *Transformations: Growth and change in adult life*. New York: Simon and Schuster.

Greif, G. 1985. *Single fathers*. Lexington, Mass.: Lexington Books.

Hansel, T. 1987. *Holy sweat: The remarkable things ordinary people can do!* Waco, Tex.: Word.

Havighurst, R. J. 1978. *Developmental tasks and education.* New York: Longmans.

———. 1953. *Human development and education.* New York: Longmans.

Hugget, J. 1986. *Growing into love.* Downers Grove, Ill.: InterVarsity.

———. 1986. The other side of loneliness. *HIS* (Jan.): 1-4.

Hunt, A. E. 1988. Unmet needs: Untapped resources. *Fundamentalist Journal* (Mar.): 34-37.

Hunt, M., and B. Hunt. 1977. *The divorce experience.* New York: McGraw Hill.

Ihinger-Tallman, M., and K. Pasley. 1987. *Remarriage.* Family Studies Text Series, Vol. 7. Newbury Park, Calif.: Sage.

Kinard, M. E., and H. Reinherz. 1986. Effects of marital disruption on children's school aptitude and achievement. *Journal of Marriage and the Family* 48 (May): 285-93.

Lamberg, L. 1986. Midlife crisis: The myths, the facts. *Better Homes and Gardens* (Mar.): 34-35.

Levinson, D. J. 1978. *The seasons of a man's life.* New York: Alfred A. Knopf.

Lewis, C. S. 1971. *The four loves.* San Diego: Harcourt Brace Jovanovich.

May, E. T. 1983. *Great expectations: Marriage and divorce in post victorian America.* Chicago: University of Chicago Press.

Mayo, M. A. 1987. *A Christian guide to sexual counseling: Recovering the mystery and the reality of "one flesh."* Grand Rapids: Zondervan.

McGrath, A. 1987. Living alone and loving it. *U.S. News & World Report* (Aug.): 52-57.

Meer, J. 1985. Loneliness. *Psychology Today* (July): 29-33.

Norton, A. J., and J. E. Moorman. 1987. Current trends in marriage and divorce among American women. *Journal of Marriage and the Family* 49 (Feb.): 3-14.

Nouwen, Henri. 1979. *The wounded healer: Ministry in contemporary society.* New York: Doubleday.

Reuben, D. 1986. *Any woman can.* New York: David McKay.

Rodman, H., and D. J. Pratto. 1987. Child's age and mother's employment in relation to greater use of self-care arrangements for children. *Journal of Marriage and the Family* 49 (Aug.): 573-78.

Rubin, L. B. 1979. *Women of a certain age.* New York: Harper and Row.

Sheehy, G. 1976. *Passages: Predictable crises of adult life.* New York: Bantam.

Simenauer, J., and D. Carroll. 1982. *Singles: The new Americans.* New York: Simon and Schuster.

Smith, H. I. 1987. *Single and feeling good.* Nashville: Abingdon.

———. 1986. *Positively single.* Wheaton, Ill.: Victor Books.

Smoke, J. 1979. *Growing through divorce.* Irvine, Calif.: Harvest House.

Stedman, R. 1987. Working smart with singles. *Leadership* (Summer): 114-19.

Stein, P., ed. 1981. *Single life: Unmarried adults in social context.* New York: St. Martin's.

Sweet, J. A., and L. Bumpass. 1988. *American families and households.* New York: Russell Sage.

Tillapaugh, F. 1988. *Unleashing your potential: Discovering your God-given opportunities for ministry.* Ventura, Calif.: Regal.

Troll, L. 1982. *Continuations: Adult development and aging.* Monterey, Calif.: Brooks/Cole.

Weiss, R. 1979. *Going it alone: The family life and social situation of the single parent.* New York: Basic.

Suggested Reading

Never Married

Allon, N., and D. Fishel. 1981. Singles' bars as examples of urban courting patterns. In *Single life, unmarried adults in social context,* pp. 115-20, ed. P. J. Stein. New York: St. Martin's.

Bence, E. 1986. *Leaving home.* Wheaton, Ill.: Tyndale.

Doudna, C., and F. McBride. 1981. Where are the men for the women at the top? In *Single life, unmarried adults in social context,* pp. 21-23, ed. P. J. Stein. New York: St. Martin's.

Douglass J., and K. Long. 1986. *Single and complete.* San Bernardino, Calif.: Here's Life.

Jeremiah, D. 1983. *Overcoming loneliness.* San Bernardino, Calif.: Here's Life.

Karssen, G. 1983. *Getting the most out of being single.* Colorado Springs: Navpress.

Mahany, B. 1986. Single Catholics: No need for solitary confinement. *U. S. Catholic* (Oct.): 22-28.

McConnell, A. 1980. *Single after fifty.* New York: McGraw-Hill.

Muto, S. A. 1985. *Celebrating the single life.* New York: Doubleday.

Purnell, D. 1986. *Becoming a friend and lover.* San Bernardino, Calif.: Here's Life.

Reed, B. 1980. *Making the most of single life.* St. Louis: Concordia.

Shahan, L. 1985. *Living alone and liking it.* New York: Warner Books.

Swindoll, L. 1982. *Wide my world, narrow my bed.* Portland, Oreg.: Multnomah.

Divorced

Adams, J. E. 1980. *Marriage, divorce and remarriage in the Bible.* Phillipsburg, N. J.: Presbyterian and Reformed.

Beeson, C. C. 1984. *Picking up the pieces.* New York: Ballantine.

Berger, S. 1983. *Divorce without victims.* New York: NAL.

Brock, A. 1988. *Divorce recovery: Piecing together your broken pieces.* Waco, Tex.: Word/Worthy.

Burns, B. 1989. *Through the whirlwind: A proven path to recovery from the devastation of divorce.* Nashville: Thomas Nelson.

Cerling, C. E. 1984. *The divorced Christian.* Grand Rapids: Baker.

Chapman, G. 1985. *Now that you are single again.* San Bernardino, Calif.: Here's Life.

Correu, L. M. 1982. *Beyond the broken marriage.* Philadelphia: Westminster.

Friedman, J. T. 1984. *The divorce handbook.* New York: Random House.

Hershey, T. 1986. *Beginning again: Life after a relationship ends.* Laguna Hills, Calif.: Thomas Nelson.

Heth, W. A., and G. J. Wenham. 1987. *Jesus and divorce.* Nashville: Thomas Nelson.

Hootman, M., and P. Perkins. 1985. *How to forgive your ex-husband.* New York: Double-day.

Joiner, E. E. 1983. *A Christian considers divorce and remarriage.* Nashville: Broadman.

Marshall, S. 1990. *When a friend gets a divorce—What can you do?* Grand Rapids: Baker.

————. 1988. *Surviving separation and divorce.* Grand Rapids: Baker.

Mattison, J. 1985. *Divorce: The pain and the healing: Personal meditations when marriage ends.* Minneapolis: Augsburg.

Morgan, R. L. 1985. *Is there life after divorce in the church?* Atlanta: John Knox.

O'Conner, N. 1985. *Letting go with love: The grieving process.* Tucson: LaMariposa Press.

Pratt, K. P. 1986. Divorce's effect on children: How the church can bring about healing. *C. E. Journal* 6/2: 34-41.

Richards, L. 1981. *Remarriage—A healing gift from God.* Waco, Tex.: Word.

Scott, C. 1981. When divorce strikes. *Moody* (Sept.): 10-16.

Small, D. H. 1986. *Remarriage and God's renewing grace: A positive biblical ethic for divorced Christians.* Grand Rapids: Baker.

Smith, B. J., and I. B. Harrell. 1983. *Divorced.* Wheaton, Ill.: Tyndale.

Smith, H. I. 1987. *I wish someone understood my divorce.* Minneapolis: Augsburg.

————. 1981. *Help for parents of a divorced son or daughter.* St. Louis: Concordia.

Smoke, J. 1984. *Living beyond divorce—The possibilities of remarriage.* Eugene, Oreg.: Harvest House.

Stein, S. B., and E. Stone. 1984. *On divorce.* New York: Walker.

Streeter, C. S. 1986. *Finding your place after divorce.* Grand Rapids: Zondervan.

Supancic, R., and D. Baker. 1986. *When all else fails.* Old Tappan, N.J.: Revell.

Swindoll, C. R. 1981. *Divorce.* Portland, Oreg.: Multnomah.

Thompson, D. A. 1989. *Counseling and divorce.* Waco, Tex.: Word.

————. 1982. *Recovery from divorce.* Minneapolis: Bethany.

Weitzman, L. J. 1985. *The divorce revolution: The unexpected social and economic consequences for women and children in America.* New York: Free Press.

Zodhiates, S. 1984. *May I divorce and remarry?* Chattanooga, Tenn.: AMG.

Widowed

Cushenbery, D. C., and R. C. Cushenbery. 1991. *Coping with life after your mate dies.* Grand Rapids: Baker.

Decker, B., and G. Kooiman. 1987. *After the flowers have gone.* Grand Rapids: Zondervan.

Kolf, J. C. 1989. *How can I help: Reaching out to someone who is grieving.* Grand Rapids: Baker.

Kubler-Ross, E. 1969. *On death and dying.* New York: Macmillan.

————. 1974. *Questions and answers on death and dying.* New York: Macmillan.

Lewis, C. S. 1976. *A grief observed.* New York: Bantam.

Manning, D. 1984. *Don't take my grief away.* San Francisco: Harper and Row.

Marshall, C. 1984. *Beyond ourselves.* Lincoln, Va.: Chosen.

Mumford, A. R. 1981. *By death or divorce . . . it hurts to lose.* Denver: Accent.

Oates, W. E. 1981. *Your particular grief.* Philadelphia: Westminster.

Towns, J. 1987. *Family guide to death and dying.* Wheaton, Ill.: Tyndale.

————. 1984. *Growing through grief.* Anderson, Ind.: Warner.

Worden, M. 1989. *Early widow: A journal of the first year.* Downers Grove, Ill.: InterVarsity.

Wylie. B. J. 1986. *The survival guide for widows.* New York: Ballentine.

Single Parenting

Arnold, L. E. 1985. *Parents, children, and change.* Lexington, Mass.: Lexington Books.

Atlas, S. L. 1984. *Parents without partners sourcebook.* Philadelphia: Running Press.

Bustanoby, A. 1982. *Ready-made family: How to be a stepparent and survive.* Grand Rapids: Zondervan.

Cohen, R. S., B. J. Cohler, and J. B. Weisman. 1984. *Parenthood: A psychodynamic perspective.* New York: Guildford.

Dolmetsch, P., and A. Shia. 1985. *Kids book about single-parent families.* New York: Doubleday.

Hobbs, N., et al. 1984. *Strengthening families.* San Francisco: Jossey-Bass.

Jacobs, J. W. 1986. *Divorce and fatherhood: The struggle for parental identity.* Washington, D.C.: American Psychiatric Press.

Johnson, C. 1989. *How to blend a family.* Grand Rapids: Zondervan.

Mayo, M. A. 1986. *Parent's guide to sex education.* Grand Rapids: Zondervan.

Parke, R. D., ed. 1984. *Review of child development research.* Chicago: University of Chicago Press.

Patton, R., ed. 1986. *The American family: Life and health.* Oakland, Calif.: Third Party Publishing.

Peppler, A. S. 1982. *Single again—this time with children: A Christian guide for the single parent.* Minneapolis: Augsburg.

Pocs, O., and R. H. Walsh. 1987. *Marriage and family.* Guilford, Conn.: Dushkin.

Porterfield, K. 1974. Surviving a custody battle. *The Single Parent* (May): 20-21.

Reed, B. 1988. *Single mothers raising sons.* Nashville: Thomas Nelson.

_____. 1982. *Christian family activities for one parent families.* Cincinnati: Standard.

_____. 1981. *I didn't plan to be a single parent.* St. Louis: Concordia.

Rekers, G. A., and J. J. Swinart. 1984. *Making up the difference: Help for single parents with teenagers* Grand Rapids: Baker.

Shelly, J. A. 1982. *The spiritual needs of children.* Downers Grove, Ill.: InterVarsity.

Smith, H. I.. 1982. *Pastoral care for single parents.* Kansas City, Mo.: Beacon Hill.

Children of Divorce

Blume, J. S. 1986. *It's not the end of the world.* New York: Dell.

Boegehold, B. 1985. *Daddy doesn't live here anymore: A book about divorce.* Berkeley, Calif.: Golden/Western.

Coleman, W. L. 1983. *What children need to know when parents get divorced.* Minneapolis: Bethany.

Dycus, J., and B. Dycus. 1987. *Children of divorce.* Elgin, Ill.: David C. Cook.

Gardner, R. A. 1971. *The boys and girls book about divorce.* New York: Bantam.

Hart, A. D. 1982. *Children and divorce—What to expect, how to help.* Waco, Tex.: Word.

Mumford, A. R. 1984. *Help me understand—A child's book about divorce.* Denver: Accent.

Ticker, M. 1985. *Healing the hurt: For teenagers whose parents are divorced.* Grand Rapids: Baker.

Vigeveno, H. S., and A. Claire. *Divorce and the children.* Ventura, Calif.: Regal.

Vigna, J. 1982. *Daddy's new baby.* New York: Concept Books.

_____. 1984. *Grandma without me.* Niles, Ill.: Whitman.

Singe Adult Lifestyle

Dominitz, B. 1985. *How to find the love of your life*. Rocklin, Calif.: Prima.

Logan, J. 1989. *Not just any man: A practical guide for finding Mr. Right*. Waco, Tex.: Word.

McDowell, J. 1986. *The secret of loving*. Wheaton, Ill.: Tyndale.

McGinnis, A. L. 1983. *The romance factor*. New York: Harper and Row.

Pearson, B., and K. Pearson. 1985. *Single again—Remarrying for the right reasons*. Ventura, Calif.: Regal.

Rinehart, S., and P. Rinehart. 1983. *Choices: Finding God's way in dating, sex, singleness and marriage*. Colorado Springs: NavPress.

Smith, H. I. 1983. *More than "I do," An engaged couple's premarital handbook*. Kansas City, Mo.: Beacon Hill.

Talley, J., and B. Reed. 1982. *Too close/too soon*. Nashville: Thomas Nelson.

Sexuality

Brown, G. 1980. *The new celibacy: Why more men and women are abstaining from sex and enjoying*. New York: McGraw-Hill.

Clark, K. 1986. *Being single and celibate*. Notre Dame, Ind.: Ave Maria Press.

Coleman, B., ed. 1985. *Sex and the single Christian*. Ventura, Calif.: Regal.

Duin, J. 1988. *Purity makes the heart grow stronger*. Ann Arbor, Mich.: Servant Press.

Hershey, T. 1988. *Clearheaded choices in a sexually confused world*. Loveland, Colo.: Group Books.

_____. 1986. Intimacy and sexuality: A gift from God. *Single Spirit* 2 (Feb.): 1-3.

Huggett, J. 1982. *Dating, sex and friendship*. Downers Grove, Ill.: InterVarsity.

Hybels, B. 1989. *Christians in a sex-crazed culture*. Wheaton, Ill.: Victor.

McIlhaney, J. S., Jr. 1990. *Sexuality and sexually transmitted diseases*. Grand Rapids: Baker.

Reisser, T., and P. Reisser. 1989. *Help for the post-abortion woman*. Grand Rapids: Zondervan.

Richardson, L. 1985. *The new other woman: Contemporary single women in affairs with married men*. New York: Free Press.

Selby, T. L., and M. Bockmon. 1990. *The mourning after: Help for the postabortion syndrome*. Grand Rapids: Baker.

Short, R. E. 1984. *Sex, dating, and love*. Minneapolis: Augsburg.

Smith, H. 1988. *Singles ask: Answers to questions about relationships and sexual issues*. Minneapolis: Augsburg.

Stafford, T. 1986. *Love story*. Wheaton, Ill.: Tyndale.

Wilson, E. D. 1984. *Sexual sanity*. Downers Grove, Ill.: InterVarsity.

Homosexuality

Cavanaugh, M. E. 1986. *The effective minister: Psychological and social consideration*. Minneapolis: Seabury.

Holloway, D., and M. Green. 1980. *The church and homosexuality: A positive answer to a current question*. London: Hodder & Stoughton.

Hurst, E., D. Jackson, and N. Jackson. 1987. *Overcoming homosexuality: Helping others in crisis*. Elgin, Ill.: David C. Cook.

Payne, L. 1981. *Broken image*. Westchester, Ill.: Crossway.

_____. 1985. *Crisis in masculinity*. Westchester, Ill.: Crossway.

Wilson, E. 1988. *Counseling and homosexuality*. Downers Grove, Ill.: InterVarsity.

Single Adult Ministry—Leadership

Dobson, J. C. 1983. *Love must be tough*. Waco, Tex.: Word.
Fagerstrom, D. L., ed. 1988. *Singles ministry handbook*. Wheaton, Ill.: Victor.
Gangel, K. 1989. *Feeding and leading*. Wheaton, Ill.: Victor.
Kirwan, W. 1983. *Biblical concepts for Christian counseling*. Grand Rapids: Baker.
LePeau, A. 1983. *Paths of leadership*. Downers Grove, Ill.: InterVarsity.
Senter, M. 1983. *The art of recruiting volunteers*. Wheaton, Ill.: Victor.

Ministry Programming

Barker, S., et al. 1985. *Good things come in small groups*. Downers Grove, Ill.: InterVarsity.
Hershey, T. 1986. *Young adult ministry*. Loveland, Colo.: Group Books.
Hunt, A. E. 1988. Unmet needs untapped resources, single adults. *Fundamentalist Journal* (Mar.): 35-36.
Jordan, C. F. 1985. Singles: The new expressions in contemporary society. *Church Administration* (Sept.): 25-28.
Smoke, J. 1982. *Suddenly single*. Old Tappan, N. J.: Revell.
Stevens, R. P. 1985. *Liberating the laity*. Downers Grove, Ill.: InterVarsity.

Career Development

Blotnik, S. 1985. Midcareer changes. *Forbes* (May 6): 140-41.
Bolles, R. N. 1990. *What color is your parachute?* Rev. ed. San Francisco: Ten Speed.
McCracken, D. 1986. Still single yet serving. *World Christian* (Sept./Oct.): 18-25.
Scanzoni, L. D., and J. Scanzoni. 1981. *Men, women and change*. New York: McGraw-Hill.

Development

Hoekema, A. 1985. How we see ourselves. *Christianity Today* (Nov.): 36-38.
Hulme, W. E. 1980. *Mid-life crises*. Philadelphia: Westminster.
Schuster, C. S., and S. S. Ashburn. 1980. *The process of human development: A holistic approach*. Boston: Little, Brown.
Troll, L. E. 1985. *Early and middle adulthood* 2d ed. Monterey, Calif.: Brooks/Cole.
Walsh, P. B. 1983. *Growing through time*. Monterey, Calif.: Brooks/Cole.

Subject Index